*Advance Praise for*

# Forró and Redemptive Regionalism from the Brazilian Northeast

"This book presents a coherent, well-researched, and highly insightful analysis of *forró*. Jack A. Draper's exploration of the workings of *saudade* in the genre, his analysis of forró's relationship to patterns of migration and assimilation, and his critical division of the current field of forró into three distinct styles are excellent. As Draper notes, forró has received less scholarly attention than other Brazilian genres of similar popularity and substance. It is a major cultural phenomenon whose growth and recombination over the past seventy years present fascinating cases of cultural vitality and variation, and it amply deserves the close critical attention it gets here."

*Bryan McCann, Georgetown University;*
*Author of* Hello, Hello Brazil: Popular Music
in the Making of Modern Brazil

"In this book, Jack A. Draper very accurately analyzes the trajectory of the musical genre known as *forró*, examining this music as one of the elements of cultural expression of the people of Brazil's Northeastern region. It is a historiographical analysis that delves into the fields of sociology and anthropology, not forgetting references from the regional literature. Draper interprets signifiers and signifieds contained in the song lyrics, exploring scenarios which present the life and way of being of the artists, of the Northeastern poets that reside in the region and of those who migrated to the great cities and have in forró their greatest reference of sociocultural identity. It is a work that deals with popular musicality from the standpoint of a researcher who left behind his habitat—the United States—to go to the field. In Brazil he experienced and witnessed Northeastern customs, habits, and traditions, but it is his object of study forró that consolidates this work."

*Expedito Leandro Silva, University of Santo Amaro, Brazil;*
*Author of* Forró no asfalto: mercado e identidade sociocultural

D0821636

**WITHDRAWN**
UTSA LIBRARIES

# Forró and Redemptive Regionalism from the Brazilian Northeast

# LATIN AMERICA
Interdisciplinary Studies

Gladys M. Varona-Lacey
*General Editor*

Vol. 18

PETER LANG
New York • Washington, D.C./Baltimore • Bern
Frankfurt • Berlin • Brussels • Vienna • Oxford

Jack A. Draper III

# Forró and Redemptive Regionalism from the Brazilian Northeast

## Popular Music in a Culture of Migration

PETER LANG
New York • Washington, D.C./Baltimore • Bern
Frankfurt • Berlin • Brussels • Vienna • Oxford

**Library of Congress Cataloging-in-Publication Data**

Draper, Jack Alden.
Forró and redemptive regionalism from the Brazilian northeast:
popular music in a culture of migration / Jack A. Draper III.
p. cm. — (Latin America; v. 18)
Includes bibliographical references.
1. Popular music—Social aspects—Brazil—History—20th century.
2. Forró—Brazil—20th century—History and criticism.
3. Regionalism in music. I. Title.
ML3917.B6D73    781.640981'3—dc22    2010024004
ISBN 978-1-4331-1076-4
ISSN 1524-7805


Bibliographic information published by **Die Deutsche Nationalbibliothek**.
**Die Deutsche Nationalbibliothek** lists this publication in the "Deutsche
Nationalbibliografie"; detailed bibliographic data is available
on the Internet at http://dnb.d-nb.de/.

The paper in this book meets the guidelines for permanence and durability
of the Committee on Production Guidelines for Book Longevity
of the Council of Library Resources.

© 2010 Peter Lang Publishing, Inc., New York
29 Broadway, 18th floor, New York, NY 10006
www.peterlang.com

All rights reserved.
Reprint or reproduction, even partially, in all forms such as microfilm,
xerography, microfiche, microcard, and offset strictly prohibited.

Printed in Germany

Library
University of Texas
at San Antonio

For Jamila, my partner in everything

**WITHDRAWN**
UTSA LIBRARIES

# Table of Contents

List of Illustrations                                                  xi

Acknowledgments                                                        xiii

Introduction: Forrobodó For All                                         1

    Chapter Outline                                  2
    Forró Etimology: Two Tales of Origin             7
    (Re)defining Tradition and the Popular           12
    A Critical Approach to the Synthetic Urge        13
    Cognitive Mapping and Psychological Resistance   15
    Forró Transcends the Synthetic Urge              17
    Forró's Multitude: Transregional and Global Connections   18

1. From Symbol to Allegory: Forró Embraces the Northeast's
    Heterogeneity                                    23
    King Luiz and Baião's Apogee                     24
    Another King: Jackson do Pandeiro                29
    From Crisis to Allegory: Forró's Resurgence      32
    Luiz, Jackson and the Next Generation            36
    Strong Lineage and a Big Tent: Forró's New Assemblages   41

2. Saudade as Diasporic Affect: Forró and Northeastern Nostalgia        43

    Material Saudade: Evoking the Presence of Nature in the Sertão   44
    Mapping Memory: The Creative Transcendence of Exile   52
    Spaces of Saudade: (Re)productions of the Northeast   56
    Saudade in University Forró: O Bando de Maria and Roberta de
      Recife                                63
    Saudade in Electronic Forró: Mastruz com Leite   73
    Saudade and Redemptive Regionalisms              78

3. The Rural-Urban Negative Dialectic: Cognitive Mapping and Forró      85

    Not in Ceará Anymore: Psychological Resistance and Regional
      Remembrance                           86
    Rural Exodus: The Sad Departure                  88
    The Patronage Politics of "Vozes da seca"        91

Relational Subalternism, Melodramatic Consciousness, and
    Critical Rural Utopia                                              93
Other Perspectives: Carioca Samba and Bahian Ballads Versus
    Música Sertaneja                                                   97
Forró's Legacy and Evolution in Urban Popular Culture                 100

4. Framing Forró's Perceptiveness: Migration Contextualized           105

Migrant Testimonials                                                  105
Migration Policy and the Sociology and History of Migration           120
The Social Psychology of Migration                                    128
Conclusion                                                            134

5. The Synthetic Urge: Brazilian Narratives of National Development
    and Dependency in Global Cultural Studies                         135

Gilberto Freyre, Fernando Ortiz and the Origins of the
    Synthetic Urge                                                    136
Contemporary Echoes: Symptoms of the Synthetic Urge at
    the Turn of the 21$^{st}$ Century                                 144
Questioning Anti-Imperialist Syntheses of Popular Culture             148
New Wave Hegemony: Samba Renationalized as
    International Symbol                                               151

6. The Synthetic Urge and Forró: Against Hybrid Totalization          155

Luiz Gonzaga in the City: A Synthesis of Rural and Urban?             156
Traditional Forró: The Duel of Urban and Rural                        160
University Forró: The Middle Class to the Rescue                      163
Electronic Forró: A Northeastern Popular-Operatic Spectacle           165
Forró and Tinhorão's Continuum of Cultural Literacy                   169
The Mediating Role of Cultural Ambassadors                            171
Negative Register of National Synthesis: Forró's Double
    Consciousness                                                     173

7. The "Changing Same" and Redemptive Regionalism in the Evolving
    Popular Musical Form of Forró                                     177

"Respeita Januário": Paying Respect to a Vital Patrimony              178
Baião, In Style and Out                                               183
Weak Messianism, Sertanejo Style                                      187

Recalling a Northeastern Prophetic Tradition 190
"Êta Baião": In the Circle with Jackson do Pandeiro 192
The Rural Remembered and Revitalized 195
Conclusion 198

Conclusion: Multitudinous Diasporic Production: Critical Regionalism,
    Global Cultural Flows, and the Case of Forró 199

    Depopularization in the Global Market: The Baião Goes
        Abroad 200
    The Significance of Diasporic, Popular Roots: A Comparative
        Review of Forró in the National-Regional Context 202
    Samba-Reggae's Repopularization: Returning the World Music
        Gaze 203
    No Thanks, Paul! : Critical Regionalism and an Emerging
        Musical Multitude 207

Works Cited 211

Musical Works Cited 215

# Illustrations

Figure 1.1.    Pernambuco forró vocalist Santanna O Cantador shows
               off his traditional Northeastern pack                        33

Figure 1.2.    A typical forró trio performs with accordion, steel
               triangle and *zabumba* drum on Calhetas beach in
               Pernambuco                                                   33

Figure 3.1.    Forró fans including the author's wife, Jamila
               Batchelder, stand at the entrance of the São Paulo
               sambódromo                                                   57

Figure 3.2.    Entrance to the São João farm in São Paulo's
               sambódromo                                                   61

Figure 3.3.    Entrance to the São João farm in the fairgrounds of
               Campina Grande, Paraíba                                      61

Figure 4.1.    Map of net migratory flows between 1991 and 2000          125

Figure 7.1.    A model "casa de caboclo [country peasant home]" at
               the Luiz Gonzaga Museum in Exu, Pernambuco                  181

Figure 7.2.    Luiz Gonzaga's musical heir Dominguinhos plays
               accordion at a concert in São Paulo                         181

# Acknowledgments

My utmost gratitude goes to Professor Alberto Moreiras of the University of Aberdeen for a true mentorship, and to Professors John French, Kenneth Surin, and Michael Hardt of Duke University for their steadfast guidance and support. Thanks also to Duke University's Center for Latin American and Caribbean Studies for funding that helped with some of my research costs, and to the University of Missouri's Research Council for assistance with the cost of publication. I have also greatly appreciated the supportive environment for research offered by my colleagues in the Department of Romance Languages and Literatures at the University of Missouri-Columbia. Thanks to the *Latin America: Interdisciplinary Studies* series editor, Professor Gladys M. Varona-Lacey, and to Caitlin Lavelle and Jackie Pavlovic at Peter Lang, as well as to my anonymous reviewers, for their helpful advice and comments as I revised the manuscript. Thank you also to my Brazilian colleagues Expedito Leandro Silva, Carlos Sandroni, and Elba Braga Ramalho for your invaluable advice, criticism, hospitality and friendship. A million thanks and best wishes for continued success to the many forrozeiros throughout Brazil whom I spoke with and whose performances and insight regarding forró I greatly appreciated, including Santanna O Cantador, O Bando de Maria, Trio Virgolino, As Bastianas, Flávio José, Arlindo dos Oito Baixos, Forrozão Pegada Quente, Chiquinha Gonzaga, Joaquinha Gonzaga, Zé and Paula Bicudo, and Mano Novo, to mention just a few. I must also express my heartfelt thanks to my family and friends for their love and encouragement. Finally, words cannot express the debt I owe to Jamila Batchelder, without whom this work would not have been possible. May it make you proud.

# Introduction

# Forrobodó For All

The Brazilian popular musical genre of *forró* has always been characterized by movement. One can broadly trace the genre's history through flows of cultural production and people throughout Brazil and beyond. Between rural and urban spaces, between regional and national loci of production, between interior and littoral, between cultural marginality and national acclaim, and between home and diaspora, forró and its artists, the *forrozeiros*, have always shuttled between some of the great antinomies of Latin American modernity. On the other hand, various cultural and political agents have often sought to cease these flows and capture forró and other cultural production in one stable space, reducing it to a tamed hybrid or a regional curiosity. As a subaltern genre produced by marginalized Northeastern workers, forró has always had to deal with such forms of cooptation by groups as diverse as Northeastern landed elites, national populist demagogues and dictators, and cultural critics within academia and without. Despite these continued brushes with various hegemonic interpellations, forrozeiros have managed to continue the vital movement that leads to diachronic innovation in, and increasingly complex allegorization of, the genre—at the same time that a synchronic, redemptive imaginary is maintained that envisions an alternative Brazil in which rural workers might no longer be marginalized and forgotten.

The analytical framework for my study of forró is primarily grounded in literary and cultural studies, subaltern studies and history. Thus the reader should not expect to find an ethnomusicological analysis of the genre. My own unique theoretical approach, as outlined in this introduction, is best at revealing the broad historical development of forró and its evolving efforts to represent the Brazilian Northeast, its people, and their large-scale migration. The genre's efforts in this vein are illustrated through analyses of lyrics, instrumentation, performance styles and performance spaces. These discourses and practices are contextualized with an array of secondary literature on the Northeastern region and the migratory experiences of Northeasterners. I also emphasize the manner in which all of these elements of representation have strategically engaged the modern Brazilian culture industry from the 1940s to the present. Further, my analysis highlights how forró's subaltern, regionalist standpoint marks the limits of some of Brazil's hegemonic national ideologies (such as the developmentalist celebration of progress qua industrialization and the promotion of Rio de Janeiro as the country's "cultural center").

**Chapter Outline**

Following the introduction in this study are seven chapters and a conclusion. Chapter One is a history of the development of the Northeastern genre of *forró* over the course of the 20<sup>th</sup> century to the present day. This chapter traces forró's progression from symbolic to allegorical representation of the Brazilian Northeast as the genre matures under the aegis of Luiz Gonzaga, the King of Baião. Utilizing Walter Benjamin's distinction between symbol and allegory, I analyze the progression from the early, symbolic form of forró called *baião*, disseminated primarily by accordionist/singer Luiz Gonzaga in the forties and fifties, to the later expansion and allegorization of the genre as forró by the generation of musicians that rose to fame in the seventies. Gonzaga himself, in his *cangaceiro* (Northeastern bandit) attire, was the national symbol of the Northeast in the early years, whereas more recently the genre has developed enough complexity to boast three main branches divided largely along class lines: *forró tradicional* (traditional), *forró eletrônico* (electronic), and *forró universitário* (university). I argue that this progression from symbolic to allegorical representation was a necessary one due to the hegemonic position of the Rio de Janeiro culture industry in the forties, which at that time could only accept forró as a fad and only later would open up to forró as a genre that more holistically represents the Northeast and Northeastern cultural production.

After examining forró's insertion into the national culture industry and its development as a genre, in Chapter Two I explore its continued loyalty to a redemptive imaginary for Northeasterners, based in a profound diasporic attachment (*saudade*) to the social and ecological environment of the *sertão* or rural interior. In general terms, saudade is the Portuguese word used to describe a profound, bittersweet nostalgia for a person, place, time or other memory from which one has been separated. Thus this concept was easily appropriated by forrozeiros for their own purposes of remembering the

Northeast and its people. I examine numerous lyrics and music written and performed since the forties that demonstrate saudade's characteristic telescoping of time and space and the related irony of celebrating and "making present" a desired place, person or lifeworld through music and dance while simultaneously recalling one's real separation from that object of desire.

In forró, saudade is uniquely developed as a collective diasporic affect. Desire is collectivized most commonly through the imaginary of a rural idyll which is a repository of traditional culture and values as well as the place in which Northeasterners' lovers, families and communities await their return. These are constant themes which are present in the genre to this day, although in electronic forró there is more and more emphasis on interpersonal romance over collective diasporic affect. I suggest that this is due to an increasing discursive convergence of electronic forró with the melodrama of urban popular culture, most famously present in telenovelas. On the other hand, university forró has developed its own unique collective saudade—in this case a middle-class nostalgia for popular authenticity.

As discussed in Chapter Three, the redemptive imaginary of saudade finds its negative corollary outside of the Northeast in forrozeiros' common resistance to cognitively mapping the social space of the Southeastern (or even coastal Northeastern) cities in which many Northeasterners now live for economic reasons. In the latter part of this introduction, I will further elaborate on my framing of this resistance and its potential as part of a negative dialectic which questions the hegemony of urban industrialization.

In Chapter Four, all of the previous discussion is contextualized in a larger analysis of the migration of Northeasterners throughout Brazil. As noted initially, forró has always been characterized by movement and this reflects the massive internal migration of Northeastern workers. In the past these were rural workers, but increasingly people have been leaving urban areas as well, as the Northeast becomes more and more urbanized. Northeasterners have migrated to all parts of Brazil, however the primary destination has been the Southeast—and within the Southeast the preferred location has been the most dynamic economy in the city and state of São Paulo. Through collections of interviews of migrants to São Paulo, demographic statistics related to internal migration, and related studies in the fields of sociology, social psychology, communication studies, history and ethnography, this chapter emphasizes the powerful accuracy and continued relevance of forró's discourse on the Northeastern migratory experience. On the other hand, the analysis also broaches some of forró's blind spots from the standpoints of gender difference, life in the diaspora, and alternate forms of nostalgia. These oversights, however, have not diminished forró musicians' key role in vividly imagining a redemptive return to the home region for Northeasterners. I demonstrate how, in recent times, an increasing amount of displaced Northeasterners are making this dream of return a reality as the economy of their home region revives. The chapter concludes with a section addressing forró's perspicacious portrayal of migrant subjectivity, along with the genre's ability to elaborate Northeastern migrants' losses and to celebrate their common cultural patrimony. Studies in the area of social psychology confirm these insights that forrozeiros have shared with, and received from, the Northeastern community since the origins of the genre in the mid-twentieth century.

Chapters Five and Six critique the synthetic urge, a rubric I use to describe the impetus behind the hegemonic international narratives attempting to position forró within some of modernity's major temporal and spatial matrices (i.e. rural-urban, modern-traditional). The synthetic urge is typically driven by a reductive notion of hybrid identity that can be found in diverse overlapping discourses in the field of Latin American cultural studies, including national-popular narratives promulgated by cultural theorists such as Gilberto Freyre and Fernando Ortiz, a related conservative nationalist anti-imperialism, the dominant post-war economic ideologies of developmentalism and urbanization, and the vulgar postcolonial hybridity theory circulating more recently in North American and Brazilian academia. The synthetic urge essentially serves to reify complex and shifting identity positions into one static hybrid. The purpose of this reification is, of course, to capture power for a certain subject position or narrative, in this case by associating said position or narrative with a certain hegemonic discourse like those four mentioned above. The synthetic urge either ignores forró in favor of culture considered more nationally representative or encourages analyses of forró that champion the genre as a synthesis of rural and urban, traditional and modern. As should be clear even from the schematic description of forró provided thus far, dialectical synthesis is a very problematic process with which to identify the antinomian tendencies of forró vis-à-vis rural and urban spaces and forrozeiros' conservation of, and innovations in, their regionally-inspired cultural production. I propose the concept of savage hybridity as one that marks what Alberto Moreiras calls the "failure of hybrid totalization," and therefore is a more adequate model for representing both forró's subaltern positionality with respect to national culture and its refusal to merge into any static hybrids developed in the aforementioned hegemonic discourses (Moreiras, 2001).

Chapter Seven seeks to explore the dynamic role of tradition in the evolving popular musical form of forró. Central to this section is a consideration of the relationship between notions of the popular and the traditional in Brazil. Romantic notions of the rural continue to define this space as a privileged repository for timeless, unchanging, authentic popular traditions. Rural popular culture can be contrasted with urban popular to reveal that the urban space is largely considered to be one of comparative innovation (with less authenticity), even within genres that have become traditions in their own right such as *carioca* (Rio de Janeiro) samba. The relationship between rural and urban popular culture can fairly accurately be mapped onto that between regional and national, or specifically in the case of forró between Northeastern and Southeastern Brazil. A major goal of Chapter Seven is to argue against the spatial and temporal ghettoization of tradition in the local and the past, using the example of forró as a strong counterexample to disprove the assumptions behind such associations. As various theorists of globalization have argued, the local already assumes and includes the global within itself, and in the case of forró we could say it includes the national as well. Accordingly I call the claim that forró as a cultural tradition is exclusively rooted in the local a *relocalization* of tradition. Such a relocalization serves to purify and thus authenticate tradition by cutting it off from the world and making it seem organic rather than ideologically engaged in a popular-historical field of discursive struggle. With the common, stereotypical spatialization of the past in rural and regional areas comes the assumption that real, authentic forró must have been created in bygone years in the Northeast while more recent production and forró by non-Northeasterners must be either derivative or degraded. Alternatively, some Southeastern musicians imagine that forró produced in the present-day Northeast will never be able to equal the music of Luiz Gonzaga and other famous musicians of the past, or even that it is no longer being produced at all in the Northeast.

From these perspectives, contemporary forró cannot be understood in its full, tripartite and transregional complexity as a genre. Forrozeiros prove through their music that subalternity, as an unstable multitudinous condition of being, resists ontological spatialization within hybrid totalizations such as the local-traditional synthesis. Out of this subalternity comes a spatially and temporally dynamic conception of tradition. Forró achieves this dynamism through its redemptive regionalism based in the epistemologies of a subaltern people rather than a hegemonic national-popular narrative. Nevertheless, the genre has at times been in danger of losing its redemptive-regionalist orientation, and has in these instances been susceptible to cooptation by regional-popular narratives championed by Northeastern elites.

The concluding chapter examines the transformation of cultural hierarchies that has taken place since forró's early days due to the global integration of capitalist markets, led by dominant capitalist countries like those which comprise the G8: i.e. the US, Europe/the EU, and Japan. In the case of Brazil, at the time of forró's birth into the national culture industry Rio de Janeiro controlled the distribution and hierarchization of cultural flows and the resultant formation of a Brazilian national cultural identity. This carioca hegemony had been established since Getúlio Vargas's rise to power and his privileging of Rio de Janeiro's samba as the representative cultural expression of the popular classes in Brazil. Vis-à-vis the international market, samba, and later bossa nova, were chosen by various cultural agents to represent Brazil's cultural riches, "poetries for export" (to paraphrase Oswald de Andrade) that played the role of counterpart to the country's industrial products and natural resources. But since trade liberalization during and after the dictatorship years of the seventies, the national product has become less privileged as representative of the people and a wave of regional cultural production has come to the fore in answer to the omnipresent influx of North American cultural flows. Successive waves of national popularity for forró, and related hagiographies of its major proponents such as Luiz Gonzaga and Jackson do Pandeiro, are symptoms of this larger rise of regionalism. Regional production need no longer be mediated through the cultural arbitration of Rio de Janeiro for the purposes of strategic representation of the nation-state in foreign markets.

Nevertheless, the concept of a direct communicational link between local realities in Brazil and those elsewhere in the world must be problematized with an analysis of the new cultural hierarchies that have replaced the old national-popular variety. One of Luiz Gonzaga's own monikers, "The Ambassador of the Sertão," provides the figure for my own analysis of

Brazilian cultural flows on the global market. In the present world economy, many flows from subordinate capitalist countries to other countries (be they subordinate or dominant) tend to be mediated through cultural ambassadors. Typically, these mediators function through personal ties between musicians and entrepeneurs in the subordinate country and musicians in centers of production in other countries. For example, one could cite Jimmy Cliff's relationship with Gilberto Gil where Gil acted very much like a state ambassador in receiving Cliff in Brazil and touring the local music scene with Cliff. A perhaps more unequal relationship would be that between Paul Simon and Airto Moreira or Milton Nascimento, both of whom helped to provide Simon with his introduction to Brazilian music that would end in Simon's 1990 album, *Rhythm of the Saints* and the participation of the Afro-Brazilian, Salvadoran drum troupe Olodum on the record. These collaborative relationships can range from the egalitarian to the extremely hierarchical. As Timothy Taylor outlines in *Global Pop*, in the cases of Simon and other global pop/rock stars like Peter Gabriel who desire to incorporate global influence into their albums (usually considered "world music"), there exists in the very process of producing the music a structural imbalance of power between the global star and the musicians/entrepeneurs from subordinate capitalist countries that is virtually insuperable (Taylor, 1997). Without an influential and persistent cultural ambassador of their own, forrozeiros are left to struggle for limited state funding to attend international music festivals and exhibitions, and to hope their music can find a place among the categories of world music, Latin music, Afro-pop, folk music, etc. on the world market. The conclusion traces the contours of these new global striations of cultural hierarchy, and the potential for alliances among forrozeiros and the multitude of other musicians excluded by the current configuration of global capital flows.

**Forró Etimology: Two Tales of Origin**

Before further introducing the discourse of forró, I find it imperative to discuss the discourse about forró. The importance of such a beginning was impressed upon me by countless Brazilians, mostly Northeasterners, who found an evidently immense pleasure in sharing with me their knowledge regarding the etymology of the word "forró." This desire to share information about their cultural heritage is representative of the typical hospitality and generosity of Northeasterners and the rightful pride they take in their own cultural history. As can be expected, not everyone tells the same story about where the word comes from. But one can divide these tales of origin into two main categories.

The first is the tale of an Anglicism that entered Portuguese to describe a popular music with thoroughly Brazilian roots in the Northeastern backlands or sertão. To understand this version, one must go back to the turn of the twentieth century when English railroad companies were laying tracks in the Northeast, connecting the isolated region to the rest of the country. These companies, so the story goes, would throw dances for the workers and the surrounding communities. To signal that it was a party with free entry to anyone in the area, the dances would be advertised with a large sign above the door inscribed with the words "For All." Thus the word "forró" is said to be a transcription of the Brazilian manner of pronouncing two English words. A variation in this version of forró's origin myth has it that those throwing the party were not British railroad companies, but rather American soldiers stationed in Brazil during World War II.

Although I have my own reservations with respect to this story's etymological likelihood (especially concerning the more recent version with American soldiers), these in no way reduce the cultural relevance of the story. In this vein, it will be quite revealing to sketch a few comparisons with the origins of the word samba. Like "samba" originally did, forró first signified a festive gathering with unique and popular-folkloric, if somewhat vaguely defined, musical accompaniment. Also like samba, the word forró has its roots in a foreign language. As opposed to an African language, it is a European one in the latter case. This difference certainly reflects the greater emphasis on African or Afro-Brazilian influence in samba, as opposed to forró's relatively ambiguous racial identifications. Another distinction from samba is that in this version of forró's origins, we can isolate the historical moment at which the neologism entered the language, as opposed to the much cloudier picture of samba's entrance. Perhaps the most important discursive effect of the clearly pinpointed entrance of the word into Brazilian Portuguese is to localize the genre indubitably within the Northeast. The story clearly relates events in this region, but it also involves an international cast. In this case, samba seems more typical of any word entering a language, with its slower, more evolutionary incorporation that is harder to pinpoint historically.

What purpose do the British (or Americans) serve in the story, though? For one, they serve to unify the Northeasterners as one people. There is no question of whether landowners or peons are going to be at the party, it is explicitly "for all." So implicitly, all Northeasterners regardless of class are celebrating together at the railroad companies' dances. The magnanimous British are the hosts, whereas everyone else who attends the event is simply a Northeastern Brazilian. This lack of hierarchy in the story is significant in the light of stories told by Luiz Gonzaga regarding parties held in the Pernambucan sertão during his youth in the teens and twenties. In Sinval Sá's biography, Luiz Gonzaga is quoted as opining:

> But there was something that bothered me about those parties. The separation of the so-called 'whites,' who isolated themselves in a room, while the tenant farmers remained out in the yard. The criterion of color varied with wealth. (Sá 2002, 50)[1]

The poorer, darker-skinned residents of the ranch were typically segregated from those at the top of the racially-inflected class hierarchy, or pigmentocracy. The "for all" origin story directly contradicts this reality in favor of an emphasis on undifferentiated Northeastern community. Thus one important functional role of the British in this scenario is to provide a space devoid of the contemporary power dynamics in Brazilian rural society. Through this deus ex machina enters the specter of a newer ideology of peaceful and harmonious coexistence between the races, known as racial democracy. If this ideology was in fact an influence upon the story, there is some historical revisionism involved here since the ideology did not become hegemonic until several decades after the turn of the century. But racial democracy was a popular ideology for much of the last century and thus may well have influenced the populist, "for all" connotation attributed to forró in this etymology.

As noted above, the presence of the British gives this story an international cast. Foreign characters make this version of forró's roots seem all the more universal. In a spatial sense, the inclusion of foreigners and Brazilians in the event is a meeting of the global and the local, transforming the Northeastern region into a microcosm of the then British-dominated

---

[1] All foreign language texts here and below, unless otherwise noted, are translated by the author.

geopolitical state of affairs. In a temporal sense, the British involvement in the Northeastern infrastructure recalls the ever-present desire for modernity, while the Brazilian attendees are a reminder of the living tradition of the local communities. The amicable fraternization between the two groups hints that Brazil, and especially the Northeast, are ready for modernization and will participate in it on their own terms. Such autonomy combined with partnership brings us back to the Brazilian translation of the English words "for all" into one word, "forró."

But of course there is an alternative history of the genre's name. This origin myth goes back to at least the nineteenth century, when the word "forrobodó" used to appear in the Recifense press (Albin 2006, 289). The word was typically used in a rather disparaging manner to refer to popular festivities, often with connotations of violence. Such festivities would include dancing and music, but were not really "for all" like the British parties. It was precisely due to the lower-class attendees that the bourgeois press looked upon the gatherings with suspicion or even disdain. This type of attitude was common among the middle class towards any popular gathering (and its associated music) where there was no clear space for mixture between classes nor deferential inclusion of wealthier Brazilians.

So according to this version, the word forró is an abbreviation of the older forrobodó, of clear origin in Brazilian Portuguese. This etymology is a favorite with more traditionalist musicians, as well as Brazilian scholars studying forró and folk music more generally. It is the preferred etymology of the *Dicionário Houaiss* of Brazilian popular music. As is the case in this dictionary's entry and others like that of the *Enciclopédia Musical Brasileira*, the "for all" etimology is not seen as a legitimate alternative origin story. The word forró is reclaimed for the Portuguese language from its supposed association with English. Thus in making the case for the word forrobodó, we can detect a nationalist or regionalist pride that fuels the desire to dispel myths around the influence of foreign languages.

During the 1960s, there was a movement among university-educated musicians to valorize the cultural production of the lower classes as a sign of solidarity with proletarian struggles (Draper 2003, Dunn 2001). It was easy to imagine this as a common struggle since the military dictatorship had been cracking down on both the freedom to organize and the freedom of speech of all classes (although much less so, in the beginning, on university intellectuals (Schwarz 1996)). I see the forrobodó etymology as a discourse within this tradition of politicizing popular music. This history of forró gives credit for the creation of the genre entirely to poor Northeasterners, who gathered together to play and dance music they had developed over the centuries with little commercial influence. The mode of production emphasized in this history, above all else, lends an aura of ethnic authenticity to the music. Adding to the aura is the long-held belief (at least since European Romanticism) that the poor, especially the rural poor, are a pure archive of any ethnicity's primitive (and thus natural) artistic development.

To begin a comparison of the "for all" and the "forrobodó" etymologies, it seems fitting to note that the former has far greater circulation. One is much more likely to hear this story than the forrobodó story, and one hears it even from people who are not forró fans and have no great knowledge of the genre. Does this mean that the Anglo-Brazilian etymology is more "popular"? Perhaps. Or perhaps this is simply a better story. A Brazilian word (especially a Northeastern word) no longer in common usage hardly makes for a fascinating tale. From a historical perspective, there is no identitarian specificity to the word forrobodó as opposed to "For All," which evokes a specific type of party with universal attendance of railroad workers, their families, their employers and their larger community.

It is also easier to relate this imaginary to the present-day status of forró as a genre of Brazilian popular music. As discussed in several of the following chapters, the present-day categories of university, electronic and traditional forró span a wide variety of musicians in terms of region, race, class and gender. This variety approaches the diversity of the Brazilian nation as a whole, thanks to the national scope forró has managed to achieve over the past sixty years. An all-inclusive party with international corporate sponsors is an origin story that certainly resonates with major contemporary forró performances throughout the country. On the other hand, recalling the word forrobodó emphasizes that forró originated from the peasant and working classes of the Northeast, and continues to trace its strong identitarian roots back to them. Here we come up against conflicting definitions of the popular. In the case of "for all," the underlying understanding of the popular is based in the acceptance of a broad national audience and wide distribution by the music industry, whereas in the alternative case it is a music considered to be "of the people," authentically produced by poor people who do not necessarily gain any commercial advantage or widespread personal recognition for their work. Defining the popular is a discursive struggle which has wider reverberations throughout the sphere of popular culture in Brazil and elsewhere, which I discuss in Chapter Seven.

## (Re)Defining Tradition and the Popular

While theorists such as George Yúdice have called for a reevaluation of cultural production through the lense of expediency (Yúdice 2003), Chapter Seven broaches some of the ethical and epistemological questions that such approaches avoid. From Yúdice or even Néstor García Canclini's perspective, forrozeiros might be using their traditional patrimony primarily for profit or to make claims for recognition from the state. They certainly do make use of culture in these ways, but forrozeiros are first and foremost performing collective affect and writing history such that they can guarantee continued psychological, social and cultural survival in the Northeastern diaspora and even within the Northeast itself. I understand this constitution of traditional culture to be something akin to Paul Gilroy's concept of the "living memory of the changing same," according to which there exists a direct relationship between a community of listeners, in this case Northeasterners, and the production of traditional music like forró, "even when the network used to communicate its volatile contents has been an adjunct to the sale of [...] popular music" (Gilroy 1993, 198). While expediency or resource management are not adequate characterizations of forró's emphasis on a collective ethos or worldview, one must also avoid the ethnomusicological tendency to marginalize or ghettoize tradition through a discourse of authenticity (involving the tracing of origins and/or sources) that chains tradition to specific localities or bygone eras. This tendency is a relocalization which purifies tradition by cutting it off from the world and making it seem organic and natural to a certain locale rather than ideologically engaged, as it is, in a popular-historical field of dialogue, debate, and performance stretching across and even beyond the Brazilian nation. In other words, forró's subalternity cannot and should not be definitively spatialized by the cultural analyst. Expediency and authenticity discourses can, of course, go hand in hand, since a reified notion of tradition qua authentic folklore (even if recognized as a commodity within a (trans)national culture industry) can easily be accommodated within a grander theory concerning the increasing usage of culture as a politico-economic resource. While forrozeiros certainly use Northeastern culture as a resource for creative inspiration and to attract state and private funding, theirs is a historical project akin to Walter Benjamin's critique of the concept of historical progress in his *Passagenwerk* [The Arcades Project] (Benjamin 1991, Vol. 5) as well as his "Über den Begriff der Geschichte [Theses on the Philosophy of History]" (Benjamin 1991, 691-704). Outside of the hegemonic ideology of national progress, forró is produced in the fullness of a "now time" that draws the meaning of the present constellation of Northeastern popular culture out of its relationship with the diasporic history of subaltern Northeasterners. While this conception of popular tradition and related cultural production goes far beyond resource management, one must also recognize, with Durval Muniz de Albuquerque Jr., that "the invention of tradition" has been a favorite occupation of the Northeastern elite, who have certainly found Northeastern culture expedient for the purposes of consolidating their own power base (Albuquerque Jr. 1999). With respect to forró, such resource management involves the elite's melodramatic identification with subaltern populations and their self-representations in popular music, for its own purposes of masking its domination and exploitation of these same populations.

## A Critical Approach to the Synthetic Urge

It is from the perspective of forró's profound rootedness in living tradition, and in some cases the related utopian rural imaginary, that in Chapters Five and Six I critique theories of temporal and spatial synthesis so prevalent in contemporary cultural studies. Urban and rural factors, as well as modernity and tradition, have not been incorporated into new syntheses but rather have much more antinomian tendencies in the context of forró's production. Urban centers of the Southeast and Northeast have been sites of production for forró since its beginnings as a popular-industrial genre. Yet this has not made urban themes enter and influence the discourse of the forró canon. Rural areas, whether in the coastal, agreste, or sertão regions of the Northeast, have remained by far the dominant spatial references for the genre. Likewise, the influence of modernity in the genre—which in this limited context refers to developments in the contemporary music industry— is largely confined to technological, and in some cases performative aspects, but is either attenuated or consciously avoided in lyrical expression. Lyrics tend to stress ties to the past, or the traditions of a vibrant community that continues to face life throughout Brazil on its own terms. We could call these terms authentic, if by this we mean the collective ownership and the stress on the continuity of the popular nature of forró—"popular" here meaning the preservation and valorization of Northeastern communities and social spheres.

Thus rural and urban, modern and traditional are addressed as antinomies that need to be carefully negotiated and cannot effectively be synthesized. My position here deviates from various forró analyses which seek to prove a synthesis of rural and urban imaginaries in forró through a process of modernization of Northeastern folk music. However, I am confident that my analysis resonates with both of forró's origin myths, which stress rural community and place the modern economy in second place, if they refer to it at all. Unlike many scholarly analyses of forró and culture generally in Latin America, these stories demonstrate no symptoms of the synthetic urge, a phenomenon I analyze at length in Chapters Five and Six.

To expand a bit further on the concept, the synthetic urge can be described as a tendency towards identitarian reification of what remain complex historical processes involving many subaltern tensions. These tensions, which are well exemplified in Brazil by the above-mentioned double negation of rural and urban utopias, are glossed over by the supposition that a synthesis has occurred. The motivating factors behind this analytical urge towards synthesis are multiple in Latin American cultural studies, including the combined hegemonic influence of disciplinary and broader societal discourses. In the case of rural and urban cultural production, and in other spatially-defined production codified as modern or traditional, these hegemonic discourses often involve a focus on hybridity. The concept of hybridity in Latin American cultural studies can be traced back to thinkers such as Gilberto Freyre and Fernando Ortiz, who theorized Brazilian and Cuban national identity, respectively, as hybrids of various local and global cultural and politico-economic influences. In my analysis, their static, reified formulations of the hybrid are proven to lead to hegemonic syntheses that mask certain forms of domination and subalternity. This problematic manifestation of the hybrid still echoes in present-day analyses of Brazilian culture and cultural production, as I demonstrate in my analysis of a recent international polemic on race in Brazil, and thereafter in a survey of some of the important literature on forró and popular music in rural and urban zones.

## Cognitive Mapping and Psychological Resistance

The two etymologies of forró, which are at the same time origin stories or myths, also have some key commonalities which are explored throughout this study. Both are clearly situated within the Brazilian Northeast. Although the term forró came to designate the genre only after it had achieved national acclaim as the baião, no one claims that the Brazilian nation or other regions have anything to do with the origins of forró. The certainty about the regional development of the genre reflects the profound affective attachment of Northeasterners to their region as well as the related dominance of a cognitive mapping of that region in the discourse of forró wherever it is produced and performed.

As discussed in Chapter Three, this cognitive mapping of the Northeast, often the rural Northeast but including urban areas, occurs to the exclusion of incorporating into forró any new discursive themes from the urban-industrial complex of the Southeast. This exclusive focus is surprising since so many Northeasterners migrated to the Southeast that one would expect forró to address the experiences of the diasporic communities of Northeasterners in São Paulo and Rio de Janeiro. But any detailed portrait of Northeastern migrant communities as such is generally suppressed in favor of preserving and valorizing affective and cultural ties to the home region. No matter what innovations occur musically and lyrically, there remains this profound need to be rooted in the region and its history. Telling stories about the derivation of the word forró is really just another way of sharing and reaffirming these roots.

Vis-á-vis the social space of the city, the researcher enters the difficult realm of political representation when faced with the task of labeling the lack of cognitive mapping in forró. Is it a failure, a resistance, or something else? The academics and artists I spoke with throughout Brazil typically rejected the word "resistance," which is very politically charged and does not seem to correspond to the subtler ways in which forró avoids representation of life in the city. When analyzing what I call the "forró canon"[2], one is certainly not

---

[2]The forró canon can be described as the general discourse of forró as mediated by and through its most influential producers, such as Luiz Gonzaga and Jackson do Pandeiro. I

faced with a conscious political project or "forró movement" against the progress of urban industrialization and the related fall in political and social status of rural areas and their residents. Of course, to call the lack of representation of the city a "cognitive failure" would be accurate in some respects but is perhaps too close to the hegemonic narrative of progress. According to this narrative, championed by both the democratically elected Juscelino Kubitschek and the later military dictatorship, Brazil's bright future depended upon rapid industrialization and urbanization (along with the national transformation of farming according to the dictates of industrial agribusiness), in accordance with the developmentalist projects of global capital and the International Monetary Fund. In terms of the psychology of the migrant worker, this narrative of progress would likely deem forró's attachment to rural life and its cognitive resistance to mapping the Northeastern worker within the urban economy as unhealthy and unproductive. For this reason it is important to emphasize that the terminology of cognitive failure need not connote that there is some kind of "successful" cognition that could have effectively integrated the migrant worker into the urban society of the Southeast. The fact remains that upon being displaced from urban and rural economies in crisis in the Northeast, Northeasterners were incorporated into the surplus labor pool of São Paulo and other industrial centers. This placed them, and continues to place millions, in a very marginal position within the national economy. Since this marginality is a systemic problem, it should hardly be designated as the responsibility of the migrant workers.

Ultimately, I have found that the hermeneutical approach that best suits the history of Northeastern migration is to frame the migrant standpoint as one characterized by some degree of psychological resistance or repression. One advantage of this approach is to avoid a verdict on whether forró's championing of the rural roots of Northeasterners in the city is conservative or progressive. Although forró discourse has certain qualities critical of hegemonic developmentalist policies, it would be difficult to regard the nostalgic visions of forró as calling for significant political change, especially not within the industrial core. What might have been considered conservative within the confines of the Northeastern communities where

---

discuss the development of the canon further in Chapter One.

forró first flourished as folk music, however, cannot be so easily categorized in the new, national context into which forró entered upon its first commodification as baião. In Chapter Three, I discuss the rural idyll of forró discourse as a utopian critique of urban modernity which "discloses the complacency of the urban celebration" and forms half of a negative dialectic (Jameson 2004, 50). The other half is, of course, the urban utopia which celebrates the city and, in Fredric Jameson's words, "exposes everything nostalgic and impoverished in the embrace of nature" (Ibid.). Therefore, although forró does not present a political program, it functions as a dialectical counterpoint to the hegemonic utopia of urban development and thereby serves as a continual reminder of rural subalternity. This reminder is all the more striking when produced by means of the technology of the culture industry, within the Southeastern urban, politico-economic core, or even within the larger coastal cities of the Northeast. Returning to the context of the psyche, if in forró's discourse we can find a psychological repression of the economic violence of urbanization, then we must also recognize that this repression acutely reveals its opposite number in urban consciousness. In this way, forró is a symptom within popular music, a return of the repressed for the urban core—the repressed being the core's reliance upon massive levels of surplus labor, displaced from more rural regions on the periphery like the Northeast.

**Forró Transcends the Synthetic Urge**

As noted earlier, in Chapter One I sketch out a history of the genre of forró, which I theorize as progressing from a symbolic to an allegorical representation of the Northeast. This analysis draws from Benjamin's discussion of allegory in his *Ursprung des deutschen Trauerspiels* [Origin of German Tragic Drama] (Benjamin 1991, 203-430). Three historical phases can be traced in forró's development: first, the apogees of Luiz Gonzaga and Jackson do Pandeiro's careers followed by a decline after the rise of bossa nova; second, a reemergence in the seventies with a second generation of artists including Dominguinhos, Elba Ramalho and Alceu Valença; and third, a splintering of forró into three subgenres after Gonzaga's retirement and death. These three genres reflect contradictions always present in forró along class and regional lines but which did not produce subgenres as long as Gonzaga's formidable presence united all forrozeiros. These phases can be periodized historically as corresponding roughly with three eras: firstly, post-war modernization/urbanization and import substitution; secondly, trade liberalization in the 1970s with a build-up of foreign debt and the transnationalization of the music industry; and finally, the post-dictatorship era in which cultural renationalization occurred through the production of regional and subaltern groups like Northeasterners and *favelados* (slum dwellers).

These periods themselves can all be related to specific synthetic urges. In the fifties we find the state's desire to at least appear to be synthesizing all regions into national development. Luiz Gonzaga helped to give the appearance of an incorporation of the marginal Northeast, at least on the cultural level. In this context synthetic symbols, like those of the rhythm called baião and the folk figure called the cangaceiro, are what most easily represented Northeastern culture and what sold in the Southeast. In the seventies, with the transnationalization of the economy and cultural industry, a space opened up for a more diverse, allegorical representation of the Northeast which incorporated some of the region's contradictions. The second generation arrived on stage and began to develop forró in São Paulo, Rio de Janeiro, and Brasília and also in the Northeast (which before had been unable to support Gonzaga and Jackson's national careers). But forró really came into its own with the return to democracy when the forces of cultural integration from the state were reduced, while at the same time a widespread regionalist cultural response to North American penetration of the national music market was on the rise. Also, as noted above, the departure of Gonzaga as a major presence defining the canon relieved the genre of his strong personal synthetic pressure, opening it up to the tripartite division of today.

**Forró's Multitude: Transregional and Global Connections**

What we now have under the genre of forró is a diverse group of immaterial laborers throughout Brazil whose future coherence might best be gauged through Hardt and Negri's concept of the multitude (Hardt and Negri 2004). To what degree do these groups collaborate democratically for the purposes of creatively disseminating Northeastern popular culture? Any sign of a departure from the horizontally-networking, egalitarian biopolitics of the multitude, that is, of the wielding of a synthetic sovereignty for the purposes of establishing a new hegemonic canonization of forró, would likely entail a decisive atomization of the genre along class and/or regional lines and the subsequent formation of new genres or mergers of certain subgenres with other pop music genres like *brega* or *música sertaneja.* (The political concept of sovereignty here is intended to resonate with Benjamin's description of the allegorical play as one in which the sovereign is absent from the stage and thus there is no one referent unifying the narrative.) There is some lack of communication between Southeast and Northeast that might threaten to result in an attempted synthetic move towards sovereignty on the part of artists in the economically dominant Southeastern industrial corridor, but presently there is enough immigration of Northeastern artists to the region, and demand among transplanted poor and working-class Northeasterners for a variety of forró styles, to maintain a transregional dialogue and a recognition of the continued flourishing of forró in diverse forms throughout the country.

Finally, the conclusion will demonstrate how synthesis is most heavily at work in the transnational flows of culture which commodify cultural production into various broad categories like Latin or World music, Afro-pop or folklore. This synthetic commodification may be a function of the lack of a destabilizing particular context, or rather the subalternization and constitutive exclusion of the particular Brazilian cultural contexts. At times music is commodified secondarily by nationality, especially in compilations, in which case a synthetic representation of a society can be presented as an introduction or background to the music. Here expediency is the perfect concept to capture the logic by which foreign, sometimes unintelligible sounds are made relevant to a listener in one of the dominant capitalist countries. The cultural imaginary of the other (nation, region, people) is used to sell its music, especially to further the consumer's incipient interest such that he or she will become conscious of the vast array of cultural production emanating from other parts of the globe, or at least aware of the other international offerings at the record store. Whatever struggles occur on the intranational level to define forró as a genre are always already elided on the world market. This state of affairs suggests a parallel between the national music market in 1950s Brazil and the present-day world market. Yet rather than the synthesizing force upon subaltern culture exercised by state-managed industrial development, in the present world market there is only the force of global musical categories as defined by the handful of megacorporations comprising the transnational entertain-ment industry. But foreign categories for forró like Latin and Brazilian, or even "Music for Maids and Taxi Drivers," do not have any noticeable effect upon the actually-existing genre in Brazil, unlike the categories of rap and rock which tend to offer up many more international comparisons and possible influences from foreign models. Not to mention that, with respect to the world market, forró is probably the least-circulated of the genres of national significance in Brazil, perhaps because it does not easily fit in with the hegemonic samba-bossa nova-MPB[3] constellation, nor does it have a famous ambassador like Paul Simon, who featured Olodum on one of his albums (thus shedding a spotlight more generally upon the Afro-Brazilian music of Salvador).

In the wake of dependency theory and recent theories of globalization, one has to recognize that, if a genre like forró does not seem to have relatively large global distribution, *by no means does this signify that it is not globally significant.* Its very absence, in fact, represents its global subalternity along with countless other genres. Indeed, we should always remember that there are many more poor musicians than artists with platinum records. From this vantage point we can recognize the danger inherent in cultural theory like that of Franco Moretti which relies excessively upon the concept of evolution (Moretti 1996). Evolutionary theory attempts to explain the lack of distribution in terms of the innate qualities of the work itself. From my study of forró in the context of Brazilian popular culture more generally, it appears that the qualities of this genre of music have very little to do with whether or not it is incorporated into global cultural flows. Sales are much more related to marketing, which is most skillfully achieved not by the musicians themselves, especially on the global level, but by cultural ambassadors and the categories of world music which provide space on the shelves at the record store and on websites. Much like Gonzaga partnered with professionals in the economically-dominant sector of Brazil to achieve national prominence, a partnership with a cultural entrepreneur or musician situated in a dominant capitalist country like David Byrne or Ry Cooder is necessary for genres produced by subaltern groups in subordinate regions to achieve any global recognition. This is a highly hierarchical relationship which raises the question of whether

---

[3] MPB is the acronym for *música popular brasileira*, or Brazilian pop music.

a global multitude of cultural "content producers" is presently possible. It is certainly conceivable as a utopian project, but what if we refer back to the national history of forró (discussed in Chapter One) as a test case for a real transregional, transclass alliance of musicians, one that utilizes but is not limited to the logic of the dominant economic paradigm? It appears that the possibility, if faint and living by the double-edged sword of creative freedom (which can yield both autonomous collaboration and isolation), does exist.

# Chapter One

# From Symbol to Allegory: Forró Embraces the Northeast's Heterogeneity

In this chapter I seek to trace the historical development of the genre of forró from its early days in the 1940s to the present. My focus is on the formal evolution of forró from its original, rather faddish commodification as the baião rhythm to its more complex representation of the whole of rural Northeastern culture, through the region's diverse array of coastal and interior musical genres. The theoretical underpinning for this evolution is provided by Walter Benjamin's antinomic discussion of symbol and allegory in his analysis of German Baroque tragic drama. Through Benjamin's critique of the symbol as fetish, we can appreciate the manner in which forró qua baião was mediated through the national Brazilian culture industry and commodified as a fad of authentic, regional rhythm and dance that drastically simplified and homogenized the complex realities of Northeastern social history. Yet the performers of forró, and their most loyal audiences of Northeastern natives and migrants, never entirely accepted this commodification, oriented as it was towards the national cultural center of Rio de Janeiro and its communications media that alone enabled national popularity for Brazilian musicians for much of the twentieth century. The centripetal force of the symbolic representation of forró qua baião, however, was a powerful commodification that maintained itself throughout the first decade of Northeastern popular music's foray onto the national market and into the national consciousness. It was only the gradual waning of the suprisingly long-lasting baião fad and its rather sudden displacement by bossa nova and a new generation of middle-class musicians that decisively shifted the genre of forró towards a less fetishized, more complex, allegorical representation of the Northeast as a region and a cultural collective.

By the time forró had passed its apogee in the early fifties, Northeastern forrozeiros such as Luiz Gonzaga and Jackson do Pandeiro could boast that they had truly found a place on the national stage and had even sparked some international interest in their music. Yet in the sixties they would increasingly be pushed into the background by the post-war generation of bossa nova, protest music, and Tropicália that featured young Northeastern stars of the emergent MPB (*música popular brasileira*, or Brazilian pop) musical category such as João Gilberto, Caetano Veloso, and Gilberto Gil. It is through an analysis of Luiz Gonzaga and Jackson do Pandeiro's complementary careers, as they went from boom in the late forties to bust in the late fifties to boom again around 1970, that we can best appreciate not only the ability of forró to survive the rise of other musical genres to prominence, but also its increasing ability to represent the Northeast in an allegorical fashion that reproduces a more complex, historical imaginary incorporating many more of the region's cultural commonalities and singularities. Jackson do Pandeiro helped to bring this democratization of regional representation about through his unique performative style that incorporated many musical styles and genres from the Northeast and elsewhere, in addition to his collegial and collaborative approach to music-making. Jackson was also the first forrozeiro to regularly perform with a female partner, Almira Castilho, thus taking the first steps away from the male-dominated early years of the genre.   Although Luiz Gonzaga was known by the monarchical title of King of Baião in his heyday, and often sought to shape his relationship with other forrozeiros as one between patron and client, he too was finally encouraged by the next generation to take a more collaborative approach and to allegorize the Northeastern identity he had so effectively symbolized in the more restrictive culture industry of the forties and early fifties. The post-bossa nova generation had taken over the music scene in Brazil, displacing Luiz Gonzaga as the one and only mediator of Northeastern popular music, to a position of authentic originator and inspiration. In the wake of Gonzaga's death in 1989, the genre achieved a level of diversification never seen before, to the point of developing three distinguishable subgenres: eletrônico, tradicional, and universitário. The Northeastern people represented by forró was an organic whole in the old symbolic imaginary, but today, thanks to these early symbolic efforts and the semantically centrifugal force provided by subsequent generations of artists, we can see in forró a people that embraces its heterogeneity.

**King Luiz and Baião's Apogee**

Luiz Gonzaga and Humberto Teixeira's first big hit, "Baião" (initially performed by Quatro Ases e Um Coringa in 1946), set the stage for the next decade of Northeastern music in the national culture industry based in Rio de Janeiro. Lyrically, the baião is presented as a close couple dance that may have some sort of connection to Northern or Northeastern Brazil, but is primarily a fad that will replace other dances:

I will show you
how to dance baião
And whoever wants to learn
should pay attention
*Morena*, come over here
Very close to my heart
Now just follow me
And I'll dance the baião […]

I've already danced *balancê*
*chamego*, samba and *xerém*
but the baião has something
the other dances don't have […]

Eu vou mostrá pra vocês
como se dança o baião
E quem quiser aprender
é favor prestar atenção
Morena, se chegue pra cà
bem junto ao meu coração
Agora é só me seguir
pois eu vou dançar o baião […]

Eu já dançei balancê
chamego, samba e xerém
mas o baião tem um quê
que as outras danças não têm […]
(Gonzaga and Teixeira n.d.)

The most famous lines of the song are in the first verse, and comprise a sort of "dance lesson" that interpellates the listener as the singer's feminine partner (who is also probably Afro-Brazilian, as the word *morena* tends to imply in forró). "Baião" has all the necessary elements to launch a musical fad: visual imagery (Gonzaga in his cangaceiro outfit), a unique dance, and the conviction that this genre is better than anything that has come before.

The aspirations of the song for success on the music market were fulfilled with astounding success. Through the mid fifties, baião would effectively challenge the cultural hegemony of carioca samba and become one of the most widely-circulated and performed genres of popular music in Brazil. As Mundicarmo Maria Rocha Ferretti illustrates, this was a unique moment in the history of Brazilian popular music, because baião was not just another Rio fad that would take the place of samba. This was the first time that popular music *qua regional* had achieved national recognition (Ferretti 1988, 51). With the help of Luiz Gonzaga's baião, the Northeast had found a foothold in the national imaginary that its natives, especially forrozeiros, would utilize to the fullest in subsequent years to further allegorize the region as a culturally pivotal area in Brazil, despite its relative economic poverty and its lack of political power. The song even includes some slight references to Northeastern accent, such as the dropped r's in the words "quisé" and "mostrá." Yet clearly "Baião" was only a first, symbolic step on the path toward allegorical representation, since lyrically the rhythm is being marketed as a dance fad and there is no representation of the collective of Northeasterners, nor even of the Northeast as a cultural region more generally. This one 2/4 rhythm of baião, which itself was originally the name given to a musical interlude for dueling *cantoria* guitarrists in the Northeast, had to stand in for (and above) all of the region's rich culture and history. It had to serve as a semantically centripetal symbol at the time since this was the only way the Northeast could effectively be commodified and find an initially small space for itself in the pantheon of national Brazilian cultural production.

By the time Luiz Gonzaga released "Tudo é baião," penned in partnership with Zé Dantas and recorded in 1952, the baião had practically achieved a life of its own, while still being intimately associated with "The King," Gonzaga. As the song details, the rhythm had become so successful a fad that people had started questioning its origins in the putatively backwards region of the Northeast, assuming that the master accordionist and singer Gonzaga had just invented it himself with his collaborators:

I will show you
Where the baião comes from […]

They're saying the baião is an invention
Whoever says this was never in my sertão

To see the blind men singing in this rhythm
And the guitarist, improvising with baião

The accordionists [...]
They play baião there in the forró [...]

In my land, everything is baião [...]

Eu vou mostrar pra vocês
Donde é que vem o baião [...]

Andam dizendo que o baião é invenção
Quem disse isso nunca foi no meu sertão
Pra ver [os] cego nesse ritmo cantando
E o violeiro, no baião improvisando

Os sanfoneiro [...]
Toca baião lá no forró [...]
Na minha terra, tudo é baião [...]
(Gonzaga and Dantas qtd in Ramalho 2000, 125)

The first lines of the song are clearly a reference back to Gonzaga and
Teixeira's song "Baião," discussed above. Yet the focus has changed from
demonstrating how to dance to the faddish rhythm to tracing the cultural
roots of the emergent regional genre, or "where the baião comes from." The
song goes on to paint a picture of a few of the traditional cultural referents of
the Northeast, including the blind troubadours found at markets and festivals
and the notorious bandit Lampião. The third verse then maps Northeastern
space much more clearly than in "Baião," with a list of place names from the
states of Alagoas, Ceará, Pernambuco, and Paraíba. The lyricists clearly find
it important to stress, in response to the incredible national popularity of
baião, that this music is not merely a strategically marketed fad produced by
the culture industry. In fact, it is a region rich in culture and history and even
its music alone cannot be adequately represented by the one rhythm of baião.
Yet ultimately, the assumption behind the song is that this one symbol, baião,
is capable of mediating the complexity of Northeastern people and their
culture for the rest of the Brazilian nation. In the words of the song, "in my
land, everything is baião." Of course, the ability of this symbol to express an
open series of Northeastern cultural referents is belied by the very necessity
of writing a song to let fans know that baião is not just an invention of Luiz

Gonzaga and his cohorts.

Another work called "Baião Grã-fino," recorded about three years later in 1955, reveals a certain preoccupuation over the possible alienation of the commodified baião (and by extension of Luiz Gonzaga himself) from the lived realities of Northeasterners:

> [...] Ai, ai, Baião, you conquered!
> But in the sertão no one forgot you
> Ai, ai, Baião, ai, follow your destiny!
> You already grew up, already forgot us
> Became so high falutin'

> [...] Ai, ai, Baião, você venceu!
> Mas no sertão ninguém lhe esqueceu
> Ai, ai, Baião, ai, siga seu destino!
> Você já cresceu, já nos esqueceu
> Ficou tão grã-fino
> (Gonzaga and Valentim n.d.)

The idea in the narrative of this song, that the Northeast remembers the baião but the baião does not remember the Northeast, is a fairly accurate portrayal of the semantic relationship established between signifier and signified in the field of regional cultural production during the forties and fifties. The fact that he recorded this song demonstrates that Gonzaga, at least to some degree, recognized the limitations of the baião symbol and its relative ineffectiveness with respect both to musically transporting Northeasterners in the diaspora back to the sertão, and to translating the sertão to the rest of the nation. Yet Gonzaga remained the King of Baião, and gladly played the role of king-maker for younger, lesser known forrozeiros.

If we take a closer look at Luiz Gonzaga's career more generally, as well as that of the other big name of the early years of forró, Jackson do Pandeiro, we can more fully realize the nature of forró's early symbolization and the subsequent beginnings of an allegorical approach to representing the Northeast. Gonzaga forced his way onto the national stage not only with the baião rhythm and dance, but with a bandit costume akin to that of his childhood hero, Lampião (mentioned in "Tudo é baião" as representative of the Northeast and its music). Bandits, or cangaceiros, are said to have developed one of forró's major musical subgenres, the *xaxado*. After seeing another performer, Pedro Raimundo, in the costume of *gaúcho* cowboys from Southern Brazil, Gonzaga hit upon the idea of dressing up like a cowboy of the Northeast, with a cangaceiro hat to recall the antihero Lampião. Gonzaga at first met with some resistance to his attempt to stylize himself as a traditional Northeastern singer. He had previously made his name as an accordion player in the early forties who played a variety of non-Northeastern genres popular at the time such as polkas and waltzes. But the accordionist then made a conscious effort to portray the Northeast through costume, rhythm and lyrics. Of course, a cangaceiro uniform, like the baião rhythm with regard to music, cannot but be a symbol that portrays the Northeast while hiding whatever people and places that do not correspond to that symbol, be they areas and workers outside the sertão, or Northeastern women more generally.

As Luiz Gonzaga became a national star, he accepted his title of King of Baião and in his relations with other musicians seemed to evoke some of this monarchic bearing. He saw fit to deem what was Northeastern music and what was not, and liked to help young musicians grow famous under his own tutelage and aegis. He assembled a group of musical royalty and nobility around him including a "queen," "baron," "prince" and "princess" of baião (Dreyfus 1996, 169, 172, 196). Rather than being primarily about his own ego, although this was probably involved, Gonzaga played the part of king and patron of forró because this type of symbolism is what he understood to be necessary to successfully commodify and circulate Northeastern culture. For it was not until Gonzaga developed the powerfully symbolic imagery and performance of the cangaceiro uniform and the baião rhythm/dance that Northeastern musicians began to be able to have professional careers as such. Gonzaga's relationship with Jackson do Pandeiro is illustrative of how he positioned himself as symbolic mediator of baião and forró during his career's apogee and also throughout its decade-long fall from national popularity in the sixties. To understand this relationship a little better, though, we must first consider some of the distinctions between these two artists' career paths as professional forrozeiros.

**Another King: Jackson do Pandeiro**

As detailed in Fernando Moura and Antônio Vicente's definitive biography, Jackson do Pandeiro did not go directly to the center of the hegemonic national culture industry in Rio de Janeiro to begin his professional career like Luiz Gonzaga did (Moura and Vicente 2001). Jackson's first involvement with the media of mass communication was as part of the cast of a radio station in Paraíba's capital, João Pessoa. Here he was allowed to perform in a two-man comedy act with a lyricist he would later write many songs with, Rosil Cavalcanti. Although comedic, the act also demonstrated the type of representations of the rural Northeast that were deemed acceptable at the time, as Cavalcanti and Jackson dressed up as two *matutos* or hicks and the jokes were accordingly related to their ignorance and backwardness vis-à-vis the cosmopolitan coastal cities. Thereafter he was soon recruited to become a member of both an orchestra and of a smaller band on the Northeast's biggest station at the time, Rádio Jornal do Commércio in Recife, Pernambuco. Once installed in Recife, Jackson's unique performance style and stunningly agile vocals gained attention and he was featured as a performer in a duet with his future wife, Almira Castilho. Jackson's signature genre of popular music was the *coco*, native to the littoral sugar plantation regions of the Northeast, however he also performed baião and various other forró subgenres and rhythms. In fact, it was during the apogee of Jackson do Pandeiro's career during the mid to late fifties that forró began to be recognized as a diversified genre encompassing many Northeastern musical rhythms and styles as it is today. The contemporaneous success of Jackson and the birth of forró as a genre indicate how Jackson do Pandeiro's performance style, his collaborative approach to music-making, and his ability and willingness to play percussion and sing to any rhythm in Brazil helped to displace the baião as major cultural symbol of the Northeast and to shift cultural producers like himself, Gonzaga, and many forrozeiros towards a more differentiated, allegorical representation of the region. As he would say in 1981 after forró had entered a more allegorical stage, "I invented forró [...] when, during a recording session, I ordered that the guitar play choro, the cavaquinho samba and the bumbo play baião" (Moura and Vicente 2001, 369). Clearly, baião would become just one of many rhythms under the rubric of forró, and even rhythms and genres that are not exclusively Northeastern like samba would be admitted or at least claimed as influences.

The allegorical shift in forró will be discussed in detail below, however we must first consider how Jackson was envisioned in the culture industry prior to the achievement of that shift. Despite his fame as a performer of coco, for years Jackson was not really seen as a performer of Northeastern music, baião, or forró as such. Rather, in Recife he was seen as a great sambista, on par with the famed musicians on Rio radio stations. Later when he was performing in Rio itself, Jackson was often portrayed in the media as an authentic matuto from the Northeast, but because he had his own personal style and did not imitate Gonzaga's cangaceiro attire, which had become symbolic of the Northeast, Jackson was viewed more as a great, authentic Northeastern sambista along the lines of Bezerra da Silva. He did what carioca musicians did, and did it well, but he was not seen as a co-progenitor of the regional musical movement over which Gonzaga reigned as king. When he was eventually crowned a "king" by the media, it was not as king of any Northeastern genre but rather as "O Rei do Ritmo," the King of Rhythm, thanks to his amazing skills with percussion instruments, especially with the *pandeiro* or tambourine from which he received his epithet. At that point in time, Jackson do Pandeiro was valued most highly as an extremely skilled and multi-talented entertainer, rather than as a representative of a subaltern region and people.

Luiz Gonzaga helped to maintain the relative lack of identification of Jackson with baião and Northeastern regional music by calling the pandeirista's music "samba de sanfona [accordion samba]." This characterization shocked famous Pernambucan percussionist Naná Vasconcelos, who must have found Gonzaga's implied exclusion of samba from the regular repertoire of the accordion rather hypocritical since the famed sanfonista himself had played many a samba and *choro* (a related carioca genre) on his preferred instrument (Moura and Vicente 2001, 330). It seems very likely that Gonzaga's need to call Jackson's music something other than "baião" or "forró" was a means of clearly staking out the territory of the symbolic realm of popular culture over which he ruled. Jackson was doing something quite different, which would eventually help to expand the boundaries of the genre and make it more flexible and open to innovation. This flexibility would lead to the diversity of today's forró, much more an allegory of the true complexity of the Northeast than a simplifying, coherent symbol. Gonzaga was understandably still holding tight to the power of the symbol he had created—viz. the baião and its related imagery and dance— which had given him and other Northeastern regional musicians a previously unheard of level of access to the national culture industry. Nevertheless Jackson do Pandeiro, by identifying himself with forró through such television shows as *O Forró de Jackson* and various Rio de Janeiro-based radio shows, would circumvent the exclusive symbolism of baião and help prepare the shift of the genre to allegorical representation.

## From Crisis to Allegory: Forró's Resurgence

In the fifties, both Gonzaga and Jackson's stardom would reach a peak and start to wane (Gonzaga's sooner since his peak was a few years earlier). Times were changing, and the bossa nova generation was just around the corner. Getúlio Vargas, perhaps Brazil's greatest populist leader and an enthusiastic supporter of Luiz Gonzaga's regionalist approach to popular culture (as he had been of carioca samba in the 1930s), had committed suicide. He had been replaced by Juscelino Kubitschek, whose developmentalist plans for import substitution and rapid industrialization were more appropriate to the sophisticated, middle-class "poetry for export" aspirations of bossa nova. Bossa nova arose out of the same Rio de Janeiro culture industry that the baião had utilized so effectively a decade earlier. It not only captivated the Brazilian middle class, but also reached larger audiences in North America and Europe than any Brazilian genre before it or since. In hindsight it seems inevitable that the baião fell from grace for those with the most purchasing power, the middle-class aficionados of bossa nova. As a symbol of the Northeast in a time when rapid industrialization was seen as paramount, the baião carried the negative association of the poverty and slow economic development of the region relative to the Southeast. In contrast, bossa nova was the "new sound" that had little or no regional associations despite the fact that one of its progenitors, João Gilberto, was Bahian. Thus the sound track to much of the Brazilian sixties would be bossa nova, not baião. But the resulting hard times on the national cultural market for baião would not spell the end of the genre, rather they became an opportunity for regeneration after which Northeastern music would reemerge on the national stage as forró, an allegory of the region and all its classes, genders, and generations dispersed throughout Brazil.

Before analyzing this reemergence in detail, we should consider the relevance of Walter Benjamin's concept of allegory for the historical shift from baião to forró. Benjamin discusses allegory most thoroughly in his 1925 writings on the German Baroque tragic drama, titled *Ursprung des deutschen Trauerspiels*. He describes allegory, in contrast to the symbol, as maintaining a primacy of thingliness (*Dinghaften*) over the personal (*Perso-*

Figure 1.1: Pernambuco forró vocalist Santanna O Cantador
shows off his traditional Northeastern pack

Figure 1.2: A typical forró trio performs with accordion, steel
triangle and *zabumba* drum on Calhetas beach in Pernambuco

*nalen*) and of the fragment (*Bruchstücks*) over the whole (*Totalen*). This rather materialist critique of transcendent subjects or totalities is contrasted with the symbol and the desire that shapes it, viz. "the will to symbolic totality" (Benjamin 1991, 362). Benjamin provides the example of humanism's image of man as an expression of this will. The perfect coherency and unified instrumentality of the healthy human body mirror that of any powerful symbol. On the other hand, Benjamin tells us, an allegorical hermeneutic approach to the same phenomenon, such as Winckelmann's "Description of the Torso of Hercules in the Belvedere of Rome," goes through the body piece by piece, part by part, not assuming a coherent and hierarchic structure and thus displacing any will to symbolic totality that might be derived from the intent of the artist or his/her specific artistic and cultural context (Benjamin 1991, 352). From a historical perspective, allegory involves sifting through the ruins of the past in order to combine fragments into a new structure that does not unite them into a whole but rather exceeds ancient harmonies *in its destroyed or ruinous state* (*Zerstörung*). To rephrase this in other Benjaminian terminology, redemption of the past is carried out by collecting ruinous forms, but with no intent of assembling a "complete" collection. The law of allegory, Benjamin states, is collection and dispersal: "things are brought together according to their meaning; lack of a shared existence [*Dasein*] scatters them again" (Benjamin 1991, 364). This method of collection assumes an open series of assembled forms unfettered by any structure that would prevent the addition of more forms to destabilize the coherence of the assemblage. No fragment or group of fragments can be privileged above the others as representative of the totality, and thus such an assemblage can open itself up to the subaltern moment. When introduced into this ruinous system, the unrepresented or excluded fragment can cause a kaleidoscopic shift in the assemblage.

Returning to the case of Northeastern music, it is clear that in the early years of baião on the national stage, Luiz Gonzaga's will to symbolic totality was the driving force behind the genre's phenomenal success. His assemblage of Northeastern popular culture was dominated by the imagery of the cangaceiro, the rhythm and dance of the baião, and the traditionally masculinist gender politics of the Northeastern *vaqueiro* (cowboy) or tenant farmer. It was from this gendered perspective that Gonzaga also portrayed the sufferings of the Northeasterners in the face of drought and their subsequent trials and tribulations when forced by the harsh climate and the underdevelopment of the region to migrate, in songs such as "Asa Branca [White Wing]," "A Triste Partida [The Sad Departure]," and "Pau de Arara"[1]. Most essential to the baião as symbol, though, was an easily recognized figure like Gonzaga in his cangaceiro outfit and a danceable rhythm, both marked by the folksy authenticity of symbolic regionalism. As noted above, Jackson do Pandeiro departed somewhat from Gonzaga's symbolism and helped to begin a shift towards allegorical self-representation of Northeasterners and their region. Towards the end of the fifties Marinês had begun to make a name for herself as the first woman to lead a forró band, thus taking the first few steps in extending the genre beyond its male-dominated discourse and imagery. Yet it was the post-bossa nova generation of musicians that finally dethroned the symbol of baião from its centripetal semantic position, pulling it out of the symbolic totality that had been created by Gonzaga and his collaborators via the national recording industry and mass communications media in the forties and fifties.

The mere fact that the baião was no longer trendy in the sixties helped to begin to destabilize it as a coherent symbol of the Northeast. Gonzaga himself left the cities of the Southeast where he had been "King" and spent most of his time during these years touring through the Northeast and in other areas with many Northeastern residents. He never lost his popularity among people from the region, and their loyalty sustained him and also eventually yielded a new generation of forrozeiros in the seventies. Also significant is Gonzaga's interaction with people throughout the region in his many travels of those years, which must have reminded him vividly and repeatedly of the real referents and protagonists of his music. Regarding the new generation, though, Gonzaga was initially somewhat skeptical. In the song "Xote dos Cabeludos," he sings sarcastically about the "long-haired ones" who do not belong in "the sertão of his godfather" (Dreyfus 1996, 239). According to Dominique Dreyfus, with this song Gonzaga hit rock bottom. He could only rise again with the help of the very generation he was mocking.

---

[1] This song's title, literally "macaw branch," references the nickname given to the primitive seating in the large pick-up trucks in which migrants would often emigrate from the Northeast.

## Luiz, Jackson and the Next Generation

Luckily, they were for the most part happy to oblige. When Gonzaga was moved by Caetano Veloso's version of his own classic "Asa Branca," recorded in exile in London, the old forrozeiro began to have second thoughts about his distaste for hippies. Clearly, new approaches could be taken to forró and the music could work in entirely different, even international, cultural contexts. Other musicians like Geraldo Vandré, who also recorded a version of "Asa Branca," saw Gonzaga as a precursor of protest music. Gonzaga's estranged son, Gonzaguinha, also saw the song "Vozes da seca [Voices from the Drought]" in this light, although he criticized some of Gonzaga's propagandistic songs like "A Marcha da Petrobras [The Petrobras March]," which praises the state-owned oil company (Echeverria 2006, 200). For Vandré and Gonzaguinha's generation, Gonzaga's critique of poverty and drought in the Northeast was an indirect means of criticizing the oppressiveness of the military dictatorship. In general, Luiz Gonzaga represented a sort of folk authenticity to the post-bossa, hippie generation, and thanks to their praise and support he was able to come back into the national limelight to some degree.

This return to fame made Gonzaga begin to see young popular musicians like Tropicalists Gilberto Gil and Caetano Veloso, as well as his own son Gonzaguinha, as knowledgeable vis-à-vis the trends of the record industry and mass media. By performing for and with members of this generation, Gonzaga was willing to allow his music to become associated with the democratic resistance to the dictatorship, thus displacing his baião from its coherent, regionalist symbolism. This was no small step for Gonzaga, since his political views had never been anti-government. Gonzaga had spoken kind words about the military regime as a former soldier, and had even performed for one of the regime's leaders, President Castelo Branco (Echeverria 2006, 199). In any case, the flexibility to produce forró in the context of the youth culture of the 1970s signalled that Gonzaga's own symbolic imagery and discourse were no longer completely central to the genre; forró could be performed as part of a political and cultural movement of a younger generation that did not want to forget the roots of Brazilian culture in the subaltern populations and their folklore. Thus even as he began to adjust his own views on musical collaboration, Gonzaga was being displaced as the prime mediator of the genre to the role of authentic originator and muse.

Besides Gil and Veloso, a whole group of Northeastern musicians, many from Gonzaga's native state of Pernambuco, would make a name for themselves in the seventies, carrying on and expanding Gonzaga's project as well as that of Jackson do Pandeiro. These artists included Elba Ramalho, Alceu Valença, Quinteto Violado, Zé Ramalho, Dominguinhos, and Fagner, among others. Many of these musicians would become consecrated along with Gonzaga as stars of "MPB," the acronym for Brazilian pop music consumed faithfully by the middle class. They have helped to make forró the diverse allegory of the Northeast that it is today. Along with his strengthening of ties to the younger generation, Gonzaga also approached Jackson do Pandeiro in 1972 to perform on the weekly forró show Jackson hosted at the time on the radio in Rio. For the first time, Gonzaga found himself in the position of needing a favor from a fellow forrozeiro rather than handing them out. Thus the two great progenitors of *sertanejo* (meaning from the sertão) and littoral forró reached a détente, and Gonzaga implicitly accepted Jackson's style as a legitimate alternative to his own within the genre. In addition to some help from his old rival Jackson, the historical significance of Gonzaga's work was emphasized by some of the performers mentioned above, such as Valença and Elba Ramalho. These forrozeiros would not only introduce Gonzaga and Jackson's repertoires to vast new audiences of the younger generation, but also emphasize the importance of the two as representatives of the Northeastern people and their history, including their subaltern culture. Ramalho continues to do so, as can be seen in her recent album and concert tour entitled *Elba Canta Luiz* (2002).

For his part, Jackson do Pandeiro was always very enthusiastic about the new generation of forrozeiros. He took many opportunities during interviews in the seventies and eighties to highlight their efforts and achievements. For instance, in 1977 he told the magazine *Amiga*:

> There are many things to be exploited in terms of folklore. We are very rich. All this richness needs to be very well disseminated so that all of Brazil sings. There are many new singers who are on our side, like Zé Ramalho, Amelinha, Alceu Valença, Fagner. The radio stations don't need to play foreign songs, they have to value that which is ours. The young people are demanding and the means of communication will obey, because there is no lack of interest from them. (Moura and Vicente 2001, 355)

In 1981, Jackson told the daily *Folha de São Paulo*:

> These young people are marvelous, they want their own things. And they don't
> content themselves with inferior things. They want to know what is theirs. This is
> right. We are the proprietors of more than fifteen original rhythms and few can
> distinguish between a samba and a coco. (Ibid., 354)

Clearly, Jackson wanted subsequent generations to delve as deeply into the popular musical traditions of the Northeast and the rest of Brazil as he had, with the aim of maintaining the living tradition of Brazilian music. In his reference to foreign songs, Jackson also brings up the issue of the liberalization of the Brazilian economy and the opening up of the recording industry to multinational corporations and of the mass media to international, particularly North American, music. In this context, forró found a new relevance as "roots" music, and the forró night clubs in the large cities, called *casas de forró*, became the popular Brazilian alternative to discotheques. In the case of these clubs, it is certainly true that the means of communication have met the demand for music inspired by the rich folkloric culture of Brazil, and continue to do so. A new generation of these clubs in Northeastern cities, São Paulo, Rio de Janeiro, and elsewhere opened in the nineties and continue in popularity to the present day.

Jackson do Pandeiro went even further than public support in his interviews for the next generation of forrozeiros, though, by participating on many of their own albums as a percussionist, many times with very little fanfare. Moura and Vicente list a few of these selfless collaborations:

> Clara Nunes, Wanderléia, Dominguinhos, Beth Carvalho, Elba Ramalho, Alceu
> Valença, Gilberto Gil, Bezerra da Silva, Jair Rodrigues, Raul Seixas, Geraldo
> Azevedo, João do Vale...There were dozens of participations of Jackson on others'
> records, just as a percussionist, or assuming the artistic direction or production of
> forrozeiros. (Moura and Vicente 2001, 334)

Jackson's biographers go on to state that this type of collaboration was often as shocking for the artists for whom Jackson was working as if João Gilberto was just playing guitar or Tom Jobim just piano on their album. I would call this approach *allegorical-multitudinous*, in that it supports an allegorical representation of the Northeast that is itself produced through egalitarian relationships between forrozeiros. The old relationship, in contrast, would have to be identified as *symbolic-patronizing*. The symbolic-patronizing paradigm is the model that Gonzaga utilized as King of Baião in order to force his way into the national market. The word force is key here—a certain symbolic violence or musical militarism was necessary in order to displace the hegemony of *samba carioca* (carioca meaning from Rio de Janeiro) in the mass media. The recognition of this necessity for hierarchic discipline was reflected, for instance, in the moniker of Marinês and her first band. In the late fifties, they were known as Luiz Gonzaga's "shock troops" (Dreyfus 1996, 194-196).

As noted above, though, Gonzaga himself was shifting to the allegorical-multitudinous paradigm of cultural production in the seventies. His attitude towards innovation in his own music and collaboration with the younger generation, however, remained somewhat ambivalent in that decade. This ambivalence seems to have found its roots in Gonzaga's consciousness, despite common regional origins, of a class distinction between himself and the largely university-educated group of forrozeiros that was on its rise to fame:

> These youths that are coming up have a lot of agility in unfolding, creating new styles, arriving closer and closer to modern things. They are renovators. Now, I have the necessity of continuing with that which I always created. I am a conserver. Those poorer ones, the manual laborers, the workers are closer to me and they feel themselves capable of imitating me. They will never reach these youths, who are in front of everything, reaching other classes, more developed, more evolved. Even so, they appreciate my work and they are the first to advise me not to change. So I won't change anything, and I will continue as myself. (Dreyfus 1996, 277)

It is important to note here that Gonzaga's hesitant attitude towards innovation is based, according to the musician himself, in a desire not to alienate his music from the subaltern population from which it stems. We should recall that Gonzaga had spent much of the previous decade on the road, touring the small towns, hamlets, and peripheral urban neighborhoods of the very workers he mentions here. Not to mention the fact that Gonzaga's father, Januário, was himself one of these workers as well as a renowned sanfoneiro in the Cariri region.

Gonzaga's attitude towards innovation in his music at this point was reflected in his major "come-back" concert in 1972, entitled *Luiz Gonzaga Volta pra Curtir* [Luiz Gonzaga Back For Good]. Gonzaga was perfectly content to play for an audience of young leftist members of the opposition to the military dictatorship, thereby associating himself and his work with their cause. He would even praise the leftist organization for the development of the Northeast, Sudene, during a later concert with his son Gonzaguinha. His performance in 1972 was received with great acclaim by the young audience, however it comprised solely a review of his classic repertoire, as opposed to new, innovative compositions. In the eighties Gonzaga would have a prolific partnership with songwriter João Silva and would collaborate with younger musicians like Elba Ramalho and Fagner to release some big hits, but he was slower than Jackson do Pandeiro in coming to the point of being able to subsume his own creative process in the new allegorical-multitudinous paradigm of cultural production.

Gonzaga's concert with his formerly estranged son in 1981, *Gonzagão e Gonzaguinha—A Vida do Viajante*, was a key step in completing his departure from the symbolic-patronizing production of the baião years. He and his son were on equal footing in the concert, performing some of the best songs of each musician and also reformulating some of both of their works so as to perform them as duets. Gonzaga had never before performed with a primarily pop (MPB) musician like his son, either, and thus was demonstrating a new level of flexibility. Furthermore, on the album produced from the concert Gonzaga incorporated the *causos* or humorous stories about quotidian Northeastern life that he would sometimes intersperse between his songs during performances, such as "Karolina com K [Karolina with a K]" and "Apologia ao Jumento [Apologia for the Mule]." Storytelling was a way of further diversifying the imagery he presented of the sertão, thus contributing further to the allegorization of forró. Finally, by this time Gonzaga was never wearing the full leather cangaceiro outfit that he wore back in the fifties, and only sometimes wore his bandit hat. In the case of the concert with his son, he dressed very similarly to Gonzaguinha, in unornamented, relatively urban garb: white pants and a white, short-sleeved shirt with open collar. The image of the cowboy or cangaceiro was no longer central to the production of forró. Gonzaga also demonstrated his openness to the evolution of the genre in his appreciation of the modern production values of the *Gonzagão and Gonzaguinha* concert tour, commenting warmly on the "atualização de tudo [updating of everything]" under his son's management (Echeverria 2006, 202).

## Strong Lineage and a Big Tent: Forró's New Assemblages

Perhaps the best example of the transformation towards allegorical representation of the Northeast is the greatly increased performance and recording of the medley musical form called *pot-pourri*. A pot-pourri, most common in live performances (which are often recorded and then released as albums), typically incorporates many forró songs into one continous stream of music, one song blending smoothly into the next. Nowadays, these pot-pourris are performed by virtually every forrozeiro at some point or another. I consider this form allegorical-multitudinous because it incorporates a diverse array of forró songs without any master narrative or symbol to unite them into a coherent whole. At the same time, any forrozeiro can sing a pot-pourri, and he or she can incorporate virtually any song into the mix, even including works outside the genre of forró. Most commonly, however, forró pot-pourris are a selection of canonical works that the forrozeiro in question can string together in unique ways. Of course, there is the danger of crass commercialization of this song form, which certainly does occur. But the ability to easily produce pot-pourris is really just a sign of how democratic the form is in terms of its accessibility to a large number of professional and amateur forrozeiros, including the workers and manual laborers Gonzaga speaks of so loyally.

In the wake of Luiz Gonzaga's death in 1989, it can only be said that the genre he played such an integral part in formulating has reached a new stage of diversification. It is as if, to use Benjamin's terms, Gonzaga's career offered the last vestige of shared existence for forrozeiros throughout Brazil, who have now scattered and come together again in new assemblages. These can be grouped into three main subgenres—viz. *forró tradicional, forró eletrônico,* and *forró universitário,* all discussed in detail in the following chapters. The production of the three major subgenres of forró will be analyzed in diverse contexts, such as that of diasporic affect, psychological resistance, and the changing same of vital tradition. But these three subgenres must always be thought out vis-à-vis the initial symbolism of baião and its subsequent allegorization over the course of the first two generations of forrozeiros. For despite the great diversification of the genre, all the assemblages of forró today continue to trace their roots back to the canon established by Luiz Gonzaga, Jackson do Pandeiro, and their collaborators.

# Chapter Two

## Saudade as Diasporic Affect: Forró and Northeastern Nostalgia

Saudade is a profound feeling and a complex cultural phenomenon. It has been expressed and examined frequently in Brazilian art, since long before the beginnings of forró as a popular genre. The word has no equivalent in English and for this reason has recently been incorporated into the English language by the Oxford English Dictionary. Generally speaking, saudade is a yearning for something, someone or somewhere that is distant in time or space or has been irretrievably lost. It is backward-looking, but always involves a bleeding of the past into the present, a reliving of past joys through memory that has grown bittersweet. The desiring subject of saudade is in much the same position as Walter Benjamin's famous angel of history, assuming the angel believes there is something of value to be salvaged from the wreckage of the past. While looking back upon the past in ruins, the angel sees things she loves among the wreckage, but she inexorably continues to be propelled forward by historical progress. Whatever the angel feels, be it horror or apathy or something else, we can be sure she must feel saudade. The pain caused us by something that is out of reach as we attempt to recover it; a tantalizing suffering.

All these aspects of saudade have been thoroughly explored in poetry, song, literature and elsewhere but forró itself makes a unique contribution to the artistic expression of this phenomenon. There is no other cultural production that so effectively *collectivizes* this yearning or nostalgia. Through this collectivization, essentially of the proletarian desire for a threatened or lost way of life, saudade is lifted out of the confines of individual affect and up into the realm of the social and even the political. While forrozeiros certainly have always sung about the suffering of being far away from one's lover and family, with only one's bittersweet memories for comfort, the implication is often that it is not just one's lover that is lacking, but an entire regional culture. This culture incorporates the rural life of the small landowner or tenant farmer and typically relies very much on visceral sensory experience of the natural environment. Rural workers' strong affective ties to the sertão have historical roots that can be traced back to at least the nineteenth century when many slaves escaped the coastal plantations or were let go during stagnant periods of the sugar industry and headed for the relative freedom of the interior to become subsistence or cotton farmers, day laborers, cowboys, ranchers, etc. (Davis 2002, 385).

Thus through comparison with enslavement on the coastal plantations, life in the sertão, an area that is often climatically and geologically inhospitable (i.e. prone to drought, lacking adequate irrigation, and generally covered with nutrient-poor soil), became identified with freedom, autonomy, and redemption from the horrors of slavery. Even taking into account the dominance of the local bosses or *coronéis* in the backlands, this was a region with a much looser hegemony of elites over workers than in the plantations where masters maintained constant supervision and surveillance over their slaves. When invoked in forró lyrics, the natural world of the sertão serves to reinforce both personal ties and the common experiences of all poor Northeasterners, especially those who have been forced to leave the former promised land of their home region over the last half-century for radically different urban environments. Songs about saudade express the desire to share sadness and lessen pain through commiseration, and also can serve the function of modeling how best to transcend, if only momentarily, the pain experienced by many migrants in exile from their idyllic Northeastern past. As the sertão once redeemed those escaping from slavery, now it again becomes a space and an imaginary of redemption for those who were forced into exile by the combination of drought and economic marginalization, and who hope one day to return to their native region when it finally receives the long-awaited replenishing rains.

**Material Saudade: Evoking the Presence of Nature in the Sertão**

To explore the ways in which saudade is both analyzed and expressed by forrozeiros, one must consider lyrics on a range of themes. One song which emphasizes sensory experience of the Northeastern region's natural environment is Nanado Alves and Ilmar Cavalcante's "Cheiro de nós." The song's title, which translates as "Our Scent," may sound rather incongruous with a love song to outsiders' ears but expresses both the great importance of sensorial memory in evoking the presence of the Northeast, and the collectivity of this experience. The composition is filled with Proustian scents that help the world of the sertão to materialize before the audience. The smell of the earth after the rain is tied to a memory of a son yelling to his father who is bringing the cattle home to be corralled. The smell of a fire burning in the stove and of an orange tree leads to the remembrance of the girls who gathered beneath the tree in the afternoon to watch the sunset. These smells then lead to more metaphorical smells of passion, love, and then the trope of an orange sun that "insists upon not setting." Clearly the songwriters are attempting to create a certain timelessness within the world of associations based in sensorial memories. A scent, something that might be quite ephemeral, is solidified through its placement within a context of related images and scents, until the midpoint of the song when the narrative is entirely caught up within the eternal, idyllic afternoon in the sertão.

None of the people and places mentioned are specifically identified, thus making it all the more easy for the listener to associate his or her own specific place of origin in the Northeast with the singer's description. It is a sign of the subtlety of the lyrics that they are able to encourage such general identification without losing the feeling of intimacy in the narrative's perspective. The penultimate verse features one smell, that of the "morena" (dark-skinned/haired woman) who is the singer's love interest. She is compared to a white lily, which of course evokes a very specific scent as well as beautiful natural imagery. In this verse, the songwriters are able to create a clear space within memory in which the pair of lovers can interact, using very simple descriptive language (essentially just two nouns and a verb beyond the lily epithet). The lovers danced at a forró in the sertão, in the "sala de reboco [white-washed room]" of a "casa de caboclo [country peasant's home]." This space makes it very clear that the singer is from a rustic, rural community where dances take place in simple adobe cottages (see Chapter Seven, Fig. 7.1 for an image of such a cottage). The owner of the house is a caboclo, which is a racial mixture unique to the Northeastern interior and the North, usually with emphasis on indigenous and Portuguese heritage with perhaps some African. As with many racial signifiers, caboclo situates the homeowner within a class as well—in this case the peasant class at the base of the rural economy.

The final verse encapsulates in the "cheiro de saudade," which in this case is a scent of nostalgic remembrance, all of the previous odors mentioned within the song. The singer tells us that the scent of saudade is one

[...] That in truth will never leave me
Has been with me since I was a boy
Accompanies my destiny
Thus makes me so happy

[...] Que na verdade nunca vai sair de mim
Anda comigo desde o tempo de menino
Acompanha o meu destino
Me faz tão feliz assim
(Alves and Cavalcante n.d.)

Here saudade is associated with the innocence of childhood memories and the carefree happiness found in the simple pleasures of the singer's youth. These pure beginnings are expanded to symbolize a chain of events that are characterized as the subject's destiny or fate. Thus in this particular song, saudade is not so much a desire to retrieve something the singer is lacking, but rather functions to call up all of the beautiful memories in the singer's life as easily as one catches the scent of the earth or a flower. As a final note, it bears mentioning that the singer in the recording I am analyzing is Santanna O Cantador (see Chapter One, Fig. 1.1), whose voice sounds much like that of Luiz Gonzaga in timbre and phrasing. This metalyrical association with the most important forrozeiro also encourages the listener to experience a saudade for forró's glorious past when Gonzaga's career was at its apogee.

Ultimately, the example of "Cheiro de Nós" demonstrates not only saudade but a sometimes opposing tendency within forró's discourse that emphasizes communal celebration and personal relationships in the present. This latter tendency corresponds more to a presentation of the direct experience of life in the Northeast, one that would be most characteristic of non-migrant residents of the region. The celebration of communal gatherings and festivities emphasizes the vivacity and movement of forró's rhythms and dance movements, placing the listener within the dance hall or rural home as the events described in the lyrics unfold. The immediacy of the narrative can also be seen in portions of certain songs featuring saudade, such as "Cheiro de Nós," since the nostalgia often functions to evoke vivid memories that transport the singer and listener into the past. The past is thus made present, and one is forced to realize the poverty of any definition of popular tradition that does not recognize its vitality and its contemporaneity with modernity.[1] "No meu pé de serra [At my foot of the mountain]", a song written by Luiz Gonzaga and Humberto Teixeira, develops a more poignant sense of saudade but also clearly demonstrates the ability of nostalgia to bring the past into the present (Gonzaga and Teixeira n.d.). It is also an example of forrozeiros' recognition of the profound importance of music in this task of alleviating the pain of spatio-temporal separation. The song was first recorded by Gonzaga in November 1946 and is firmly established within the forró canon. The lyrics begin with the word "lá," there, which immediately places the backlands setting in the high sertão at a distance from the singer's perspective. The singer reveals that he has left his heart at the "foot of the mountain," a trope for the rural interior of the sertão. This naturally leads him to have profound "saudades" for his beloved home, and in the next line he sings of his decision to return there, "to my sertão." So a distance from the sertão is established in time and space, a distance which produces saudade and the desire to "kill saudade," as the popular expression goes. The singer says that he will return to the sertão to kill his saudade, but having sung this, the lyrics then shift to the imperfect tense to describe life the way it used to be there, at the foot of the mountain. An ambiguity is established by this transition between actually returning to the sertão and returning there in memory through music, specifically forró. This ambiguity is only reinforced by the remainder of the lyrics. After describing how although he had to work hard on his piece of land, he had everything he could want, the singer recalls the musical gatherings in the sertão. The lyrics then explain to the listener that there used to be dances every Thursday featuring sanfona (presumably the eight-button accordion that rural musicians like Gonzaga's father played), and *xote* (a rhythm originally derived from the German *Schottische* folk dance) was played all night.

The mentioning of xote leads to the final section of the song, colored by another transition in verb tense to the present. The present tense underlines what is evident from the lyrics, that singing about the sertão is more than just an artistic endeavor, it is also a means of bringing everyday life in that region into the collective consciousness of Northeasterners in exile. Since Luiz Gonzaga had a project of introducing Northeastern music to the rest of the

---

[1] I expand upon this line of thought at length in Chapter Seven.

country, the description of xote here also serves the didactic purpose of demonstrating a Northeastern musical genre to Brazil:

> […] The xote is good [clap clap]
> To dance [clap clap]
> We stick to the cabocla without fail
> One step there [clap clap]
> Another here [clap clap]
> While the accordion is playing,
> Weeping, crying,
> Whimpering, complaining without stopping

> […] O xote é bom
> De se dançar
> A gente gruda na caboca sem soltar
> Um passo lá,
> Um outro cá
> Enquanto o fole tá tocando
> Tá gemendo, tá chorando
> Tá fungando, reclamando sem parar
> (Gonzaga and Teixeira n.d.)

This final section features much shorter lines than the rest of the song, separated by periodic claps on the recording. The claps emphasize collective participation in dancing the xote, and also break down the rhythm which the singer is demonstrating step by step. Gonzaga was known to call radio audience members on stage to teach them to dance to his music, as can be seen in some of the earliest video footage of his performances in the fifties. Thus it is clear that the song has shifted gears from the initial lines, which feature explicit feelings of profound saudade, expressed with longer phrases and more poignant vocal emphasis on certain key words like "pé de serra" and "saudade." The final section is very much a celebration in the moment of a certain Northeastern rhythm and dance style. The metalyrical discussion of music in the song, specifically the xote rhythm of forró, is mirrored by a (re)enactment of Northeasterners' quotidian experience of that genre through lyrical emphasis on bodily movement to the sounds of the accordion (mediated as always through Gonzaga's personal experience and his career objective of nationally marketing Northeastern music). At the same time, the telescoping of spatio-temporal distance is achieved through subtle transitions in verbal tense up to the point of a fully present dance in the final lines cited above. The power of music to kill saudade is skillfully demonstrated by bringing Northeasterners back "there," to their sertão, at the same time that the sertão is brought "here," to Rio de Janeiro where Gonzaga is performing and making the sertanejos' (that is, natives of the sertão) dance accessible to Southeasterners.

But it must be said that even in this final section of the song, in which the immediacy of dance and musical celebration are emphasized, a note of sadness remains. Luiz Gonzaga helped to make the accordion the instrument with which forrozeiros most identify, since it is the foremost (and often single) melodic instrument in forró. Gonzaga himself first made his entrance into the music industry as an accordionist and only later became a singer as well. Thus when Gonzaga sings of the accordion's weeping and crying, it is reasonable to associate these expressions of sadness with the singer himself. They are ironized somewhat by the whimpering and complaining of the accordion, but a bittersweet lyrical note remains at the song's culmination. Musically, there is nothing emphasizing this bittersweetness in the song, yet it is characteristic of saudade that even in its more wistful or happily nostalgic iterations that an underlying sadness can be detected.

As already demonstrated to some extent in my discussion of "Cheiro de Nós," the natural environment of the sertão is a profoundly important medium for forrozeiros. Through nature, they paint a picture not only of the idyllic beauty of their home region, but also of its potential productivity. The latter image helps to combat stereotypes of the Northeastern interior as a barren wasteland. The sertão suffers periodic droughts, which in the past drove many poor Northeasterners out of the region, but it can also be very beautiful and green during the rainy winter months. However, perhaps the most common trope in forró lyrics is to metaphorically associate nature with the lover whom the singer left behind in the Northeast. All of these elements can be found in the baião entitled "Minha Fulô" first recorded in November 1954 by Luiz Gonzaga, who wrote it in partnership with fellow Northeasterner Zé Dantas (Gonzaga and Dantas n.d.). "Minha Fulô" means "my flower" in the dialect of the sertão ("fulô" being a transcription of the regional pronunciation of "flor"). Dialect is another one of the discursive means that Gonzaga and other forrozeiros frequently use to evoke the regional culture of the Northeast. Here the vernacular pronunciation of flower, or the "natural" way of speaking in the sertão, anticipates and then underlines the natural environment of the sertão described in the song through its flora and fauna.

The lyrics of this song begin with the eponymous exclamation "Minha fulô!" and then "Ai! Que saudade! / Ai, ai que dô [Oh! What saudade! / Oh, oh, what pain]," setting the wistful tone of the lyrics (Gonzaga and Dantas n.d.). In the first verse, the singer names four different flowering plants common in the sertão—the *pau d'arco, pau pereiro, canafista* and *muçambe*. He remarks upon their beautiful appearance as well as their lovely smell, anticipating the importance of scents and imagery in the more recent "Cheiro de Nós." The song continues to expand this archive of the sertão's natural wonders in the following verse, in which four different kinds of bees are mentioned. These bees make a honey from the aforementioned flowers "that is admired." Thus in these two verses we have natural elements forming an allegory of beauty, industriousness, and productivity. Of course there are obvious gendered overtones to flower and bee imagery, and it is not by chance that the women of the sertão are often described as beautiful in forró lyrics, while the men are depicted as hard workers. While the singer is clearly nostalgic for the beauty of nature in his home region, the allegorical character of the lyrics transforms this saudade into a larger longing for Northeastern community and values (especially gender roles and relationships). The metaphorical references of the flora and fauna become clear in the final verse, in which the singer remarks that upon seeing the bees "kissing the flowers," he just remembers the "sweet honeycomb / of the kisses of my love" (Ibid.). Here nature is personalized and the common trope of comparing nature's beauty, bounty or sweetness to one's lover is employed. When the "my flower" chorus is repeated after this last verse, the flower has been imbued with an array of allegorical associations that gives it a more rich symbolic quality, beyond the hackneyed use of flowers in many love songs. The flower is a single, beautiful entity that encapsulates the entire world the singer dearly misses.

The most famous song featuring saudade is another Luiz Gonzaga tune, "Asa Branca," this one coauthored with Humberto Teixeira in 1947. The natural environment of the Northeastern interior is also extremely important in this song, which is often referred to as the "hymn of all Northeasterners" because of its centrality in the forró canon and in that of Northeastern popular music in general. The Asa Branca is a type of bird that leaves the sertão during times of drought, and thus serves as a clear symbol of the plight of Northeasterners displaced from their homes and often from their traditional occupations of small-scale or subsistence farming, or raising cattle, in the rural interior. "Asa Branca" begins with a detailing of a long series of afflictions of the dry sertão. These exist to such a severe degree that the singer suggests the drought is a punishment from God: "A Deus do céu, ai / Pru que tamanha judiação [Oh God in the sky, oh / Why such great torment]" (Gonzaga and Teixeira qtd in Ramalho 2000, 94). The migrant awaits the return of the rains that will bring life back to the sertão and allow him to return to his lover there. She is closely associated with the singer's plantation through this striking trope: "Quando o verde dos teus óio / Se espaiar na prantação [When the green of your eyes / Disperses into the plantation]." Again, woman, nature and the rural economy are all profoundly intertwined by the nostalgic, traditionally male desire of forró discourse. The song ends with a promise to return which is brought closer to fruition in a sequel piece appropriately titled "A volta da Asa Branca [The Return of the Asa Branca]."

This sequel was first recorded in October of 1950 by Luiz Gonzaga and written by him in collaboration with Zé Dantas. The return of the Asa Branca occurs, of course, when the rains begin to fall again after the drought. These same rains allow the narrator of "Asa Branca" to make good on his promise to come home. Now, as opposed to the fiery imagery of drought in the first song, its sequel emphasizes the rain and the wetness of the land. The Asa Branca sings, joining the voice of the forrozeiro, and the first repeated lines, in the third verse of the song, emphasize the happiness of the Northeastern people that reverberates in the exuberance of nature: "Ha! Hai, o povo alegre, Mais alegre a natureza [Ha, ha! The people happy, More happy nature]" (Gonzaga and Dantas qtd in Ramalho 2000, 127). The inclusion of the people ("o povo") at this point in the song is significant, since it comes prior to the expected lines about the singer's lover and is a new element. The happiness of the people, reflected in their natural surroundings, provides a vivid contrast to the "sad solitude" of exile previously described in "Asa Branca." In fact, there is no explicit mention of the people in "Asa Branca," so this added element in the sequel does not parallel the original song. Rather, it makes explicit the importance of the collective of Northeasterners that could only be inferred symbolically in the original. The general happiness of the sertanejos, as already noted, comes prior to the singer's personal happiness in the song. The following lines about the singer's lover, Rosinha, can thus be easily assimilated into the larger joy of all the migrants who can return to their homes, families, and lovers. Rosinha is described as "A linda frô do meu sertão pernambucano [The beautiful flower of my Pernambucan sertão]," an epithet which ties the woman to nature as the people are connected to it in the previous verse (Ibid., 127). Of course there are many flowers in the newly abundant growth of the rainy season, some of which were catalogued in the song "Minha Fulô" discussed above. Thus the metaphor suggests that every Pernambucan migrant has a flower waiting for him back in the sertão. Saudade for one's land, one's lover, one's people—in short, for Northeastern culture—is resolved collectively, if at all.

Considering "Asa Branca" and "A Volta da Asa Branca" together, one must recognize that in these canonical works of the forró genre, feelings of saudade are externalized and made concrete through descriptions of the state of the natural environment. Exile from the Northeast, particularly the sertão, is associated with the searing heat and dryness of the drought that afflicts the land. The sadness of saudade is a burning wound that can only be healed by God's hand and the balm of rain he will send when his "torment" ends. Saudade in forró can thus be described as an epistemology of the displaced peasant. The affect encapsulated in the concept of saudade, especially as expressed in this important pair of songs, is a psychic response to the painful marginalization inflicted upon the peasant class by infrastructural problems in the Northeast and wealth disparity throughout the country. Through an inability or unwillingness to address political power dynamics directly, the peasant consciousness displaces responsibility into the hands of God, who punishes the sertão and sertanejos for some unspecified crime, only to forgive them by returning the rains after a period of expiation. This expiation, and the dream or reality of eventually extinguishing the fires of saudade, is clearly a collective experience of the Northeastern peasant class, composed of cattleherds for hire and subsistence or small-scale farmers. In this case, saudade is not only a suffering but also a collective redemptive drive to actualize, or make present, an idyllic communal and personal life that has been shattered by climatic and economic factors. The redemptive drive is made all the more acute by the perception that its object, rural-regional life, has been inevitably and inexorably relegated to the past.

**Mapping Memory: The Creative Transcendence of Exile**

The song "Lamento Sertanejo [Sertão Lament]" expands upon the intense feeling of displacement and alienation experienced by sertanejos in urban exile. This work was written by Gilberto Gil and Dominguinhos and was recorded by the two on Gil's soundtrack album for the film *Eu tu eles*. In Gonzaga and Teixeira's "Asa Branca," there was virtually no mention of the city where the singer is forced to live as he sings a song of saudade for the life he left behind in the sertão. "Lamento sertanejo" is an example of the negative side of saudade, the counterpart to the redemptive rural utopia presented in many of the songs discussed in this chapter. The song's discourse cannot accurately be called a dystopia since there is no attempt to directly represent or critique the social structure of the city.[2] Rather, the lyrics are a representation of absolute anti-cathexis and depression vis-à-vis the urban center.

The first lines of the song present the singer's origins in the rural sertão. They focus on the wildness of the sertão, citing the well-known forests and shrubland called *caatinga*. The environmental origins of the singer are not distanced temporally by the past tense, but rather attached quite literally to the singer's being, or his "ser de lá," his being-from-there (Gil and Dominguinhos 2000). Because of his being-from-there, the singer lives only very marginally in the space of the city that is his current residence. He is "almost not" able to remain there, but obviously is forced to stay there by his desperate situation as an economic refugee (Ibid.). The refrain of "almost not" surviving in the city is repeated throughout the song in different ways, all of which serve to emphasize the narrator's extreme marginality in the social milieu of urban exile. He almost does not go out, he almost has no friends, he almost does not speak, he almost knows nothing. The song culminates as the singer relates that he feels marginal to the point of being subhuman, a wandering steer among a multitude like him, going nowhere. The song has a slow tempo, and is performed by Gil and Dominguinhos in such a way as to make it one of the more melancholy and despairing works of the forró genre, which usually tends towards mitigating the acute suffering of saudade through danceable rhythms.

Luiz Gonzaga and Hervé Cordovil's "A Vida do Viajante [The Life of the Traveler]," is another poignant song, this one emphasizing the migrant's incessant journeys through Brazil (Gonzaga and Cordovil qtd in Ramalho

---

[2]See Chapter Three regarding the lack of cognitive urban mapping in forró.

2000, 127). The song is a *toada* (ballad) first recorded by Gonzaga in 1953. The singer's very life "is to walk through this country/ to see if some day [he] will rest happily" (Ibid.). In his migrations, he carries with him the memory of "the lands through which he passed" and "the friends that he left there" (Ibid.). Saudade is precisely this memory that the migrant in question carries with him, a memory that makes him feel less lonely on the road. Due to circumstances beyond his or her control, the migrant cannot settle down in one place for his/her lifetime. However, she will still carry saudades with her for the people and places she has gotten to know along the way. Saudade is the melancholy or bittersweet paradigm through which all these memories are linked and organized. In this epistemology of lack hides always a profound hope for a return to an idyllic origin, or at the very least to a place one holds dear. As opposed to the anti-cathexis (or de-linking from the surrounding world) encouraged by saudade in "Lamento sertanejo," "A vida do viajante" stresses the affective links produced by saudade and the continuity which feelings of nostalgia provide even to someone whose experience is spatially scattered. Over and across time, saudade creates a continuity that ameliorates the vagrant condition. The song also has a personal resonance for Luiz Gonzaga, who for much of his life traveled throughout Brazil to share his music with Northeasterners and the nation as a whole. Thus it was also the song that he sang upon announcing his retirement from regularly performing and touring, to enjoy the peace and quiet of his ranch in his native Exu.

"Qui nem giló" is the final song from the forró canon that I will discuss here, as it offers an explicit evaluation of saudade and its potentialities (Gonzaga and Teixeira n.d.). This baião was written by Gonzaga and Teixeira, and first recorded by Gonzaga in 1950. A giló is a fruit used in Northeastern cuisine, which could be compared in shape to a small eggplant, but has a reddish-green color and a distinctive bitter flavor. Thus the bitterness of the native fruit is used to characterize the suffering that saudade can cause for Northeasterners. However, the song begins with a different perspective—saudade can be good if we remember in order to savor past loves and the happiness they once gave us. After all, the root cause of saudade is a pleasant stimulus in one's memory, so perhaps it need not necessarily bring with it negative associations. But this first phrase of the song is, not surprisingly, followed by a caveat, for saudade is never quite that simple and always occupies a very ambiguous space between the more straightforward feelings of joy and sadness. Saudade is bad, sings Gonzaga, if it makes us "dream/ about someone that we desire to see again [sonhar/ com alguém que se deseja rever]." The lyrics continue, "I cast this [painful saudade] from me [Eu tiro isso por mim]" (Ibid.).

Yet the chorus that follows seems to undermine this rejection of the tantalizingly agonizing side of nostalgic longing. The first two lines cite the perspective of someone suffering from an acute longing for reuniting with his/her love, "Ah if only some one would allow me to return/ to the arms of my sweetheart [Ai quem me dera voltar/ Para os braços do meu xodó] " (Gonzaga and Teixeira n.d.). The next two lines then explain that this longing is more bitter than any giló. However, the final lines of the chorus suggest that the singer himself is not immune to this sort of bittersweet yearning, and  must find other means to sooth the anguish of separation:

But no one can say
That he saw me sad and crying
Saudade my remedy is to sing [repeat]

Mas ninguém pode dizer
Que me viu triste a chorar
Saudade meu remédio é cantar [bis]
(Ibid.)

These lines sum up the powerful potential of forró to combat feelings of sadness and alienation in exile. Rather than merely repress the complicated and sometimes heartbreaking emotions described by the word saudade, the singer chooses to sublimate his suffering through the musical genres of his home region. Thus saudade becomes the very raison d'être of forró in the diaspora of Northeasterners in the Brazilian South. It serves a dual function as both the source of artistic inspiration for forrozeiros and their target in their attempts to lessen the suffering of exile or "kill saudade." Since they are inevitably unable to eliminate this great lack, both for themselves and for Northeasterners as a whole, forrozeiros find saudade to be a continuous source of musical productivity, a neverending desire. As "Que nem giló" concludes, saudade can be mitigated by singing and the associated musical gatherings, but it can never be extinguished and of course reestablishes its powerful hold once the song and the celebration end.

## Spaces of Saudade: (Re)Productions of the Northeast

Certain celebrations of Northeasterners, especially within performance spaces of the Southeastern diaspora, deserve special attention as examples of this simultaneous manifestation and mitigation of saudade. São Paulo's Centro de Tradição Nordestina (Center of Northeastern Tradition or CTN) is one such example. This center is a permanent space in the Northern zone, which is the part of the municipality closest to São Paulo's large populations of transplanted Northeasterners. Throughout the year, Northeasterners can visit the CTN in their leisure time and take part in a reenactment of the way of life in the Northeast through food, religion, music, and dance. Within the substantial boundaries of the center, one can find an outdoor stage fronting a large dance floor where Northeasterners of all ages enjoy dancing forró. This space lies adjacent to various booths that serve typical Northeastern fare to groups of friends and families watching the dancers and listening to the bands. Behind these booths one finds various stalls with standard carnival games, and a few meters further brings one to the entrance of a functioning church. On the Saturday in March 2004 I visited, the church was packed with worshippers, singing to the music of an electric guitar strummed by an enthusiastic young priest. The church contains relics related to Frei Damião, since it was built on the site of a visit of the popular Northeastern priest to the CTN. Miracles are said to have occurred to the life-size statue of Frei Damião, such as nails growing out of the toes. As one can tell from these various spaces within the CTN, the designers put much effort into reproducing the experience of common pastimes and of the cultural happenings in a Northeastern town or settlement. The fact that such a location is primarily frequented by Northeastern immigrants to São Paulo only furthers the intended effect of transporting one back to the home region. Clearly, one of the primary reasons for building the CTN was to kill saudade, or at least to offer a place for easing one's homesickness and at the same time to sell Northeastern food, music and other products.

The elements brought together here could be found in many towns and smaller villages in the Northeast, the only difference being precisely the absence of a surrounding downtown area, where one usually finds diverse architecture and infrastructure necessary for daily life including roads, residences, businesses, fields, factories, transportation, etc. Usually these other elements are interspersed within or around outdoor spaces for forró in

Figure 3.1: Forró fans including the author's wife, Jamila
Batchelder (m), stand at the entrance of the São Paulo
sambódromo

the Northeast, making the music and related celebration themselves seem more organically a part of the surrounding community. The CTN, however, is located in an area zoned homogeneously for warehouses and industry, and is thus fenced off and isolated behind a parking lot and next to a large freeway. It is clear that one is surrounded by São Paulo, but of course the São Paulo of the Northeasterners, who often work and live near these industrial zones. Nevertheless, the sense of community is similar to that which this researcher experienced in equivalent event-spaces in the Northeast. This sense exists in marked contrast with the atmosphere of forró night clubs in São Paulo, which are clearly much more oriented towards the youth culture of the city. At the CTN, the structural plan for the space resonates with the collective saudade felt by attendees. People come together there both to (pro)claim their saudade and to mitigate it through celebrating the Northeast with their peers.

Another similar event-space is worth discussing since it has only very recently been claimed for forró and Northeastern cultural production more generally. This is the sambódromo, a sort of fairground built in the early nineties to hold São Paulo's major carnival parades (Fig. 3.1). The space was obviously built as an answer to Rio de Janeiro's eponymous structure. Now, however, São Paulo has begun utilizing the space in response to some of the

Northeast's larger São João celebrations. In the Northeast during the entire month of June, the largest São João celebrations are held in the towns of Caruaru and Campina Grande. São Paulo, with no apparent desire to compete with these famous spaces for forró, scheduled an "anticipatory São João" in the sambódromo for the month of May 2004. In preparation, advertisements astutely rechristened the event park as the "forródromo." This was the first event of its kind to take place in the Southeastern metropolis, and drew around 100,000 visitors during its 4-day span, despite cold, rainy weather (Anhembi Turismo e Eventos 2004).

The name given to the event was indeed replete with saudade, "São João of the Northeast in São Paulo." The event was sponsored by the municipality, some private corporations, the federal cultural ministry, and the local media including radio stations and a satellite television station. Upon entering the forródromo, one encountered a vast open area, approximately 500m². For the São João event, organizers had positioned a row of tents along the side of the entrance, each tent representing one of the states of the Northeast. These tents served a dual purpose of promoting tourism to the respective states and performing a sort of "roll call" of the Northeast, affirming the presence of representation from the entire region at the festival. Adjacent to these tents were various stalls where one could find sundry souvenirs for sale, all more or less related to the Northeast. Many of the merchants present had traveled to São Paulo for the occasion from the Northeast to sell toys, musical instruments, clothes, popular art, traditional food (*comida típica*), etc. They were able to use the occasion to promote their local businesses in the Northeast, under the assumption that many of the *paulista* (São Paulo) Northeasterners attending the celebration would visit the Northeast at some point, perhaps for the upcoming São João season in June. These merchants are an example of the pride Northeasterners take in circulating and marketing their own cultural production, and also prove that saudade can manifest itself through consumerism—a premise that of course provided one of the major incentives to hold this paulista "anticipatory" São João in the first place. One way of assuaging saudade seems to be to purchase a remembrance from the home region. These souvenirs were also given out as prizes at some of the forró performances and by at least one major drinks vendor (the most common prize was a sertanejo cowboy hat).

At the margins of the vast open area were some performers on a large, parked truck. This stage was reminiscent of some of the moving trucks of the *trios elétricos* in Salvador's carnival (electric guitar-based bands now also seen elsewhere such as in Recife). There appeared to be little interest in this stage, possibly due to its out-of-the-way location and poor lighting. The performers were primarily the flamboyantly-dressed dancers typical of forró eletrônico, who perhaps clashed too jarringly with the adjacent merchants selling traditional crafts. In any case, the primary interest of attendees in this area seemed to be in the Northeastern merchandise for sale.

Moving deeper into the event-space, attendees were invited to walk down a long runway about a third the width of the vast entry area. First one passed large, bigger than life-sized puppets representing some of the famous popular figures of the Northeast, like forrozeiros Luiz Gonzaga and Jackson do Pandeiro, as well as the anti-hero bandit Lampião and his lover, Maria Bonita. These puppets were movable, and some event-goers took the opportunity to shake their giant hands or roll them around a bit. Their size relative to the adults in attendance seemed to encourage the adoption of an attitude of childlike wonder towards the event. Such a framing of consciousness taps into saudade for the mythical stories Northeasterners and even other children are told in their youth about the pantheon of Northeastern popular culture. All these figures play a large role in the forró canon, so they were an appropriate group of greeters to welcome the audience to the space behind them—the main stage.

Here, on one side of the long runway lies the stage, and on the other a long section of bleachers going up several dozen rows. Over the course of the festival, famous forró bands from throughout the country (although mostly based in the Southeast presently) performed here, including Petrúcio Amorim, Dominguinhos (see Chapter Seven, Fig. 7.2), Elba Ramalho, and Frank Aguiar. Other regional music was also played, including calypso from Pará (in the North) and música sertaneja from the interior of São Paulo and parts further west. This line-up integrating forró and other genres reflects the musical interests of Northeasterners throughout Brazil, which span from the self-consciously Northeastern forró to other regional genres with themes and rhythms similar to electronic forró. For instance, música sertaneja does treat the theme of saudade, usually with reference to separation from a lover, but the attire and instrumentation of these musicians is much closer to North American country music. But although these genres share the same stage and even mix musical styles somewhat, especially in São Paulo, it was clear that forró was the core genre of the event, as it is in the Northeastern *festas juninas* (June harvest festivals).

Nevertheless, as a percentage of the overall major performances, the other regional genres were certainly better represented here in São Paulo than in the São João celebrations of the Northeast. This departure, perhaps one of the most significant made in the forródromo from the established festas juninas, demonstrates the ability the organizers had to orient the shows towards the broadest possible market. Regional genres as a whole, even among Northeasterners, have a far larger market share than forró alone. In the Northeast, the festas juninas are an established tradition and therefore have a responsibility to represent (and hire for performances) those who are seen as traditional Northeastern musicians and their legitimate musical heirs. Música sertaneja and calypso would be considered out of place in such a cultural context, especially to the extent that they were present in São Paulo. Perhaps to make up for this difference, at the end of the runway past some food booths was the "forró tent" where lesser-known forró bands were playing throughout the event, providing the music for couple dancing. As a continuous space for forró where event-goers could dance to forró rhythms, this large tent-roofed area was more like what one would find in the Northeastern festivals. Like the crafts and souvenir booths near the entrance, the essence of this space allowed for the collective assuaging of saudade.

Many of the forró bands performing in the tent would be considered electronic forrozeiros and the musicians tended to be relatively young. The older musicians playing traditional forró and other Northeastern music like *pífano* and *cantoria* could be found in the most saudade-inspired space, located behind the bleachers mentioned above. A desire for folkloric authenticity was in evidence as one approached this section, where one first arrived at a wooden fence surrounding a reproduction of a typical "casa de caboclo," or humble back-country home (Fig. 3.2). Hanging from the eaves of the house was a sign designating this space as the "Sítio São João," or the São João farm. In the São João festival of Campina Grande which took place a month later, a very similar farm reproduction was situated in the main celebration area at the center of town (Fig. 3.3). São Paulo's own "Sítio São João" is thus a case of multiple levels of saudade converging in one space. The original "Sítio" in Campina Grande is intended as a remembrance of rural simplicity and religiosity (containing various relics of popular religion and basic hand-made furniture). But in Campina Grande, a Paraíban city located in the midst of a large agricultural and cattle-ranching area called the

Figure 3.2: Entrance to the São João farm in São Paulo's sambódromo

Figure 3.3: Entrance to the São João farm in the fairgrounds of Campina Grande, Paraíba

agreste, the virtual farm is not far removed from its actual, rustic "original" inhabited by poor Northeastern rural workers. In São Paulo, on the other hand, a similar farmhouse takes on another level of saudade. Not only does the house recall rural simplicity, but it also serves the didactic purpose of presenting to *paulistas* (São Paulo residents), themselves far-removed from the original, what humble rural abodes look like in the Northeast. This didactic purpose also fulfills a desire to experience the "real" Northeast, a desire which in this context could be called the second or more abstract, collective, diasporic level of saudade that we have seen so well described in the forró lyrics above. This diasporic saudade also manifests itself as a desire to experience the São João festival itself as it is experienced in the Northeast, thus explaining the existence of a space evoking the Campina Grande São João (of course this desire applies most poignantly for those who have been to the festas juninas of Campina Grande or similar events in the Northeast).

The "Sítio de São João" of São Paulo was actually a far more extensive space than its Campina Grande equivalent, in keeping with the didactic effort of presenting a working farm to the paulista public. In addition to several small rooms filled with everyday items and relics of popular religion (such as a small shrine to Frei Damião), upon leaving the house one entered a backyard where various authentically-clad employees of the festival demonstrated the workings and handicrafts of a typical farm, such as the making of rope from native plant fibers, and the milling and sifting of corn into corn flour. Continuing on, there was a small barn with a few live farm animals inside, a storeroom and a small, rustic chapel. The aforementioned traditional forrozeiros and other folk musicians performed in the sideyard of the little house. Near these performers was a table selling *literatura de cordel*, which are booklets filled with folk poetry related to traditional tales and figures in the Northeast as well as some current events. The poets selling these books were based in São Paulo, as were many of the musicians at the event. On one night, a typical forró trio performed here and the audience danced on the dirt-covered surface of the sideyard, as if this were just a small event among friends on a ranch in the sertão. In the end, the effect of the "Sítio São João" at the forródromo was to recreate, on this small scale, Northeastern culture as an entire rural way of life and to associate this way of life with certain folkloric artistic forms, especially music like that performed by the traditional forró trio. The isolated location of this area off to the side behind the bleachers only further contributed to the feeling of being in another world, far from the vast urban metropolis of São Paulo and its parade grounds. This virtual sertão dwelling and its environs were the most powerful examples at the festival of how saudade can both manifest itself and be mitigated through a combination of spaces, structures and performances appealing to all the senses.

## Saudade in University Forró: O Bando de Maria and Roberta de Recife

Having discussed the more traditional treatment of saudade through various lyrical examples from the forró canon, as well as through the event-spaces of the Northeastern diaspora in São Paulo, we can now turn to some more novel expressions of this unique feeling by university and electronic forrozeiros. In the case of forró universitário, saudade often is explored through an anthropological lens that recalls the didactics of the "Sítio São João" in São Paulo. University forrozeiros pay tribute to a previous era when Gonzaga was the reigning King of Baião and forró had first achieved national prominence. Especially outside of the Northeast, although there too among the middle class, university forrozeiros consider Gonzaga's heyday a forgotten era and in need of retrieval, or "resgate." The era needs to be rescued from oblivion so that young music fans can recognize forró's unique importance within the pantheon of Brazilian popular music. The desire to rescue forró, especially the forró canon and its aura of authenticity, is a middle-class saudade for the seemingly timeless popular culture of rural Brazil. In the case of traditional forró, the saudade for a rural utopia was developed as a means of giving hope to poor Northeasterners in exile that they might some day return to the idyllic land of their birth described in the lyrics. University forró has developed a different kind of utopia based on the originality of a past rural, Northeastern locus of production that the musicians themselves may well never have directly experienced. This utopia is not primarily spatially-oriented as in the case of traditional forró, but rather exists as the limit of saudade for folkloric authenticity. The Northeastern region is not so much the referent for authenticity as one expression among others of this middle-class feeling of saudade. The manner in which the rural or the natural qua authentic is developed differs based upon whether the band is from the Northeast or São Paulo.

At this point a few examples should bear out the uniqueness of saudade in the university forró context throughout Brazil. An example of a band from

São Paulo is O Bando de Maria. This is a band of six young forrozeiros who are mostly from the interior of the state of São Paulo (the exception is the lead singer, Maria Paula Godoy, who is Argentinian but has lived in São Paulo state since her childhood). Most of the band members have no connection to the Northeast, except for the accordionist, Jonas Virgolino Dantas, who was born in São Paulo state but is the son of a Northeastern forrozeiro who emigrated there. This band performs primarily in the state of São Paulo, has no plans to tour in the Northeast, but is attempting to participate in international festivals in Europe and the United States (Author Interview, 22 March 2004). Yet, as the triangle player of the band told me, they have a desire to "channel" traditional music and musicians for their young audiences in paulista forró clubs (Interview with Fernando "Teflon" Ricardo Xavier da Silveira, 24 March 2004). This desire is echoed by the forró clubs themselves, such as O Canto da Ema in São Paulo where O Bando de Maria often performs. Around the dance floor are hung large photographs of famous forrozeiros such as Marinês, Luiz Gonzaga and Jackson do Pandeiro, encouraging the young dancers beneath them to learn and respect the forró canon. In some sense, the idea of channeling is to create a saudade among music fans who may have no preexisting personal connection to the Northeast or to its music. These young residents of São Paulo thus may well lack adequate knowledge of Northeastern history and of the various sagas of Northeasterners in order to recognize the related cache of authenticity associated with the folkloric music of the region. University forrozeiros like O Bando de Maria see themselves as representing and creatively dialoguing with a legitimate though undervalued part of the national cultural patrimony. Their saudade is for a time when young people like their fans in São Paulo were more cognizant of forró's worth and the genre had not yet been diluted by the putatively inauthentic influence of electronic forró. This saudade is thus transformed into the underlying project of the group beyond pure entertainment, an anthropological or ethnomusicological project of respectful analysis and representation that ultimately is transformed through performance into a didactics of appreciation for subaltern cultural production. The creative process of the group is to develop their own archive of canonical LPs, and by listening to these LPs to learn how the songs were traditionally played. Stylistic innovations can then be made from this basis, by means of the electric guitar, the rock and blues-inspired vocal stylings of the lead singer, and unique lyrics.

O Bando de Maria does in fact lyrically echo the feelings of saudade expressed by canonical forrozeiros in a song called "Terrinha" by bandmembers Thiago Mazzilli and Celso Rocha (Mazzilli and Rocha n.d.). But the saudade is expressed only through the band members' own experiences, and thus although it makes reference to a rural idyll akin to the Northeast, the object of saudade is actually a small, rural town located in the Southeastern region of the country. "Terrinha" is a song about the town of Itaúnas in the state of Espírito Santo, a town beloved to several members of the group. According to the band's website, Itaúnas is known as the "berço do forró" or cradle of forró, despite its location in the Southeast (O Bando de Maria 2004). This privileging of Itaúnas as an authentic site for forró production is confirmed by a study of the university forró scene in the São Paulo neighborhood of Pinheiros (Braga 2001). In fact, this study reveals that the belief is a widely held one amongst the fans and musicians of the university forró community outside the Northeast. One should note here that this community thereby seems to be creating its own origin story for forró, one that is distinct from that of Luiz Gonzaga and other traditional, Northeastern forrozeiros. Apparently forró is very popular in the small coastal town of Itaúnas, and the residents have a great appreciation for it (as Fernando "Teflon" Silveira puts it, "the kids run around in the streets with triangles") (Author Interview, 24 March 2004). The lyrics of "Terrinha" ("My little land") walk the listener through the beautiful natural environment of Itaúnas and a typical day exploring the simple outdoor pleasures to be found there.

As the singer narrates the experience of the dunes, the river, the feeling of timelessness, the good people, the natural pools on the beach, and the sunset, one is reminded of the many forró songs describing the redemptive rural imaginary of the Northeast. The day ends with a forró and the singer recounts, from the male perspective of the lyricists, dancing xote with "the most beautiful princess" and returning home to make love to her. Along with a slightly greater level of explicit sexuality than in traditional forró, there is an ironic contrast that occurs in many of the group's songs, since the female lead singer has the strongest stage presence but is usually singing songs written from the perspective of the male members of the band. The band seems to find the gender-bending unproblematic, a sign that sexual politics are certainly different among university forrozeiros than among traditional musicians. (Nevertheless, it is still the men in the group who are writing most of the original lyrics.) The gender-bending mirrors the region-bending discourse of "Terrinha," which seems to follow in the footsteps of songs like the canonical "No meu pé de serra" and the traditional "Cheiro de nós" discussed above, but is not celebrating the sertão nor even the Northeast. The displacement of the object of saudade to the Southeastern region (if still north of São Paulo) is a good indicator of the significance of Silveira's notion of channeling to the band—while "channeling" the spirit of saudade in forró tradicional and its profound attachment to the rural-natural landscape, the band is able to frame this desire within its own experiences as avid visitors of Itaúnas.

As a comparison within the university forró subgenre, we could consider the singer and accordion player Roberta de Recife. She performs under this name because she is the daughter of a famous Recifense musician, Robertinho do Recife, who has been making music in the city since the late sixties. Robertinho began his career trying to develop a Brazilian rock band and was part of a musical avant garde in Recife that resembled the more famous contemporary movement called Tropicália started by musicians from Salvador. Roberta's father also serves as her producer and arranges many of her songs, although he is not a full-time forrozeiro. Roberta de Recife started out with an album that could be categorized more generally as Brazilian pop music, or MPB, but in her most recent album she has decided to focus on forró and to school herself as an eight-button accordionist (the instrument is called the *sanfona de oito baixos*) (O Diário de Pernambuco 2003). Accordingly, she now lives in Rio de Janeiro and is learning the sanfona under Audrin de Caruaru, an experienced Pernambucan player of the instrument who she brought down to live with her as a "partner and professor of sanfona" and who is "affiliated with Dominguinhos," another of Roberta's mentors (Alzugaray 2000).

Roberta de Recife was raised not in Recife but in Rio de Janeiro, a fact which only serves to make her epigraphic name choice more significant. In a move that captures the tensions inherent in university forrozeiros' entrance into the genre, she feels the need to lay claim with her name not only to the fame of her father with the appendage "of Recife," but also to the aura of authenticity that arises from belonging in and to the Northeast. "De Recife" can also mean "from Recife" as in coming or being from the city, but in this context it more likely just means "of Recife." As in the English "of," the

Portuguese *de* can function as a subjective or objective genitive, and thus Roberta de Recife ambiguously means either that Roberta belongs to Recife in some way or that she has some kind of ownership claim on the city. There is actually a subtle change from the father's music business name, Robertinho *do* Recife, to the daughter's, Roberta *de* Recife. The article from the Recife daily *O Diário de Pernambuco* cited above actually ignores this change, calling her Roberta *do* Recife, as does the title of an earlier article from another Recife daily (*Jornal do Commércio*) discussed below. *Do Recife* would mean from Recife in this case, that is, that she had been raised there and not in Rio de Janeiro. As is clear from this slip as well as the full text of the article in question, the local press and fans are happy to claim her as a native Recifense despite her actual biographical connection to Rio. But by performing as Roberta *de* Recife, she really lays claim to a more metaphysical and aesthetic attachment to the city that echoes her desire to "always sing forró, as well as other Northeastern rhythms" despite the danger of being "pigeonholed as a singer of forró" (O Diário de Pernambuco 2003). Ironically, though, she also establishes a certain distance between her and the city since the more common way to form the name in Recife itself would be the way *O Diário de Pernambuco* expresses it, that is, Roberta do Recife. Whether her choice of name represents a conscious attempt not to claim too much, or whether it is a symptom of Roberta's literal and epistemological distance from the city, this one semiotically unstable preposition reveals much about the struggles of university forrozeiros to find their own legitimate place in the genre.

In another article in a Recife newspaper after Roberta's release of her second album (*Nordestina*), the important music journalist José Teles felt the need to defend her authenticity as a true representative of Recife and the Northeast. Apparently there was initially some suspicion that her shift towards a forró focus was just the opportunism of a "loira carioca [blond Rio girl]" taking up a regional trend currently in fashion (Teles 2000). In this context, the issue of the name "Roberta de Recife" came up because Roberta had originally performed under the name "Roberta Little" (her birth name is Roberta Little Cavalcanti de Albuquerque). Thus after recalling her familial and musical connections to the Northeast, Teles tries to put to rest the question of why she changed her name. But the explanation he quotes from Roberta only really explains why she gave up the name "Roberta Little," not why she chose "Roberta de Recife" as her new stage name (no one could pronounce Little, and in music stores her CDs were being placed in the foreign music section) (Ibid.). In fact, the article even gives a reason why she might *not* want to have a stage name similar to her father's, since she experienced some "prejudice for being the daughter of a renowned producer" (Ibid.). My reading here is that the Recifense journalist expects the reader to assume it is self-evident why she would pick the name, in other words that Roberta de Recife is a completely natural choice. All the more so in contrast to the alternative, Roberta Little, which includes a foreign word that many Brazilians cannot pronounce and that has nothing to do with forró or the Northeast. The understanding of Roberta de Recife's name as a natural one is precisely rooted in an understanding of diasporic saudade. She can be welcomed home to the Northeast as a prodigal daughter because, through the very discourse and ideology of traditional forró, Northeasterners understand the desire to return to one's regional roots, no matter how long one has been in exile.

There is still the issue of Roberta's other musical influences, though, which contributed to accusations of inauthenticity. Roberta de Recife, like most of the members of O Bando de Maria, made a transition in her career from rock or pop music to being a full-time forrozeira. Such a resumé is common among university forrozeiros, but unheard of among traditional musicians who typically either have performed the music since childhood or only begin their career as musicians once they have learned to play or sing forró. Their previous attempts at rock or pop music certainly give forrozeiras like Roberta a creative sensibility that colors their efforts at producing a forró rooted in folkloric authenticity. This pop sensibility is shared with electronic forrozeiros, however musicians oriented towards university forró are far more reticent about departures from folk tradition than those belonging to the electronic subgenre (pace any more conservative listeners' opinions about university forró's inauthenticity). Following Alberto Moreiras, we could identify O Bando de Maria and Roberta de Recife's attitudes as the "reticent version" of cultural hybridity which "dwells in skepticism or in the memory of a loss" (Moreiras 2001, 293). While forró eletrônico does not reach the level of the "transgressive version" of cultural hybridity which seeks the resolution of the aporetic stand-off between the modern and the traditional, the electronic subgenre certainly is tending in this direction.[3] University

---

[3]See my discussion of forró eletrônico in Chapter Three.

forró, on the other hand, must carry the burdens of resgate and the necessity to disprove middle-class alienation from the subaltern base of the forró genre. Thus we find among these forrozeiros the saudade for a truly authentic locus, means and manner of cultural production—despite their knowledge of the latest musical trends and/or experience producing pop music. Taken as a whole, then, university forró develops a double saudade wherein the nostalgia for the rural idyll in traditional forró is refracted through the university subgenre's own "memory of a loss"—that is, the middle-class musician's saudade for being an organic intellectual of the Northeastern lower classes.

Having said this, there are several factors which distinguish Roberta de Recife from her colleagues in O Bando de Maria. Obviously, she has a real, personal and professional connection to Recife and the Northeast in her father and family. She made sure to publicize this connection through her name, and through the name of her second album, *Nordestina* (Northeasterner). To school herself in traditional forró, Roberta researched old forró vinyls like O Bando de Maria did, but then she progressed to actually taking on a mentor accordionist from Caruaru. This is a step beyond "channeling," whatever the power dynamic in their relationship might be. After all, although Aldrin de Caruaru may be her dependent while living in her house, publicly she calls him her mentor and professor. On the other hand, or perhaps precisely because she feels these other attributes guarantee her regional authenticity, Roberta feels no need to establish her *nordestinidade* [Northeasternness] with her lyrics in her latest effort, *Aquela estrela*. She allows the music and instrumentation (produced by her father and backed up by some traditional forró musicians) to invoke the aura of the forró canon, while staking her major claim for authenticity in her struggle to develop a unique aesthetic mastery of melodic and poetic phrasing (O Diário de Pernambuco 2003). This effort is of course spatially rooted by her training in the sanfona de oito baixos, as well as the regional ties indicated by her name, but the major emphasis in the original songs of the album is on turning her own personal experiences into an authentic creative voice.

This project, informed by a dialectics of authenticity but attempting to transcend it through personal creativity, can be better understood with reference to two of Roberta de Recife's songs. "Aquela estrela" [That star] and "Quando um amor" [When one love] both deal with feelings of saudade for a lover, but in markedly different ways (Recife n.d.; Recife and Simões, n.d.). The two songs do share a lyrical similarity in that the lover is not explicitly situated in the Northeast or associated with any specifically identifiable space, in fact the focus of the songs is primarily the experience of coping with saudade rather than lamenting one's loss. From here the songs go in different directions discursively, however it also is important to note that stylistically they have much in common. As one might guess from the title, the internal economy of "Aquela estrela" is saturated with natural, celestial metaphors. While this song deals with the melancholia of remembering a failed romance, "Quando um amor" addresses the progressive step of moving on to other loves, with the chorus "When one love goes, another one arises." The narrative is a much stronger, more active one, and accordingly this song has a strong, quickly pulsating beat reminiscent of techno music and studio effects that increase the volume and resonance of Roberta's vocals. The rapid, Caribbean-style percussion is also a departure from the traditional, zabumba-led xote beat that one hears in "Aquela estrela." But the base guitar beat in "Quando um amor" played by Roberta's father Robertinho do Recife is a recognizable baião beat, maintaining the song's ties to forró. On the other hand, "Aquela estrela" itself has a beat which is by no means languishingly slow, despite the melancholy lyrics, and Roberta's voice still projects a certain strength and rings out clearly above the instrumentation. This latter ironic contrast between lyrics and musical expression is also characteristic of traditional forró, and much folk music in general, and can be found in songs such as "No meu pé de serra" and "Asa branca" discussed above. Thus in a stylistic sense, both of the songs could be categorized as attempts to "kill saudade" through engaging rhythms and strong, melodic vocals.

Nevertheless, with the nod towards techno in "Quando um amor," Roberta de Recife signals that this song is taking a different position vis-à-vis the pathos of saudade. The song's lyrics focus on renewal, with lines like "I will give myself again/ Cry I will not cry anymore/ Nor suffer for anyone [Vou me dar é novamente/ Chorar não vou mais chorar/ Nem sofrer por mais ninguém]," and the final lines "I won from life/ much more than I hoped for/ I learned to love/ and also to forget [Ganhei da vida/ Muito além do que esperava/ Aprendi o bem querer/ E também a esquecer" (Recife and Simões n.d.). Here it must be stressed that forgetting is the antithesis of saudade, a word which captures the eternal preservation of the utopian objects of one's desires. Saudade relies upon presence, while forgetting relies upon the erasure of presence or oblivion. The song's chorus, repeated many times in the studio recording, presents this antinomy of saudade and oblivion as a horizon of possibility for the lover's affect—when one love goes, another will arise. Significantly, the vocal emphasis is placed upon the the first pole of the antinomy, as Roberta expansively sings "When one love, when one love, when one love goes [Quando um amor, quando um amor, quando um amor se vai]," and then quickly ends the line with a staccato, falling "another will arise [Um outro vai surgir]." To a certain degree, the song's discourse does echo the genre of self-help literature that has become so popular in Brazil, with its emphasis on psychological health and recovery from trauma and depression. To learn to forget is a skill nominally valorized in the final words of the song, however Roberta's performative approach struggles to hold on to saudade while recasting it in a more affirmative, active light. The canonical forró vision of desire as expressed through saudade remains a strong presence that does not allow for any easy forgetting. Saudade is maintained as an affective force through Roberta de Recife's subtle usage of a typical musical tactic in forró—singing a song against the grain of its lyrical discourse. This is a form of irony related to that of simultaneously killing and celebrating saudade. This ironic voice does not seek to distance the listener from the lyrics, but rather to chart a complex, contradictory, and ultimately aporetic or antinomic representation of the waxing and waning of affective attachment through disjunctures in textual and performative expression.

As mentioned above, "Aquela estrela," at least lyrically, takes a different approach to feelings of saudade for a lost love. There is a focus on the natural metaphors of celestial bodies and moonlight representing a past love and the memories thereof, respectively:

[…] Seeing that star from a distance
In order not to cry from saudade
I don't even open the window
The light of the moon enters […]
It illuminates my life
But does not bring anyone back

[…] Avistando aquela estrela
Pra não chorar de saudade
Eu nem abro a janela
A luz da lua entra […]

Ilumina a minha vida
Mas não traz ninguém de volta
(Recife n.d.)

This song is produced in such a manner as to sound more like a typical forró love song than the partly techno-inspired "Quando um amor." Accordingly, the lyrics present a more passive, stereotypically feminine subject who is waiting for someone to return that may never come. One could imagine the lover Rosinha featured in Luiz Gonzaga's songs "Asa branca" and "A volta da asa branca," discussed above, waiting for her lover to return from the Southeast with a similarly passive, melancholy affect. The line "it illuminates my life" emphasizes the continuous presence of the past in the desiring subject's consciousness that is so characteristic of saudade as a structure of feeling, especially as represented in the forró genre. A departure from the genre is evident, however, in that both this song and "Quando um amor" notably do not link this structure of feeling to a larger diasporic experience. This may be partly because Roberta de Recife is comfortable in the Southeast, having been raised there and having launched her career there. But another, perhaps more important factor alluded to above is that Roberta de Recife has a notion of authenticity that diverges somewhat from the forró canon's regional rootedness. While O Bando de Maria has a couple of songs which hail the Northeast as the privileged site for representing the marginal, displaced, rural subaltern in forró discourse, Roberta de Recife maintains her lyrics almost exclusively within the realm of interpersonal romance. In this sense she is closer to electronic forró, but would never be categorized as such since she is a solo performer, does not emphasize spectacle, and still valorizes authenticity through her name and personal ties to the Northeast. But if she is performing a resgate or recovery of cultural patrimony, it is only through a very personal creative approach to the traditional forró theme of love and saudade.

**Saudade in Electronic Forró: Mastruz com Leite**

On this note, it is appropriate to transition to an analysis of saudade in another latter-day subgenre of forró. As explored in Chapter Three, the general lyrical emphasis of electronic forró is on interpersonal romance and sexuality. As such, electronic forrozeiros represent the closest thing to an urbanization of forró that has yet come about in the history of forró as a national genre of popular music. Romance and sexuality were always a part of forró, but the extent to which they appear in the lyrics in electronic forró, along with the fact that the romance is often unconnected to the history of the Northeastern diaspora, reflects a sensibility similar in some sense to that of producers within urban popular culture genres like television soap operas and brega music. The repercussion of this approach to urban popular culture has rather unpredictable results upon any single lyrical creation by electronic forrozeiros. The issue is further complicated by the fact that electronic forró groups are often enthusiastic to perform songs by traditional lyricists and musicians, who could not be accurately designated as organic intellectuals of the electronic subgenre.

I will consider an important forró eletrônico band at this point to further examine the treatment of saudade in this final type of forró. Mastruz com Leite [Herb with Milk] is a band from Fortaleza, Ceará that was put together by the famous producer Emanoel Gurgel and his Somzoom Studio. It is inarguably the most famous and longest-lived electronic forró group, its career having spanned the decade of the nineties and continuing to the present day. The band owes its great longevity at least partly to one of the defining characteristics of electronic forró groups—their enormous and replaceable cast of performers. Mastruz com Leite and their producer helped to define the standard structure of an electronic forró group, with upwards of fifteen performers including musicians, dancers and singers. No emphasis is placed on any one individual, so the group is seen as a collective of which any single member could be replaced without affecting the whole. During performances and in their recordings, the group continually reminds its listeners of their collective identity by singing or shouting the band's name. This self-identification, too, has become standard practice among electronic forrozeiros.

Thanks to the collective identity of forró eletrônico groups, one could not expect the same level of biographical or intimate personal connection to the lyrics that one finds in the work of a performer like Roberta de Recife. Yet the bands do make use of lyrics presenting profound expressions of saudade. On many albums, one can find one or two songs which relate to the more traditional association of saudade with the rural interior of the Northeast, such as "Meu pé-de-serra, minha vida" [My foot-of-the-mountain, my life] (Filho and Juarez n.d.). Above all, these songs speak to the roots of electronic forró in the non-electronic, rural interior which produced an important genre like forró despite its economic and political marginality in Brazil. Thus this kind of expression of saudade can serve a parallel function to the saudade of resgate in university forró, however the difference in the latter case is the element of anxiety over class alienation. Electronic forrozeiros, on the other hand, do not express this anxiety since they are generally not from the middle class and most of the famous ones hail from the Northeast. They share their humble origins with Luiz Gonzaga, the founder of the canonical strain of the genre. The inclusion of nostalgic songs about the Northeastern interior in the electronic forró repertoire serves the function of paying respect to the artistic heritage of the genre as well as to the continued importance of rural subalternity in the imaginary of forró in general.

"Meu pé-de-serra, minha vida" demonstrates a profound connection to the tradition of forró songs that express saudade for the Northeast through a dual desire for the rural interior and the lover one has left there. The song takes a male perspective and describes the beauty of the land at night under an enchanting moon. The verb tense is almost entirely in the imperfect, the tense of saudade par excellence. The narrative makes reference to the sanfona, an important instrument in canonical forró and also electronic forró's primary instrumental link to the canon. This lyrical reference is reinforced by the strong presence of the accordion on the recording. Aside from the accordion, the song features primarily traditional forró instruments such as the zabumba and triangle. The base guitar is also included—an instrument ubiquitous in electronic forró but which also has a relatively long history of use in forró going back to the seventies (Luiz Gonzaga himself made use of the instrument in his performances at the time). The latter half of the lyrics are devoted to the singer's lover, a morena (dark-haired and/or dark-skinned woman) whose kiss and scent he remembers. Although by no means graphic, the lyrics here become more sexually explicit than their equivalent in the forró canon, representing an accomodation to the demands of the current market for popular music. The singer remembers making love to his morena on the banks of a reservoir, and then ends with two lines recalling the promise to return at the end of Gonzaga's "Asa branca" discussed above: "I am still returning to the arms of my loved one/ And on a moonlit night I will return to love you [Eu ainda volto pros braços de minha amada/ E numa noite enluarada voltarei a te amar" (Filho and Juarez n.d.). Considering that the song begins with the line "How much saudade I have for my foot-of-the-mountain [Quanta saudade eu tenho do meu pé-de-serra]," the piece ends with a marked ambiguity relating to the narrator's object of desire (Ibid.). Is he referring to the beloved land (*terra*), or to his lover, the morena? Most likely the answer is both, since the song strongly associates the two and thus follows the canonical treatment of saudade for life in the Northeast.

However, the electronic forró genre more often presents saudade in a much less regionalized context. Like the songs considered above by Roberta de Recife, electronic forró usually deals with saudade in the context of interpersonal romance and sexuality, without embedding this structure of feeling in the history of the diaspora of Northeasterners. While not necessarily a departure from the forró canon per se, since forró has always included romance on the individual level in many of its lyrics, the degree of exclusive focus on interpersonal romance is a newly developing trend. As discussed in Chapter Three, this trend is symptomatic of forró's hesitant discursive entrance into the sphere of urban popular culture. But perhaps one of the greatest departures from canonical forró in these romantic ballads can be found in the treatment of saudade. A song on the same album as the discursively traditional "Meu pé-de-serra, minha vida" bears this point out. "Vou tentar te esquecer" [I will try to forget you] is a recording that places its primary emphasis on killing saudade, without the corresponding celebration of saudade that exists in so many of the songs analyzed above (Nascimento n.d.). While Roberta de Recife's "Quando um amor" takes an ironic stance towards learning to forget while recognizing the importance of coping with grief, Mastruz com Leite's "Vou tentar te esquecer" is limited to a strong affirmation of the necessity of forgetting a loved one from whom one has been estranged. Accordingly, the latter song is filled with verses related to psychological recovery from grief that one would never see in a traditional forró song or within the forró canon. Examples include such phrases as "These things happen, one can never tell [Essas coisas acontecem, não se pode programar]" and "Today I live the reality, of not having you [Hoje eu vivo a realidade, de não ter você]" (Ibid.). The final three verses confirm the overall message of killing saudade and not looking back:

It's not worth it, since you don't love me anymore
I'm going to search for another dream
And never turn back

Não vale a pena, pois você já não me ama mais
Vou em busca de outro sonho
E não mais voltar atrás
(Ibid.)

The very fact that the singer recognizes the desire of the former lover in question, and then decides to accept it, is a new element. In all the songs discussed above, mostly from a traditional male perspective, there is little contemplation of even the possibility of a desire outside the realm of the narrator's own, let alone acceptance of such a desire. This lacuna is understandable since such a consideration would naturally destabilize the lover as an object of saudade. If the lover might not share the same affect, then she or he becomes an impure object for the nostalgic, desiring subject. The opportunity to consider and come to terms with the desire of the other may be provided in this case by the female singer and her perspective in the song. In addition, the discourse of self-help literature is certainly an even stronger influence here than in Roberta de Recife's work. The narrative clearly demonstrates that to continue desiring someone after rejection is psychologically unhealthy and should be avoided at all costs. All these variations on the theme of saudade are backed up by instrumental variation from the canon, including extensive use of keyboards and saxophone and the accordion opening and closing with a rapidity uncharacteristic of canonical forró songs about separation from a lover. The singer and songwriter, Bete Nascimento, performs the song with a pop sensibility and a strong vocal attack that leave no room for ambiguity about the resolve to leave the lover behind that dominates the narrative. The utopian desire for a perfect love that we have seen in many of the forró lyrics above is maintained, though, as the singer resolves to "search for another dream." She has not necessarily dispensed with saudade altogether, but rather is taking a realistic, therapeutic attitude towards her unrequited love.

The will to "never turn back" recalls the myth of Orpheus, who lost his love Euridice and was condemned to be separated from her precisely because he could not risk the temptation to turn back and gaze upon the object of his desire. Up until the last decade, saudade in forró has represented this turning back, not only to one's lover but to an entire rural way of life. Forrozeiros, and by extension Northeastern migrants, would not wait patiently to transfer this entire way of life into an urban context, nor could they dispel it from their consciousness while working in the metropolises of the Southeast. But recent songs like "Vou tentar te esquecer" take Hades's admonition to heart, recognizing the chance for a renewal of desire if one keeps one's gaze on the path ahead. As a comparison of the post-Orphean "Vou tentar te esquecer" with a canonical work, one might consider Luiz Gonzaga and Humberto Teixeira's "Juazeiro" (Gonzaga and Teixeira n.d.). One can see a clear epistemological departure in electronic forró compositions from this classic song.

"Juazeiro" consists of an address to the juazeiro tree, a tree native to the Northeast that provides shade and thus also becomes a place for a lovers' tryst. The male singer asks the tree where his lover has gone, the same lover who carved his name alongside her own in the trunk of the tree: "Tell me, juazeiro/ where is my love?/ Juazeiro, be frank/ Does she have a new love?/ If not, why are you crying/ in solidarity with my pain? [Diz, juazeiro/ onde anda o meu amô?/ Juazeiro, seje franco/ Ela tem um novo amô?/ Se não tem, por que tu choras/ solidário à minha dó]" (Gonzaga and Teixeira n.d.). The final line, "I prefer to die in you [Eu prefiro inté morrer]," sums up the logical conclusion of an unrequited yet irresolvable romantic attachment—to die of a broken heart (Ibid.). Saudade always marks the limit of desire, but in the forró canon this is a limit which can only mirror the subject's desire back to him as suffering and can only be expressed aesthetically through alternately joyous or melancholy identification with the natural world. Thus when the human object of this desire is not receptive, the natural world loses its own gendered, overdetermined abundance and is reduced merely to a potential graveyard. Orpheus himself had an idyllic love affair with Euridice, and his love was so powerful that it extended beyond the mortal world after she died. For this very reason, Orpheus could not resist the morbid temptation to pursue this love into a netherworld where he was placed under an injunction by death. Like Orpheus, who failed his test of faith, the singer in "Juazeiro"—who was brought to the tree by his memory of idyllic love— is plagued by a perverse mixture of doubt and desire that ultimately yields a death drive. As his final act, the despairing lover wishes to eternally inscribe his suffering and desire within the context of the natural environment that was an allegory for his relationship.

In the case of Mastruz com Leite's "Vou tentar te esquecer," there is no mention of the natural world as the lyrics frame grief in an entirely psychological space framed by dreams and reality. Saudade certainly marks the limit of desire in this song, however it is a limit that the singer well knows must be transcended or forgotten through facing "reality," and thereafter pursuing "another dream," with the ultimate result of a new cathexis. The rupture of romantic desire away from the politico-economic realities of the diaspora results in a new episteme, within which mourning is, with difficulty, transcendable, and according to which one can pursue one's own personal desires in such a manner as to approximate the ideal, psychologically healthy life of an autonomous and authentic individual, free of anxieties about alienation from one's region and one's people. Such is the organic standpoint of a subaltern consciousness slowly but surely emerging, as its Orphean forebears never quite could, into the urban sphere of popular culture.

### Saudade and Redemptive Regionalisms

In the end, the entirety of the forró discourse completely belies the contention that migrants are compelled into their nomadic state by a desire to find an imagined utopia. This contention, as expressed by Malcolm Bull in a review of Slavoj Žižek's *The Fragile Absolute*, relies on the belief that migrants carry with them "narcissistic fantasies" which pull them towards their final destination (Bull 2001). In Northeastern popular culture generally, and more specifically in the forró canon, itself arguably the most representative of migration among the major genres of Brazilian popular music, there is little lyrical evidence of utopian hopes for endless opportunity in the megalopolises of the South, either before or after the major migrations to Rio de Janeiro and São Paulo in the wake of the Second World War. Michael Hardt and Antonio Negri are closer to the truth of migration chronicled by forrozeiros when they recognize that

> Certainly most migrations are driven by the need to escape conditions of violence, starvation, or depravation, but together with that negative condition there is also the positive desire for wealth, peace, and freedom[...]Migrants understand and illuminate the gradients of danger and security, poverty and wealth, the markets of higher and lower wages, and the situations of more and less free forms of life. (Hardt and Negri 2004, 133-134)

The songs analyzed in this chapter have certainly proven that the voices of migrants can illuminate the displacement of marginal populations and the attendant social inequalities and domination which are not only the root causes of these displacements but also tend to be reproduced on a grander scale by these mass movements of the poor. Hardt and Negri are also right to emphasize the ambivalence of the migrant's consciousness, split as it is by the "negative condition" of social marginality and the "positive desire" to escape this condition. But the examples we have considered from forró tend to invert this part of Hardt and Negri's schema: the positive desire expressed by forrozeiros is for the return home and the redemptive rural utopia imagined there, while the negative condition in forró is migration as such, which entails only unavoidable suffering and a profound sense of homelessness called saudade. Music functions both to express saudade and to alleviate the melancholia of this diasporic affect through a sensorial and sentimental telescoping of the spatio-temporal distance from home.

To emphasize this real inversion of Hardt and Negri's conceptual schema contrasting negative condition with positive desire, we can look at the question of migration in a broader hemispheric context. The example of Mexican immigration to the United States seems particularly cogent in the present day. Many Mexican workers travel to states from California to North Carolina, leaving small towns and rural areas from Sinaloa to Oaxaca. According to Juan Romualdo Gutierrez Cortez, head of the Binational Indigenous Oaxacan Front:

> Migration is a necessity, not a choice—there is no work here[...]If a student sees his older brother migrate to the United States, build a house and buy a car, he will follow that American dream (Bacon 2004).

It may appear from this observation that the migrants' positive desire is the "American dream" which leads them to settle in the United States and leave behind the negative condition of their lives in Mexico. But it would be more accurate to say that the negative condition is migration itself, *through which* these Mexicans achieve their dreams. At issue here is the Mexican rural worker's conception of the American dream, which involves a mapping of the imaginary of North American prosperity onto his or her routes of migration. The rural laborer's dream of opportunity to work and accumulate or improve his or her house and property does not involve leaving his or her community in Mexico, but rather creating a better life for him or herself *here*, at home. What is a petit-bourgeois dream in the United States is in Mexico more like a peasant's dream to move him or herself into the class of the small farmer. To achieve this version of the American dream it is necessary to go *there*, to the dominant capitalist country in the North, to find a job. First the migrant begins to send money home from this job, to sustain those he or she has left behind, and after the harvesting season is over, or after an adequate amount of money has been earned, the migrant returns home. It is only through the journey to find relatively well-paid work that the negative conditions at home can be ameliorated, or at least so goes the logic of the dream.

Yet migration per se does not depart from the negative condition, since it is very much a part of the system which sustains poverty. Perhaps this idea is most understandable in the words of Gutierrez: "Migration helps pacify people. Poverty is a ticking time bomb, and as long as there is money coming in from the United States, then there is peace" (Bacon 2004). These words echo Sulamita Vieira's critique of migration to São Paulo, discussed in Chapter Three, as a Northeastern safety valve for unemployed rural workers that might otherwise destabilize the regional latifundist hegemony. In the case of Mexican migrants, we can see that migration not only employs these Mexicans in distant locales, but also reactivates many local economies in Mexico, creating positive conditions, or improved standards of living, in economically marginal areas. On the macroeconomic scale, the entire process relies on the exploitation of wage and cost-of-living differentials between dominant and subordinate countries. Thus from a migrant's point of view, one must pass through the alienating, *unheimlich* condition of exodus in order to return to a more firmly established home, now a piece of the American dream.

Cathy Ragland has argued convincingly that this process is most closely represented in music by the *norteña* genre. She describes *música norteña* as the "musical format for constructing a distinct Mexican migrant history and identity, particularly for the undocumented worker" (Ragland 2009, 60). Not surprisingly, there are many similarities between norteña and forró, just as there are many parallels between the migratory histories of Northern Mexicans and Northeastern Brazilians. The American dream from the standpoint of the Mexican poor and working classes described above is detailed in various norteña songs, such as Los Tigres del Norte's "El mojado acaudalado [The Wealthy Wetback]," in which a poor migrant finds success in the US but remains loyal to his regional heritage and home community in Mexico (Ragland 2009, 185). The discourse of this song released in 1997 bears a striking resemblance to that of the forró classic "A volta da asa branca," recorded in 1950 and introduced in Chapter Two. The Brazilian song, like its Mexican counterpart, emphasizes the migrant's desire to return as soon as it is economically possible and thus to put an end to the negative condition of migration.

The major distinction to be noted here is of course that the Mexican migration featured in música norteña is international, while the Brazilian migration chronicled in forró is interregional but intranational. Taking this difference into consideration, it is striking to note that nostalgia (qua saudade) seems to be thematized to a greater degree in forró lyrics than in those of norteña. Comparing Ragland's study with my own research on forró lyrics, it seems that a greater proportion of forró songs emphasize nostalgia for the region left behind, even though the Mexican migrants that are the heroes of norteña must leave their country to travel—often illegally and with great hardship—into a foreign land with significant linguistic and cultural differences from their own. In fact, Ragland states categorically that norteña "is not considered to be [...] nostalgic" (Ragland 2009, 30). One possible reason for this distinction between the two genres is the linguistic difference; that is, the fact that Lusophone literature and music have a centuries-long tradition of celebrating or lamenting saudade, while there is no equivalent nostalgic tradition in Spanish for Mexican popular musicians to draw on. Another possibility is that, in place of a greater focus on nostalgic reminiscence on the home region, the act of border-crossing migration itself takes up much more lyrical space in norteña's discourse. The greater prominence of this theme can be explained by the fact that migration has only become more difficult over the past century due to increasingly anti-migratory US juridical and law-enforcement regimes. In contrast, the act of migration has actually become logistically (if not always financially) easier for Northeastern Brazilians thanks to improved means of transportation, combined with the fact that they are still primarily migrating within the confines of one nation-state. Thus migratory travel itself is a less important lyrical subject today in forró than in norteña, while saudade for the Northeast continues to be a principal theme of the Brazilian genre.

As forrozeiros describe in their lyrics, there were and continue to be negative conditions of economic marginality in the Northeast. But as "A volta da asa branca" attests, poor Northeasterners also have their own American dream which involves a positive, utopian desire to return to an idyllic rural home. Furthermore, real social conditions in the Northeast are abstracted into the climatological disasters of the periodic droughts which afflicted the region throughout the twentieth century. These droughts were indeed natural causes that contributed to the critical impetus for migration. Drought could of course be called a negative condition, but the only positive condition imagined in forró is the return of the rains and thus the possible return migration to the edenic imaginary of the redemptive rural utopia. Clearly these redemptive dreams of the migrant are based on significant disregard for or ignorance of the grave problems faced by rural workers in subordinated capitalist countries. As in Mexico, the migrants from rural areas in Brazil are not resolving the social inequalities at home, but rather attempting to transcend them through migration to an economically dominant region with the ultimate goal of returning home in triumph.

But if we consider forró as the rural half of a negative dialectic, as outlined in Chapter Three, then rural utopia can be seen as a desire for redemption that is also a critique of marginalization in the city. Urban utopias that might outline or imply critiques of systemic rural and regional domination and marginalization are left for the many genres of urban popular music to develop. With regard to nostalgia for life in the Northeast and the sertão, many migrants felt more free as peasants (in their sense of autonomy through rootedness) than they did as workers in the informal economy or as surplus labor in the South. Descendents of the Northeasterners who had once escaped the slavery of the *zona da mata* (coastal plantation region) for the relative freedom of the sertão were now being forced into the often more terrible "freedom" of the surplus labor pool in the Southeast. Whether or not they ever returned to the Northeast, its rural culture would be remembered fondly in song as a repository of a stable, holistic ecology encompassing nature, kinship ties, gender roles, and of course music and folklore. This sense of freedom qua redemption through autonomy and rootedness in rural ecology has become all the more evident in the past two decades on a national scale through the successful efforts of the Movimento dos Trabalhadores Rurais sem Terra (the movement of landless rural workers,or MST) to redistribute arable land to the poor for small-scale farming. The steadily increasing popularity of music like forró is a related postnationalist phenomenon that points toward renewed interest in exploring the authenticity of popular, regional roots. At the same time it must be said that millions of Northeasterners did decide to stay in São Paulo and Rio, while "São Paulo" and "Rio" themselves are all the more evident within the Northeast in the form of urban centers that are home to modernization akin to that of the Southern giants: secondary and tertiary industrial growth (and decline), including cultural production for national and international consumption, as well as the all-too-familiar marginalization of the poor encapsulated by the megaslums or favelas. These developments delineate the contemporary spatio-temporal matrices for popular culture that are beginning to be addressed, without doubt at a tentative and painstaking pace, in the works of diverse universitário and eletrônico groups like O Bando da Maria, Roberta de Recife, and Mastruz com Leite. Nevertheless, as the undiminished popularity and influence of forró tradicional attests, echoes of collective saudade continue to reverberate and find resonance in an era in which displacement and diaspora have become all the more global conditions of being.

# Chapter Three

# The Rural-Urban Negative Dialectic: Cognitive Mapping and Forró

The city is an inconceivable totality for the discourse of forró. Upon beginning migration to the city, the backland (sertão) is portrayed as a place of great lack and misery. Every step of the way, the migrant remembers the rich potential of his home region, praying that it will rain so he can return to his lover and greener pastures. Meanwhile the city is only a distant, alien destination of last resort. We are presented with two backlands, two sertões, one of which embodies the desperate poverty displacing the rural subaltern masses, and the other which is a space of desire and saudade, a bittersweet yearning for a return to better days. The city is only portrayed negatively vis-á-vis these two deeply symbolic faces of the backlands and more broadly, northeastern Brazil.

There is a complex interplay between the two sertões, a dynamic most famously captured in Luiz Gonzaga and Humberto Teixeira's 1947 masterpiece, "Asa branca." The sertão is a paradise lost, but there is almost always the sense that it is retrievable. This retrievability is not limited to the physical return of the migrant and his reintegration into the local rural economy (enabled by the end of a drought as described in "Asa branca" and "A volta da asa branca"). In the song "Pau de Arara" (1952), for instance, there is a clear cognitive mapping of the journey away from the sertão which hints at the ability to return affectively through music. The journey to the southern metropolis is presented as a sort of penance ("Eu penei, mas aqui cheguei [I suffered, but I made it here]" is sung as a monotonous mantra), but the penitent has brought with him in his sack the forró instruments which will allow him to recall the diversions and joys of his home region. In "No meu pé de serra" (1947), already discussed in Chapter Two, there is a telling shift from reminiscing in the past tense about the beloved sertão at the foot of the mountains (*pé de serra*) to a present tense description of dancing to xote played on an accordion. Wherever a forró (in the sense of a musical gathering, celebration and dance) might be held, the diasporic communion of those who remember the good times in the Northeast will be able to diminish the distance in time and space between that gathering and the edenic sertão. This telescoping effect only emphasizes the lack of affective attachments to the city. The Northeastern migrant's existence, as portayed in forró lyrics and performances, is circumscribed by a redemptive desire for return to the rural homeland.

## Not in Ceará Anymore: Psychological Resistance and Regional Remembrance

Portrayals of city life and cityscapes are few and far between in forró lyrics. "No Ceará não tem disso não" (1950) is an example of a song which touches negatively on life in the southeastern metropolis (Morais 2000). It is typical in that it reveals very little other than the fact that the city holds many dangers for the Northeasterner that are not to be found in his native region. Ceará is portrayed as free of the exploitative "sharks" of the Southeast, with the help of a regional expression—"Ceará doesn't have any of this"—reminiscent of the phrase "we're not in Kansas anymore." This is a world filled with things that, for a Northeasterner from Ceará, have no explanation ("Não existe explicação"). Most revealing of the alienation experienced by the migrant in the city are the lines "Nem que eu fique aqui dez anos/ Eu não me acostumo não/ Tudo aqui é diferente/ dos costumes do sertão [even if I stayed here ten years/ I still wouldn't get used to it/ Everything here is different/ than the customs of the sertão]" (Ibid.). As a result, the singer decides to catch a ride on the first truck back to his land ("minha terra"), presumably in Ceará.

Another song which mentions a specific city, "Adeus Rio de Janeiro" (1950), describes the singer's sadness upon leaving Rio (Gonzaga and Dantas quoted in Ramalho 2000, 93). However, the only descriptive elements in the song are brief references to Rio's famous beach neighborhood, Copacabana, and its "morenas" (dark-haired and often dark-skinned women). Compared to the intricate descriptions of life in the sertão and the Northeast (not to mention the oft-lauded Northeastern morenas) which comprise the bulk of forró discourse, this xote to Rio turns out to be a rather superficial tribute. Indeed, the final verse emphasizes that the singer's Northeastern lover, Rosa, is "em primeiro lugar [in first place]" (Ibid.). The singer of this song, too, will go back to his native region, even though he seemingly had a much more positive experience in the Southeast than the protagonist of "No Ceará não tem disso não." What is happening here? Why does the migrant's cognitive mapping through musical creativity stop short of representing his or her existence in the city, even when the songs in question are explicitly about life in the city and reasons for leaving it behind? The answer may involve a repression of the severe alienation experienced by Northeasterners in the metropolises of the Southeast. The failure to provide a mapping of urban space and social structure can be seen as a subaltern psychological defense against forced migration. All affective energy is placed into the redemptive space of a phantasmagorical Northeast waiting for the migrant's return as soon as conditions allow. This exclusive gaze necessarily involves a turning away from the new, harsh realities of urban life.

Here my reading diverges from much of the analysis of Luiz Gonzaga's musical production. The work of Sulamita Vieira is emblematic in its portrayal of forró as an aid to the migrant in orienting himself within the new urban environment. Vieira cites the song "Baião de São Sebastião" (1950) in an attempt to demonstrate that Gonzaga was chronicling the moment at which "a cidade 'se abre' ao migrante que nela procura uma forma de inserção [the city "opens itself" to the migrant who is seeking a form of insertion within it]" (Vieira 2000, 243). But it is problematic, without significant qualification, to generalize from this song about the experience of the migrant. It is true that there are parallels with many other forró songs that detail the migrant's journey out of drought and his or her fear of an unknown city. However, the focus of the song is Gonzaga's attempt to popularize Northeastern music in Rio de Janeiro, and his gratitude to the city for eventually accepting his music and granting him great national success through its influential recording industry. Indeed, the only "opening" mentioned in the song is Rio opening the bellows of the singer's instrument. Certainly Gonzaga could be seen here as a role model for other Northeasterners, one who has the courage to say to the culturally hegemonic metropolis "stop the samba for three minutes/ for me to sing my baião" (Gonzaga and Teixeira quoted in Vieira 2000). But does this really represent an insertion of the migrant into Rio de Janeiro? Gonzaga's story is in fact an exception to the rule. As Vieira herself relates, Northeasterners were faced with great prejudice in Rio de Janeiro and São Paulo, and if they were able to survive economically, often did so with great difficulty.

The larger point here is that within the discourse of forró, this story of the migrant's life in the Southeastern metropolis is not being told. Much like Benjamin's angel of history, Luiz Gonzaga and other forró musicians are propelled forward by the winds of uneven development while fixing their gaze upon its ruins. Composing music out of this vision is by no means a fruitless task, as Gonzaga's rich oeuvre demonstrates, and neither is it work which models assimilation or acculturation of the Northeasterner in the Southeast. The consciousness developed in forró is more radically subaltern than that.

Vieira understates the case when she makes the point that the transition of the *retirante* (Northeastern migrant, literally a refugee) into the city is not a "simple transference" (Vieira 2000, 243). But she is quite right in emphasizing that although the migrants could bring some of their traditions with them, they could not bring along the social organization of the Northeast. This in fact made it an extremely difficult, often failed transference which involved leaving behind much of the rural, Northeastern way of life, the culture of the sertão. Within the new economic centers of gravity in the industrializing Southeast, there were no systematic attempts made in the private sector or by the government to incorporate the internally displaced masses into the urban economy. The retirantes were only so much fodder for developmentalism, surplus labor which helped keep wages low until the military coup of 1964 was able to do so through arms. It was in 1964 that militancy over land reform reached its zenith, with alliances between peasants, the Catholic Church, urban labor unions and student groups taking shape. Not coincidentally, this is both the year of the coup and the year which brought the forró song that most brutally and at greatest length depicts the forced migration of Northeasterners into São Paulo.

**Rural Exodus: The Sad Departure**

The song to which I refer derives from Patativa de Assaré's poem "A triste partida," which would later be given its most memorable musical rendition as a toada by Luiz Gonzaga. The song is a long, slow lament in which a chorus repeats Gonzaga's sighing, desperate plea "my God, my God" and cries pathetically "ai, ai, ai, ai" at the end of each verse (Assaré n.d.). It is of epic length for a forró song, lasting about nine minutes, with no refrains other than the chorus's cries. The work describes a family in Ceará that, in the event of a severe drought, is forced to move to São Paulo in search of economic opportunity. Although the song provides a very moving and detailed account of the onset of the drought and the family's struggle against leaving their native Ceará, what is most pertinent about the song in the current discussion is what it fails to relate. It is not until near the end of the song that the family's experience in São Paulo is broached, so ultimately the epic verse has only three stanzas about life in São Paulo, whereas there are fifteen verses exclusively about life in Ceará and departure from the family's native land. There remains one concluding stanza/verse which I will discuss further below.

Within the three verses about life in the metropolis, a picture of privation and complete alienation is developed. The family arrives without money, with no knowledge of how to make their way in the city, searching for a "patrão," a boss who can serve as their protector and help them establish themselves. But the family "Only sees strange faces, of the ugliest people/ Everything is different/ than the dear farmland [Só vê cara estranha, da mais feia gente,/ Tudo é diferente/ Do caro torrão]" (Assaré n.d.). Apparently some sort of work is found by the father of the family, but we are not told what, and the job only drives the family further into debt, thereby indefinitely forestalling plans to return to Ceará:

He works two years, three years and more
And always he plans
To return one day
But he never can, he just lives in debt
And in this way he suffers
A torment without end

Trabaia dois ano, três ano e mais ano,
E sempre no prano
De um dia inda vim.
Mas nunca ele pode, só vive devendo,
E assim vai sofrendo
Tormento sem fim.
(Ibid.)

The third verse in question essentially repeats the plight of the family as described in the second, emphasizing even more how the father and his family are trapped in a limbo of indignity and debt, far from a home to which they will never return. The sum total of these three verses is an image of the family stranded and then trapped in a strange land where everyone and everything is foreign. The patrão clearly offers them no significant protection, only sinking them further into debt. These are the only representations of São Paulo in the work, and even they are more than offered by the most famous forró toada, "Asa Branca" (1947), which offers no details at all about the destination of migration other than that it is "many leagues" from home, where the singer of course wishes to return. But although there are three stanzas devoted to life in São Paulo in "A Triste Partida," we really know next to nothing about the migrants' lived experience, the material conditions of their existence, or the contemporary state of São Paulo's socioeconomic base and superstructure, including the number of other migrants and degree of interaction between them, and just what sort of patrons are available to immigrating Northeasterners.

The last stanza of "A triste partida" attempts a synthesis of some of the salient themes of the work, explicitly expanding the reach of the song to include all "nortistas," or Northerners (i.e. Northeasterners). The second line emphasizes that although the Northeast is dry, it is still good land. The next two lines then present one of the most powerful tropes in the song—the migrant is "Exposed to the rain/ To the mud and the morass [Exposto à garoa/ À lama e ao paú]" (Assaré n.d.). The connotations of this figurative language are overdetermined, forming a complex web of associations. The author, Patativa de Assaré, has been attempting to describe the migrant's alienation in São Paulo for the last few stanzas, and is still situating the Northeastern protagonist as "distant from the land [distante da terra]" (Ibid.). Yet the language depicting exposure to the elements is most likely a reference to the torrential seasonal rain and floods of the sertão (See Vieira 2000, note 204). This mixture of references to Brazil's North and South leads the poem into its ending lines, "It pains the nortista.../ to live as a slave/ in the North and in the South [Faz pena o nortista.../ Vivê como escravo/ Nas terras do su]" (Assaré n.d.). The transition within the last six lines of the final stanza is quite coherent, moving from a chain of associations, North—exposure—alienation—South, to the more explicit political critique stating that the Northerner, although "so strong and so brave [tão forte, tão bravo]," lives like a slave throughout Brazil (Ibid.).

Some confusion arises, however, when we compare this conclusion to the general structure and narrative content of the entire poem/song. The song seems to be telling us, down to the second line of the last octave, that although the Northeast is dry, it is "good land" to which the migrant family would gladly return. The only force that is depicted driving the family out of their native region is drought, so it is difficult to perceive any agent that will or might currently be "enslaving" the father and his dependents in the North. In any case, enslavement in the North is left completely unthematized throughout the nineteen stanzas of the poem. The most convincing explanation for this new element of Northern slavery in the final line of the poem is that the two lines about exposure to the elements brought to mind, for the poet, the broad, national scope of the systemic exploitation of small landowners, peasants, farmhands, and their migrating families. But it is the two lines of the poem, "Exposed to the rain/ The mud and the morass" that best encapsulate the song as a whole, rather than its concluding line. The Northeasterner, due to a complete lack of cognitive mapping of the city, must resort to the natural, descriptive language of the sertão to critique the exposure and vulnerability he feels in São Paulo. There is also a cruel irony here in that the Northeastern family can only be exposed to rain figuratively, for the sertão itself continues to be stricken by drought. The trope is thus portraying a profoundly unnatural event, a cataclysm which involves the warping of the dream of replenishing rain into a diluvian nightmare. Economic opportunity in the Southeastern metropolis turns out to be a very mixed blessing.

**The Patronage Politics of "Vozes Da Seca"**

Another song which addresses drought-related hardships is the toada-baião "Vozes da seca [Voices from the drought]" (Gonzaga and Dantas n.d., 17). Rather than a biographical narrative of migrants' iterations, this work addresses more explicitly the relationships of dominance and dependency between the Northeast and the South. The song could be called a cognitive mapping of power, but it will become clear that the mapping fails to take urban immigration into account, nor does it address the full complexity of the system that exploits poor sertanejos. The singer emphasizes that Northeasterners do not want paltry handouts (*esmola*), which just shame or corrupt the noble man of the sertão. Such language, combined with the fact that the song is addressed to a powerful man in the South, makes it abundantly clear that women do not enter into these networks of power relations. One might recall a similarity here with "A triste partida," in that the standpoint of the mother of the family featured in that song is never mentioned. Thus gendered, the Northeasterner proceeds in "Vozes da seca" to request "protection" from someone he addresses with the honorary title of "doctor" and describes as a "man chosen by us for the reins of power [Home pur nóis escuído para as rédias do pudê]" (Ibid.). Such a description of the "doctor" figure reveals that this could be a member of the Northeastern elite who is a federal representative in the South, or it could just as well be the president, secretary of agriculture, or someone from another region in a position of power. All of these figures are interchangable to the sertanejo, and would simply be addressed with the honorific "doutô," to emphasize their evident education and their related position of privilege in the fledgling Brazilian democracy. There is an implicit subaltern recognition here that, as a class, the Northeastern elite has more in common with the Southern elite than it does with the struggling peasants of the sertão. There is no perceived need to differentiate across such a gulf of power. The singer proceeds to ask for a program of public works to give the Northeastern interior a system of reservoirs that can make it less prone to the economic devastation brought by drought.

How this aid might actually be acquired from the federal government is not even raised as an issue. In the end, the voice of "Vozes da seca" is simply trying to reaffirm a direct relationship of dependency in order to receive protection from a patron. The song fails as a mapping of power precisely because it does not recognize the more complex network of hegemony in which regional patrons may well be taking advantage of peons in the sertão. In what came to be known as the "drought industry" (*indústria da seca*), Northeastern landlords and political bosses would profit from federal government funds by asking for public works like those requested in the song, only to have them built on private land or to skim money from the project budgets (Vieira 2000, 195). The political bosses' control over essential projects could also be used to manipulate local peasants into voting for them, thus calling into question the singer's claim that the "doctor" was really "chosen" by the sertanejos to take the reins of power. As mentioned above, the song does not deal with urban immigration. But, as in "A triste partida," the Northeastern rural imaginary overwhelms any conceptualization of the urban, industrializing South, even though there is a recognition that the reins of power are held precisely there. Power relations are perceived from the standpoint of the Northeastern peasant, and thus it his provincial, clientelistic worldview which highlights both the authenticity of the song and its blindness to the social totality of Brazil, now dominated by rapidly industrializing urban centers in the Southeast and the nascent central plateau of Brasília. The inability to map urban social structure, or even to formulate affective attachments which might lead to a partial cognition of a cityscape, is symptomatic of a failure to connect the experience of migration to the broader, systemic alienation of rural workers in Brazil. But forró's portayal of this cognitive failure provides a painfully vivid image of the tragic circumstances of the migrant in the city, a sort of photographic negative of the real no-man's land that São Paulo and the South were for so many former subsistence farmers from the sertão.

**Relational Subalternism, Melodramatic Consciousness, and Critical Rural Utopia**

Forró attempts to portray that which is essentially untranslatable into the city—Northeastern, (particularly rural) subalternity as such. To clarify this point, it should be emphasized that I am deploying the concept of subalternity here strictly in terms of what Alberto Moreiras calls a "relational subalternism." Relational subalternism is

> an understanding of the subaltern position in merely formal terms, as that which stands outside any given hegemonic articulation at any given moment. [Moreiras continues:] Relational subalternism can perhaps...offer a sort of abyssal ground for a critique of the social able to see beyond some crucial ideological narratives of the present... (Moreiras 2001, 267)

The lyrics I have been discussing all seek to trace a fissure in the grand, hegemonic narrative of modernity. In Brazil, this narrative was represented by a utopian developmentalism that would make Brazil achieve "fifty years' progress in five," in the infamous words of Juscelino Kubitschek, Brazil's president from 1956-61. The manner in which Brazilian government and big business conceived of the modernization of Brazil did not provide any place at the politico-economic table for the subject position that forró represents, rural workers. The only space left open to many rural workers (who would soon become lumpen or "landless," as their political movement is dubbed today) was the non-space of surplus labor in the burgeoning urban economies. One might assume that this new urban lumpenproletariat would fall prey to the melodramatic consciousness Louis Althusser describes, in which

> the motor of [the lumpens'] dramatic conduct is their identification with the myths of bourgeois morality: these unfortunates live their misery within the arguments of a religious and moral conscience; in borrowed finery. In it they disguise their problems and even their condition. In this sense, melodrama is a foreign consciousness as a veneer on a real condition…[such a consciousness] must still be lived as *the* consciousness of a condition (that of the poor) even though this condition is radically foreign to the consciousness. (Althusser qtd in Moreiras 2001, 50)

A foreign consciousness as a veneer on a real condition. A cognitive dynamic of this nature is at work in the consciousness represented by forrozeiros, but not in the manner one might initially imagine. Since they represent migrants coming from a subject position firmly rooted in the rural economy, forrozeiros do not assume in their works that they are equal participants in the bourgeois modernity of urban elites. Immigrants to the cities necessarily identify with the myth of economic opportunity upon first arriving in the metropolis, however forró takes the perspective of the rural subaltern's clash with the falsity of this myth and his or her cognitive failure to imagine the possibility of creating an alternative space by altering the course of Brazilian modernization.

As noted above, forró is thus tracing a fissure in the narrative of development, a trope which in one sense represents the place where subalterns fall through the cracks of (inter)national capitalism. But in another sense, narrative fissure

> might guard a critical potentiality having to do with the unfathomable excess of singularity itself: the moment at which a narrative, any narrative, breaks into its own abyss is also a moment of flight in which subjectivity registers as noncapturable; indeed, it is a moment of pure production without positivity that will not let itself be exhaustively defined in the name of any heterogeneity. (Moreiras 2001, 56)

The hegemonic narrative of modernity in Brazil is a nationalist one which seeks to interpellate the subaltern, and if successful in this endeavor, to articulate a new synthesis that eliminates the subaltern as such, coopting the subaltern subject position into a hybrid national identity. In its almost complete refusal to situate itself within the context of the city, forró maintains its subaltern subject position vis-à-vis the hegemonic narrative of modernity in Brazil and the rest of the so-called "developing world." The reader will remember, however, that I stated that forrozeiros do present their listeners with a foreign consciousness as a veneer on a real condition. It is just that their consciousness is *made foreign* by their displacement in Brazil—that is, it is the alienated consciousness of forced migration and exile. Like exiles, forró musicians are always dreaming of return to their native land. However, these dreams do not just symbolize the most ardent desires of migrants, rather they make up the entirety of forró's worldview. This is the perspective from which forró is indeed a melodrama, projecting a rural, Northeastern consciousness upon a real, urban and Southeastern condition. It is the consciousness of the peasantry from an only primitively mechanized rural economy, put to work producing music about life in a rapidly industrializing urban economy. Or defensively failing to write music about it, and merely, powerfully producing a chronicle of subaltern occlusion at the brink of modernity's exclusionary abyss. And of course a chronicle of the incredible redemptive desire for flight, for escape to the irretrievable refuge of country life. The consciousness behind forró remains a refugee consciousness since the migrant finds no safe harbor in the city.

My reading of forró's lack of urban cognitive mapping as a failure should be distinguished from the dominant discourses of hybridity within Brazilian and Latin American thought throughout the past century and within North American academia since at least the advent of cultural studies (in Chapters Five and Six I critique the hegemonic discourse of hybridity which I have labeled the "synthetic urge"). The failure I am describing is not a failure to synthesize the urban and the rural, the national and the regional, or modernity and tradition. Relational subalternism, in fact, offers us a chance to avoid the hegemonic articulation and resolution of these dialectics of uneven development, which would be a betrayal of the productiveness forró realizes in its own failure. Having distanced ourselves from such an articulation, it becomes clear that there is no apparent desire for synthesis in most lyrics of the forró canon. There is simply a failure to cognitively map the lived experience of urban life, to thematize the migrant's attitude towards that life and its necessity.

But I would like to argue more thoroughly at this point that this failure also marks the realization of a powerful subaltern critique of the city, which is itself seen negatively through the hermeneutic lens of rural utopia. In this sense, as a conscious or unconscious refusal to map urban space and social structure, forró's failure becomes a rejection of synthesis, of hegemonic articulation within the Southeast, the city. We are dealing here with what Fredric Jameson calls a *negative dialectic* in his essay on the politics of utopia. In his discussion of rural and urban utopias, he describes the value of utopian thinking vis-à-vis country and city as "differential," that is,

> it lies not in its own substantive content but as an ideological critique of its opposite number. The truth of the vision of nature [or the country, the rural] lies in the way in which it discloses the complacency of the urban celebration; but the opposite is also true, and the vision of the city exposes everything nostalgic and impoverished in the embrace of nature...If dialectical, then this one is a negative dialectic in which each term persists in its negation of the other; it is in their double negation that the genuine political and philosophic content is to be located. But the two terms must not cancel each other out; their disappearance would leave us back in that status quo, that realm of current being which it was the function and value of the utopian fantasy to have negated in the first place; indeed...to have doubly negated. (Jameson 2004, 50-51)

The discourse of forró lies in the ambiguous terrain of a rural subalternity within a city whose raison d'être negates all that it stands for. If forró is a rural utopia, it is all the more a utopia par excellence, one that encompasses the recognition of the incommensurability of modernity and its other, the no-place of subalternity within a hegemonic narrative of developmentalism. This narrative does not correspond to the reality which forró sings—in other words, forró marks the fissure in the ground of Brazilian modernization. We could also frame this tracing of fissure in Walter Mignolo's terms as "a radicalization of the interplay between 'local histories' and 'global designs' on the grounds of their mutual incommensurability." Moreiras explains that such a radicalization "might lead into new determinations for thinking historically and geopolitically that would not appeal to identity/difference or to its domestication as hybridity as a primary referent" (Moreiras 2001, 268). This is a similar line of thought to Jameson's insistence upon upholding rural and urban utopias as such, and not resolving their radically differential nature in a synthesis. In the case of political utopias such as the rural idyll of forró and the developmentalist panacea of urbanization, it is precisely from their polarity as antinomies that each pole gains its critical power.

## Other Perspectives: Carioca Samba and Bahian Ballads Versus Música Sertaneja

To explore a contrasting vision of the city which will highlight forró's unique utopian vision, we can look to the musical genre of samba. The first samba to be registered with Brazil's National Library was "Pelo telefone," by Donga. Donga was an Afro-Brazilian musician living in Rio de Janeiro, and he registered the song in 1917, having stylized the folkloric music developed in gatherings and parties of Rio's Afro-Brazilian bohemians, especially those held at the house of the famous patroness of samba, Tia Ciata. Although at this point samba had roots in the rural Northeast much like forró did, with Tia Ciata herself and many musicians hailing from Bahia or other Northeastern states, the first registered samba is probably based on an anonymous, eponymous work that explicitly references the chief of police, a telephone call, and the gambling occurring on a certain street in Rio (Sandroni 2001, Chp. 5). Since telephones were still only available to the elite at the time, and gambling was only being policed at the houses that catered to poorer customers, one can see even without more specific details that the song is evoking the social totality of the city, including its socioeconomic strata and the power structures through which they are maintained.

Carlos Sandroni's discussion of "Pelo telefone" points out that some of the references in the song are to two different newspaper reports in 1913 and 1916, respectively (Sandroni 2001, 121-122). Thus this early samba (the anonymous version of "Pelo telefone") also demonstrates a savvy awareness of the important news events of the city and of Rio's newspapers. This kind of discursive integration of the song's lyrics into the social totality of the city could hardly be more different than the subaltern resistance of forró against interpellation into any urban narrative. In its unpublished, anonymous variation, "Pelo telefone" represents, from a subject position firmly rooted in the urban popular classes, a witty and subtle critique of the urban elite and police corruption. Perhaps thanks to a more gradual migration to Rio de Janeiro, the support of Rio's already-existent Afro-Brazilian community, and/or a familiarity with the urban environment of Salvador in Bahia, those immigrants from the Northeast associated with samba were able to express a degree of integration into city life in their lyrics.

Highlighting another artistic imaginary which contrasts with that of forró, Bryan McCann provides a revealing juxtaposition of the regional perspectives of two Northeastern migrant musicians, Luiz Gonzaga and Dorival Caymmi (McCann 2004). McCann argues that the latter musician's lyrics and self-presentation, saturated with the Afro-Brazilian popular culture of Salvador, Bahia, present a harmonious vision of Brazilian society akin to that of Gilberto Freyre.[1] Caymmi's lyrics envision a hybrid society combining rural and urban elements, and of course a fusion of European- and African-descended cultural influences. In comparison with Caymmi, McCann demonstrates that Luiz Gonzaga outlines a much stronger, more distinct regional identity for the Northeast—based largely in the rural popular culture of the sertão. Thanks to this strong regional element and his narratives of economic exile from the region, Gonzaga's work has often been pointed to as representative of the dignity and struggles of the rural poor and the Northeastern working classes. McCann notes appropriations of Gonzaga's work by the organizers of the liberation theology-inspired "cowboy masses" of the 1970s as well as, more recently, by members of the MST (McCann 2004, 124-125).

On the other hand, Caymmi's oeuvre has not been politically associated with the struggles and aspirations of marginalized sectors of the Brazilian populace. Instead, Caymmi's music and image have been "pressed into service to conciliate and pacify" the real antagonisms within Brazil's unevenly developed society (McCann 2004, 127). Thus, although not exactly structured on a rural/urban polarity like Jameson's negative dialectic, McCann presents a kind of dialectic between Gonzaga and Caymmi, centered around a dialogue between their relatively resistant and conciliatory regionalisms and the various appropriations thereof. Like the urbane popular musicians behind the rise of Rio's samba, Caymmi—a middle-class musician from the city of Salvador—developed his music in the Rio-based culture industry without addressing the severe alienation of the rural poor and of the many millions of migrant workers. For this reason, his music is more properly considered Bahian than Northeastern, or as McCann puts it, Caymmi is the "ur-baiano [Ur-Bahian]" while Gonzaga is the "ur-nordestino [Ur-Northeasterner]" (McCann 2004, 98). Although both musicians were

---

[1] See Chapter Five for a discussion of Gilberto Freyre's paradigmatic imaginary of Brazil as a uniquely hybrid nation.

partially of African descent, for most of his life Gonzaga identified racially as a nordestino, while Caymmi emphasized his Bahian, Afro-Brazilian roots (Ibid., 117). Thus we can see that Caymmi's perspective, along with that of the Bahian-influenced perspective of early samba musicians, provides a clear contrast with the Northeastern regionalism of forró. Clearly the carioca and Bahian musicians could not be considered to be aligned with forró in its negation of urban developmentalism from a rural-regional standpoint.

However, there is a more recent trend in popular music which could be said to engage alongside forró in the negative dialectic between rural and urban utopias. This is the Central-Southern genre of música sertaneja, most thoroughly analyzed by Alexander Dent (Dent 2007). Dent invokes Walter Benjamin's redemptive approach to history[2] (and his concept of messianic time) to describe the framing of temporality in Central-Southern rural music:

> [...] *música caipira* [a predecessor to música sertaneja] and *música sertaneja* explicitly oppose their idea of messianic time—where modernization becomes a corrupting influence—to that of mainstream Brazilian culture's notions of historical, or linear time, where the present is the result of ineluctable progress. Rural genres question the inevitability of progress at every turn precisely through the lamination of time and space that kinship executes. (Dent 2007, 486)

The mainstream belief in ineluctable progress noted by Dent is, of course, the utopian urban developmentalism that functions as one half of the negative dialectic I have outlined. Música sertaneja musicians stand with forrozeiros in opposition to this urban celebration, imagining a redemptive rural utopia that disrupts the hegemonic conception of Brazilian modernity. Dent also cites the work of Judith Irvine on language ideology to suggest that, within a given historical moment, temporalities exist in opposed pairs (Ibid.). This schema of opposed rural and urban temporalities mirrors the rural-urban negative dialectic and provides further support for the idea that música sertaneja and forró share the ideological and epistemological perspective of the rural half of this dialectic.

Regarding Dent's discussion of kinship, though, it should be clarified that there are significant thematic differences between forró and música sertaneja. Música sertaneja emphasizes the trope of brotherhood to a much

---

[2] In Chapter Seven, I discuss Benjamin's theoretical approach as it relates to Northeastern prophetic traditions and forró's related conception of the relationship between past and present.

greater degree in its performance style and lyrics. This emphasis is reinforced by the fact that the genre is usually performed by a pair of male singers who are often biological brothers. Based upon this evidence in the música sertaneja genre, Dent argues for the thematic and epistemological importance of kinship and that "the brother form increasingly shapes the performance of Brazilian rural music" (Dent 2007, 471). This statement may well be true of música sertaneja, however one should be careful not to generalize about all Brazilian rural music. Forró has no such emphasis on brotherhood, nor is it characteristic of this Northeastern genre to see brothers perform together or hear brotherhood thematized in the lyrics. When kinship is evoked by Luiz Gonzaga, it is in reference to his father Januário. This father-son relationship is usually not incorporated into Gonzaga's or other forrozeiros' performance styles, rather, it serves the purpose of symbolizing contemporary musicians' profound respect for the traditions they have received from previous generations of artists.[3]

## Forró's Legacy and Evolution in Urban Popular Culture

Although forró initially reflected the absolute alienation of rural Northeasterners in the Southeastern metropolises, is it possible that the musicians producing forró lyrics will begin to cognitively map urban space and society once Northeasterners are more permanently settled in the city? To begin to address this question, it should be noted that I have limited my analysis of forró thus far to standards which still make up the majority of songs played by many bands and are widely considered the most authentic to the genre in terms of lyrics and performance (see Chapter One on the forró canon and its development). But what of more recent trends, such as that of forró eletrônico? One might expect that forró eventually began to incorporate a cognitive mapping of the city as Northeasterners became settled in the Southeast and as the urban centers of the Northeast themselves swelled in population. But this is almost universally not the case, not even in the lyrics of the most popular performers in urban markets like Caviar com Rapadura, Mastruz com Leite, Limão com Mel and Walkyria Santos. Although these

---

[3] See the discussion in Chapter Seven of Luiz Gonzaga and Humberto Teixeira's "Respeita Januário" for more on the symbolism of the father/son relationship in traditional forró.

bands all have very pronounced pop sensibilities and accordingly most have achieved major sales to urban audiences, they fail to imagine the social totality in which they perform and their audience lives, just as Luiz Gonzaga and the earliest generations of popular forró were unable to map the city. This in part reflects a reification of certain aspects of the forró canon, especially the sentimental love songs filled with bittersweet yearning for a distant lover. This reification is amplified by elements of Brazilian pop culture that the above-mentioned bands are utilizing.

The developments in recent forró vis-à-vis the city are a bit more complex than this, however, and deserve to be analyzed more specifically in their two main iterations. The first present-day trend in forró involves bands like those just mentioned, categorized by many fans and critics as forró eletrônico. Lyrico-discursively, forró eletrônico focuses on individual subjectivity and sexuality, with themes like passion, betrayal and nostalgic yearning or saudade. This kind of focus, as mentioned, is not alien to previous forró but is much influenced by other hegemonic elements in contemporary Brazilian pop culture such as bestselling popular music like brega and música sertaneja, as well as the most popular cultural phenomena, television soap operas. Brega, in particular, deserves special mention since the performative and lyrical sensibilities of forró eletrônico artists seem to overlap very much with this new genre. The word brega originally was used derogatorily and meant kitsch, but in the last few decades has been embraced by many musicians as a symbol of the unabashed expression of sentimentality and desire in their music, along with the lack of any grounding in established Brazilian musical genres. Forró eletrônico follows this discursive example, and also reflects brega performance styles with the pop appeal of large stage productions including emphasis on lighting, dance and a large number of young performers in fashionable and often sensualized attire. Instrumentation is generally more complex and modern, with emphasis on electric instruments like guitar, bass and keyboard; the canonical sanfona and zabumba are thus relegated to a secondary role. So it could be said that there is a stylistic synthesis with an essentially urban pop sensibility in forró eletrônico. However, this synthesis does not depart significantly from the forró canon in terms of the discursive absence of the urban imaginary. And many of the new elements follow in the vein of earlier innovations in forró— for example, the large number of performers could be considered as a natural extension of the chorus in the call-and-response format of some forró standards by Gonzaga and Jackson do Pandeiro. The absence of the city is, however, only a trace of the subalternity affirmed in earlier forró, thanks to the strong influence of pop music upon this subgenre. Thanks to this influence, it is conceivable that forró eletrônico will begin to develop a cognitive mapping of the city at some point in the future, though it may come at the price of a decisive break with the forró canon.

On the other hand, the two other main subgenres recognized in contemporary forró, universitário and tradicional (AKA pé-de-serra), follow very much in the tradition of the Luiz Gonzaga-inspired canon. Forró pé-de-serra is simply the reaffirmation of the canon in the present day, with a strong emphasis on authenticity that leads precisely to a similar subaltern subject position from which the narrative failure and alienation of modernity are traced. The saudade or nostalgia in such music is all the more poignant and utopian since the rural world it longs for has experienced significant upheaval over the six decades of popular forró's lifespan. But bands that would fall under the less traditionalist forró universitário category often place even more emphasis on the rural idyll, even though these bands sometimes play other music that is not at all resistant to cognitive mapping of the city (and the related articulation of subjectivity within the totality of urban modernity).

Some examples of forró universitário bands that one might deem most likely to thematize urban life are those that have been involved in the "new music scene" indigenous to the northeastern city of Recife, such as Cascabulho and Mestre Ambrósio. In fact, the opening song of Cascabulho's forró album, *Fome dá dor da cabeça* (*Hunger Gives You a Headache*), invokes some major bus routes and the poverty evident in the parts of Recife along these routes. However, this song is unique to the album in its departure from forró into a much more urban, samba-inspired sound. The lyrics and instrumentation of forró songs which comprise the majority of the album tend to emphasize rural life and forrós (in the sense of cultural happenings or parties featuring forró music) in the interior and coastal rural zone where Northeastern music exists in its most folkloric, and thus "authentic" form. As Daniel Sharp notes,

Many of the songs on the recording use the same instrumentation and syncopation as Jackson do Pandeiro's accordion driven *côcos* and *forrós*. The main difference lies in the more aggressive vocal attack and stage presence of the band, which, in the wake of Chico Science's success, borrows subtly from rock and hip-hop. (Sharp 2001, 74-75)

So there is still an urban stylistic influence as in forró eletrônico, but it is offset by a strong emphasis on traditionalism and folkloric roots. These roots are particularly important to many young Pernambucan bands, since they see themselves as inheritors of the musical tradition passed down by the most famous Pernambucan musician, Luiz Gonzaga, as well as Jackson do Pandeiro, another famously talented Northeasterner from the neighboring state of Paraíba.

Another band in the new music scene, Mestre Ambrósio, composed a song whose title, "Pé-de-calçada," invokes a synthesis between traditionalist forró pé-de-serra and the city, as represented by the sidewalk (*calçada*). Yet the lyrics, instrumentation and rhythm themselves are very much within the bounds of the forró canon (the instrumentation is characteristic of Mestre Ambrósio, somewhat richer than a typical forró trio but using mostly canonical instruments). In fact, the city is just invoked with the single trope of the sidewalk, only to be discursively disappeared or swallowed up by magical forró instruments and the timeless rural imaginary in the final lines: "Old rabeca don't abandon me/ Earth-shaking zabumba, eat the ground/ In the hour when time disappears/ Transform the sidewalks into the foot-of-the-mountain [pé-de-serra]" (Siba 1998). These lyrics make explicit, and accentuate to the point of postmodern mysticism, the main utopian desire driving much of the canonical discourse in forró. As if to emphasize this flight into a postmodern beyond, the song ends with a few seconds of a piano playing a mysteriously muffled, electronically-distorted arabesque. I discuss this song further in my analysis of forró's relationship to tradition in Chapter Seven.

Returning to Jameson's negative dialectic of utopias, how can we address these newer developments in forró? Clearly many of these variations in the genre still adhere to the pole of rural utopia and the jaundiced view of the city (to the point of absolute cognitive disassociation) derived from that subject position. This continued adherence reflects the profound influence which the Gonzaga-dominated canon still has upon the more and more diverse field of forró music. The main divergence from the canon is the lyrical focus of forró eletrônico, yet this focus follows in the vein of the sentimental ballads common to canonical forró. However, in closing it is worth mentioning that there is indeed a significant departure within the context of sentimentality, involving the treatment of saudade.

Saudade, as a nostalgic longing or yearning often associated with a distant loved one, is a very common theme in all of Brazilian music, popular and otherwise. Its popularity as a theme in music and literature goes back at least to the Romantic poetry and novels of the nineteenth century which evoked pure, folkloric origins for the Brazilian nation. As discussed in Chapter Two, forró took this theme and made it over on its own terms, tracing the longing and frustrated desire of the migrant as he or she is forced apart from his lover by economic hardship and necessity. So saudade comes to represent in forró not only the migrant's most fervent desires, but also his or her utter alienation in an urban setting far from the possibility of their fulfillment. Forró eletrônico departs from this framing of saudade by detaching the theme from any grounding in the expressivity of the subaltern migrant. In other words, saudade is merely a personal phenomenon in much forró eletrônico, limited to the privacy of individual subjectivity. If the lyrics tell a story of missing and yearning for a lost love, then the split from that loved one is portrayed as a result of infidelity or some other form of personal betrayal and abandonment. Thus the eletrônico treatment of saudade is very much akin to its treatment in other popular culture media like brega and soap operas. In such a manner, the urban environment within which forró continues to flourish has begun finally to enter its discourse, if only symptomatically.

# Chapter Four

# Framing Forró's Perceptiveness: Migration Contextualized

How well do recent forró lyrics and the general imaginary presented within the forró canon depict the real migratory experiences of Northeastern Brazilians? How does the discourse of forró relate to larger trends of internal migration of Northeasterners in Brazil? In this chapter I seek to answer these questions through an overview of testimonials of Northeastern migrants as well as studies from the fields of social psychology, ethnography, media studies, history, and sociology that analyze migratory movements and the lived experience of migration from the Northeast to São Paulo, Brazil's largest metropolitan region. Through consideration of these studies, interviews, and testimonials, it should become clear that overall, forró provides an impressively accurate aesthetic production chronicling the Northeastern migrant perspective. Of course, forró musicians cannot capture every aspect of the migrant experience due to their primary focus on ties to the Northeast and the diasporic affect of saudade. Thus we should also consider facets of migration not addressed by forrozeiros and the reasons for their exclusion from the scope of the genre's imaginary.

## Migrant Testimonials

First, we will turn to various interviews and testimonials given to scholars by Northeasterners who have migrated to São Paulo and the Southeast over the course of the last century. The interviews considered here were published in Brazil as part of municipal or state-funded archives or within individual scholarly research projects at universities in São Paulo and elsewhere. One common topic in these interviews is the migrant's description of his or her first journey from the Northeast to São Paulo. Especially for those who migrated in the mid-twentieth century or before, and/or those who came from isolated rural regions, this journey was very memorable due its length and the difficulties they had to overcome to arrive at their destination. For example, we can consider the story of Maria Odete de Lima, a migrant from Senador Pompeu in the state of Ceará. She migrated to São Paulo with her husband and children when she was eight months pregnant in 1942. She describes her journey in great detail many decades later:

> Saímos do sítio no lombo de burro. Viajamos eu, meu marido, as crianças e minha irmã Creusa. Depois nós pegamos um pau de arara e seguimos viagem até pegar um vapor que transportou a gente pelo rio São Francisco até chegar em Minas Gerais. A gente teve que fazer muitas baldeações e ficávamos nas calçadas dia e noite esperando a próxima condução. A viagem foi muito difícil e as crianças sofreram muito. Em Minas Gerais nós embarcamos em um trem que chacoalhava muito. Eu estava grávida de uns oito meses e já não agüentava mais aquele balanço. Ao todo a viagem durou dezoito dias até chegarmos em São Bernardo do Campo. Sofremos muito durante a viagem. O Valmir, que tinha pouco mais de um ano, ficou doente. [We left the farm on the backs of donkeys. I, my husband, the children, and my sister Creusa were traveling. Next we took a truck and continued the journey until we took a steamboat that took us down the São Francisco river as far as Minas Gerais. We had to make a lot of transfers and we were staying on the streets day and night waiting for the next transport. The journey was very difficult and the children suffered a lot. In Minas Gerais we boarded a train that shook a lot. I was around eight months pregnant and I couldn't stand that shaking anymore. In all the journey took eighteen days to arrive in São Bernardo do Campo. We suffered very much during the journey. Valmir, who was just over one year old, got sick.] (Santo André 2000, 24)

The length and difficulty of this journey is typical of that faced by mid-century migrants, especially those coming from the rural interior of the Northeast. Maria Odete de Lima describes her family taking at least four different modes of transportation to get to their destination over the course of almost three weeks. This is a journey that can now be completed in two days or less by bus or car, and faster still by catching a plane. The family was clearly desperate to find economic opportunites in São Paulo, since they chose to travel despite the fact that the mother of the family was in her third trimester and they had very young children. Tragically, both the one-year-old child, Valmir, and the soon-to-be born infant, Osmar, would die in São Paulo due to the rigors of the difficult journey and the lack of adequate health care facilities for migrants in the destination city.

Real experiences like these are given epic resonance through the stories of migrant families sung by forrozeiros. One classic example is Patativa de Assaré's poem, "A triste partida," which in its original musical version would be performed by Luiz Gonzaga. As discussed in detail in Chapter Two, this lyric details the arduous journey of a family from the rural Northeast to São Paulo in search of work. In fact, they come from the same state as Maria Odete de Lima's family, Ceará. The emphasis on the endurance of great suffering seen in the passage above, from the perspective of a real migrant, is very much akin to that in the fictional rendition of the migrant experience in "A triste partida." Indeed, the primary difference between life and art here lies not in the material conditions and experiences described but in the point of view. Generally, in traditional forró and Northeastern popular poetry the perspective of the singer or poet is gendered male. This interviewee is a woman and a mother and thus we see things a bit more from her perspective, with her concern for her children and her pregnancy taking center stage. "A triste partida" does tell the tale of an entire family's migration, however the emphasis lies on the perspective of the father as head of the family and breadwinner. Thus this interview also shows us that women migrants' standpoints were being overlooked to some degree in traditional forró. This is all the more true of a song like "Asa branca," which assumes the viewpoint of a male migrant migrating alone and leaving his beloved "Rosinha" behind waiting for his return. As one can start to see from the case of Maria Odete de Lima, even in the 1940s it was not uncommon for Northeastern women to migrate, especially in the company of their families. This fact qualifies some of the iconic male figures emphasized by traditional forró, but does not diminish the importance of forrózeiros' ability to accurately and powerfully portray, both lyrically and musically, the refugee (*retirante*) experience of many poor Northeasterners.

Forrozeiros have also addressed through their music the forces that historically expelled people from the Northeastern region in search of work or simply of means for survival. Elsewhere in this study I discuss Luiz Gonzaga and Zé Dantas's "Vozes da seca [Voices from the Drought]" as well as Flávio José's "Utopia sertaneja [Backland Utopia]." These are important examples of songs which take on, in more or less direct ways, the causes behind the displacement of Northeastern migrants in an effort to imagine a solution for, or transcendence of, this displacement. The earlier work, produced in the mid-twentieth century during forró's golden era, addresses drought as the primary driving force behind migration. As discussed in Chapter Three, the singer of "Vozes da seca" has a somewhat naïve belief in the ability and willingness of regional or national elites to address the poverty and drought in the Northeast. The song assumes that merely shining a bright light on the problems of the Northeast will cause real reform to be instituted. The recent work, "Utopia sertaneja" (2004), recorded by Paraíban musician Flávio José, has a more jaundiced view of the political and economic elites, explicitly stating that the sertão needs to "stop seeing in power a friend that will be true" and calling for a move towards self-sufficiency with the aid of improved education (see Chapter Seven for the relevant lyrics). The regional perspective over the five decades between these songs has continued to include a desire for redemption, but the possibility of that redemption is sought more in the region itself and its own economy, environment, culture, and people. This shift, essentially determined by continually failed state policies regarding Northeastern poverty, is mirrored in comments made by migrants to São Paulo in their interviews given in recent decades. For example, one Northeastern migrant cum successful São Paulo industrialist was very critical of the so-called "drought industry" (see Chapter Three for further discussion) in the Northeast and the corruption among regional elites. This migrant called for a halt in federal funds destined for the region due to this perennial embezzlement (Medina 1989, 110). Such comments, in tandem with some recent forró lyrics such as those of Flávio José, certainly mark a shift in perspective since Luiz Gonzaga first performed "Vozes da seca," a song in which the singer places his faith in more aid from the federal government for his region.

Upon arriving in a Southeastern metropolis like São Paulo, it is not surprising that a Northeastern migrant would experience a certain amount of culture shock. This shock tended to be greater in the past when the Northeast was more isolated (in terms of communication and transportation), and continues to be greater for those who are emigrating from more rural regions of the Northeast. In Chapter Three, I outlined how this shock is typically represented in forró discourse—namely, through a refusal or failure to cognitively map the geographical and social cityscape. Instead, as detailed in Chapter Two, forrozeiros have tended to focus on the imaginary of the Northeast left behind, maintaining ties to the region through the diasporic affect of saudade. But one can imagine that the singer of "Asa branca" and the family of migrants in "A triste partida" did not find it easy to adapt to the rhythms of life in the Southeast. Even though there is not much detailed description of the migrant family's life in the destination city, we can get some sense of culture shock upon arrival in São Paulo from the following verses in "A triste partida," which describe how the family "Only sees strange faces/ of strange people" and how "Everything is different/ than the dear farmland."

Interviews with real migrants reveal similar feelings of alienation or culture shock when migrating from the Northeast, or even when returning to São Paulo from visits with family in the Northeast. A common framework amongst the interviewees for considering the differences between the Northeast and São Paulo is the distinct "rhythm of life" in either region. São Paulo is typically described as "agitado" or hectic while the Bahian pace of life, for instance, is more "calm" (Oliveira 1982). In addition, the Northeast and especially its natural or agricultural landscapes are seen to be far more beautiful than the vast, sometimes jarring cityscape of São Paulo. This appreciation of the pace of life and beauty of the Northeast can be found in many forró classics, such as Humberto Teixeira and Luiz Gonzaga's "Estrada de Canindé." As discussed further in Chapter Seven, this work compares the slower pace of life and natural, rural landscape of the sertão favorably to the frenetic urban lifestyle of the Southeast. While not exactly an ode to nature, Gonzaga and Teixeira's "Juazeiro" also merits mention here since it demonstrates a profound identification with, and anthropomorphization of, a common tree in the Northeastern interior.

Two other important factors that contribute to culture shock for Northeasterners in São Paulo are differences in language and cuisine. The difficulties with language have not so much to do with communication as with stigmatization. The effects of a heavy Northeastern accent upon a listener in São Paulo can perhaps be compared to that of a Southern U.S. accent in New York. The Northeasterner may well be labeled with the stereotype of being a hillbilly or country bumpkin, i.e. the pejorative sense of *sertanejo* (or *matuto*). Thus some interviewees speak of facing social discrimination due to their regional accent (Santo André 2000, 8). For instance, one Paraíban who migrated as a child remembered suffering cruelty from his schoolmates, who teased him for his origins (Medina 1989, 110). Forró singers beginning with Luiz Gonzaga have fought stereotypes about the Northeast's putative backwardness and, linguistically speaking, have tried to maintain and valorize the characteristic Northeastern accent through its continued usage in their performances and recordings.

In terms of cuisine, Northeasterners tend to miss the regional dishes and ingredients that are less common in São Paulo (Santo André 2000, 86).

However, this saudade is mitigated somewhat by the so-called "Casas do Norte" that have popped up in virtually every Northeastern neighborhood of São Paulo. These stores sell supplies for making Northeastern cuisine trucked directly from the region, and sometimes prepared foods as well. Forró songs like Luiz Gonzaga and Miguel Lima's "Penerô xerém" reflect this affection for regional cuisine. In this work the singer calls for a certain Dona Chiquinha to "grind up some corn...for canjiquinha" and to make other dishes beloved in the Northeast (Gonzaga and Lima, n.d.). The song's title refers to the sifting of corn and the word "canjiquinha" is itself an affectionate reference to *canjica*, a popular Northeastern corn stew. The harvest festival of São João is very important in the Northeast and corn is featured in the typical São João delicacies as one of the most important food crops of the region. As discussed in Chapter Two, this winter festival is also celebrated by Northeastern migrants throughout the country, who prepare the traditional corn dishes that help to assuage nostalgia for the home region during a time of year when thoughts turn to the Northeast.

The non-cultural factor of climatic change can sometimes be the most difficult for Northeasterners outside of their region. The shock in this case is primarily caused by the relative cold of the Southeast. The warddrobe that migrants bring with them often seems inadequate to deal with the cooler climes, especially combined with a lack of heating in their new abodes. As an example, the migrant from Ceará quoted above, Maria Odete de Lima, complained that her entire family suffered from the cold upon arriving in São Paulo (Santo André 2000, 25). Indeed, one collection of interviews from Northeasterners featured so many complaints about the cold and rain in São Paulo that the weather is referenced in the title, *Forró na garoa* (Medina 1989). *Garoa* is the fine, misty rain for which São Paulo is famous, or in this case infamous. The reader will note that the title also references forró, using it as a symbol for the presence of a Northeastern diaspora in São Paulo. The attitude about the weather in São Paulo in these interviews is mirrored in the general negative perspective on the Southeast as a place of exile in forró lyrics. With regard to culture as well as to weather, the interviewees are primarily focused on negative change—in this instance, the painful differences in climate from their home region.

As argued in Chapter Three, the destination of migration is primarily utilized by forrozeiros as part of a negative dialectic. This dialectic criticizes a society in which Northeasterners are forced out of their home region by uneven development and the resulting inequalities between regions and social classes. In the case of the discourse of Northeasterners and the Northeastern artists who attempt to represent their common experiences, the negativity is primarily focused on the alienation of Northeasterners from the sertão who have sought to make a living in a Southeastern urban environment. From the various interviews analyzed for this study as well as this author's personal conversations with Northeasterners, it seems that Northeastern migrants from a variety of areas and backgrounds can identify with this alienation to a greater or lesser degree, whether or not they come from the sertão, a small town, or even a larger coastal city. Canonical forró songs tend to focus on migrants from the sertão (or Northeastern rural interior), such as the classics "Asa branca," "Pau-de-arara," and "No meu pé-de-serra" discussed elsewhere. The experiences of these sertanejos, though, epitomize the sense of loss, displacement, and of course nostalgia or saudade felt to some degree by all Northeastern migrants. The evidence from interviews of Northeasterners demonstrates that even well-adjusted, well-employed migrants in the Southeast can feel a strong sense of saudade (Santo André 2000). For example, one migrant to the São Paulo area from Bahia managed to become a successful lawyer but still agreed with the playwright Luís Alberto de Abreu that "[the migrant's] body is here but his soul remains in the place of origin" (Ibid., 18). For many migrants, São Paulo is considered a good place to get an education or to make a living, but it never equals the significance of the Northeast in terms of regional-cultural and ethnic identity.

Saudade itself is a common topic of conversation for Northeastern migrants and also a favorite theme for forrozeiros. As analyzed in Chapter Two, it is of course the converse of the culture shock experienced by migrants, a feeling of continual attachment to the home region and a desire for return to that familiar and beloved place of origin. One interviewee explained that migrants were always trying to live "in the two places at the same moment—one in presence and the other in thought" (Oliveira 1982, 34). This is the "jeito" or trick of saudade that allows the Northeasterner to live outside of the Northeast without giving in to melancholy or despair. Certainly the genre of forró itself plays a key role in enacting this *jeito*— collective celebration with forró lyrics, music and dance in the diaspora evokes, for migrants, the lived experience of the Northeast and the region's culture and leisure activities in particular. Forró thus makes the Northeast's presence felt throughout Brazil, momentarily "killing" the saudade of those who feel far from their origins of kinship and culture.

But there are many for whom the saudade is too much, or for whom life has become too difficult in the Southeast for one reason or another. These Northeasterners choose to return. According to the estimates of major bus companies in the late 1980s, three thousand Northeasterners were departing from São Paulo for their home region daily (Medina 1989, 72). During the same period, one reporter interviewed the passengers on a bus to the Northeast and found that no one on the bus was sad to be leaving São Paulo. Instead, they complained of feelings of alienation, a lack of solidarity and a high cost of living in São Paulo as negative forces driving them out of the city. On the other hand, saudade for their "terrinha" or place of origin in the Northeast exerted its own positive attraction upon some. The poorest of these migrants were also being influenced by São Paulo migration policies, since the state was paying for their tickets, as it does for any indigent migrants who wish to return to their place of origin (Medina 1989, 72).

Forró as a genre focuses on the motivation of saudade as the key factor bringing migrants back to the Northeast. Canonical works such as "A volta da asa branca" and "No Ceará não tem disso não" rejoice over the possibility of imminent return and implicitly or explicitly valorize life in the Northeast over that in the Southeast. "No Ceará" in particular outlines, in a light-hearted manner, a sense of alienation and bewilderment with respect to life in the great urban centers. Taking into consideration the other factors such as lack of economic opportunity and influence from state migration policies, we can see that there is more at work than just the affective force of saudade to propagate return migration. Forró's canonical narratives are a simplification that emphasize the agency and desires of Northeasterners over systemic political or socio-economic influences. In fact, there is yet another significant phenomenon in this context that falls out of forró's lens. Various migrants to São Paulo relate a feeling of saudade for the Southeastern city after returning to the Northeast for visits. These are typically migrants who consider themselves "paulistas" or São Paulo locals at the same time as being Northeasterners (Medina 1989, 112). Some famous examples of paulista Northeasterners are Luiza Erundina, who grew up in the sertão of Paraíba and eventually became the mayor of São Paulo in 1989, and of course Luiz Inácio "Lula" da Silva, a migrant from Pernambuco's interior who would be elected president of a steelworkers' union in São Paulo in 1975 and as federal deputy for São Paulo in 1986 (and ultimately president of Brazil in 2002 and 2006). A few Northeasterners who have found success in São Paulo do not even wish to return to the Northeast to visit and identify exclusively as paulistas (Sarno 1965). Based upon the discourse of forró, the identification of Northeasterners as paulistas is quite a surprising development. It is hard to imagine the singer of "Asa branca" or "Pau-de-arara" giving a second thought to a Southeastern city if able to return to their home region. But considering the fact that many Northeasterners have spent years in São Paulo and Rio de Janeiro and have developed an entire social and kinship network there, and in many cases have realized their entire professional careers there, it seems understandable that they would foster affective ties to that space in addition to the Northeast.

As explained previously, the hyperdevelopment of Southeastern Brazil has attracted Northeastern migrants for decades. São Paulo itself has sustained most of its population growth over the last century through migration rather than birth rates (Berlinck and Hogan 1974). Of course, these data for the last century include migrants from other regions and countries. However, by the 1950s the evidence suggests that the vast majority of migrant arrivals in São Paulo were Northeasterners (Sarno 1965; Berlinck and Hogan 1974; Santos 1994).[1] All of these people were coming to the Southeast because there were real economic opportunities there and as a result it came to be known as a land of opportunity to Northeasterners. The establishment of a population of Northeasterners in the vicinity of São Paulo and Rio de Janeiro only encouraged further migration there, as word of mouth advertised the jobs to be found in the region to family and friends left behind. At the same time, forrozeiros like Luiz Gonzaga were developing a counterdiscourse that warned against seeing the Southeast as a utopia for Northeastern workers. Songs like "Asa branca" and especially "A triste partida" emphasized not only the pain of leaving the Northeast behind, but also the often harsh circumstances waiting to greet the migrant upon his or

---

[1] According to the documentary *Viramundo* (1965), 1,290,000 Northeasterners migrated to São Paulo in the decade 1952-1962. Berlinck's (1974) data indicate that in the decade 1950-1960, São Paulo's population increased by about 1.6 million. Santos (1994) provides data indicating that the migratory component of São Paulo's population growth in the fifties was 65%, which would be about 1,040,000 people. Thus the number of Northeastern migrants who arrived in the city in that decade exceeded the total population growth from migration by several hundred thousand.

her arrival in São Paulo or other parts of the region. There was no attempt by these musicians to reproduce narratives about successful migrants or in any way to encourage emigration from the Northeast. As mentioned above, if anything the greater part of the forró canon tends to valorize return migration to one's original community. Many Northeasterners have come to recognize the wisdom of these songs that encourage realistic expectations about the economic benefits of migrating to the Southeast. In the final decades of the twentieth century, migrants have continued to hear tales of São Paulo as the "land of success" or "of money," and these tales continue to attract them to the city and its vicinity (Santo André 2000, 27). Yet like the Northeasterners departing from São Paulo by the busload, those who do migrate are recognizing more and more that they will not likely achieve any significant social mobility through migration.

On the other hand, thanks to the establishment of large Northeastern migrant communities throughout the metropolitan region of São Paulo, it is not necessary for most migrants from the same region to immediately find economic success in order to survive in the city. This ability to survive without immediate formal or even informal employment is due to the social networks created by Northeastern migrants throughout São Paulo and elsewhere. Anthropological and ethnographic studies like that of Baptista as well as sociological work such as Durham's landmark study all emphasize the continued and increasing importance of these social networks (Baptista 1998; Durham 1978). The most important of these networks tends to be that of kinship. It is a truism that family is very important to Brazilians, and this is all the more the case for Northeasterners and Northeastern migrants. Baptista's study focusing on the favela of Jardim Colombo in São Paulo (inhabited by a Northeastern migrant majority) demonstrates well how kinship networks are essential in allowing migrants looking for work to survive in the city for months or more while living with various family members.

The importance of these social networks becomes clear when one considers the current economic situation for migrants to the Southeast. Entry-level jobs in the formal economy have become scarcer (especially in the previously booming industries of construction and manufacturing) since 1980, while the reserve workforce continues to grow (Jannuzzi 2000). Jannuzzi among others also confirms that skilled labor has a greater and greater advantage in terms of employment and social mobility. These conditions make the job market very difficult to penetrate for many poor, unskilled Northeastern migrants and even second- or third-generation Northeastern residents of São Paulo. Nevertheless, many are able to survive life in the big city and eventually find some sort of full- or part-time work, most often in the tertiary sector, due to the aid of their relatives who have already established themselves in São Paulo. In poor neighborhoods like Jardim Colombo, it is also common for Northeasterners from the same small community in the home region to settle in the same community in the Southeastern diaspora. This atmosphere contributes to a neighborhood social network of support as well. One other important social network beyond that of kinship and neighborhood demonstrated by Baptista is that of religious communities. With examples from her interviews with migrants, Baptista argues that these religious social networks can be of particular help to women, giving them psychological support and social assistance with common familial problems of domestic and alcohol abuse (Baptista 1998, 213). This argument is confirmed by John Burdick's analysis of religion's empowerment of Afro-Brazilian women in the Southeast, a group that shares a similar, often identical socio-economic position with Northeastern migrant women (Burdick 1998). Finally, one evangelical migrant explained that he had no difficulty in adapting to life in São Paulo (Santo André 2000, 30). This particular case demonstrates that, independent of gender, religious communities can help Northeastern migrants feel at home outside of their native region.

Thus, in general terms, the solidarity of Northeasterners in the diaspora has allowed them to survive and at times thrive in cities like São Paulo, on an economic and even a political level. However, the woes of emigration from the Northeast catalogued in the forró canon remain relevant and are becoming increasingly more so as the job market worsens in São Paulo, especially for low-skilled workers. We have seen the evidence of return migration as a sign that many poor and working-class Northeasterners would agree with the singer of "Asa branca" that their home region is really the best place for them to be. Nevertheless, when considering the evidence above about social networks in São Paulo, we should refer back to Chapter Three and the phenomenon in forró discourse of resistance to cognitively mapping these same social spaces of the Southeast. In so doing, we can see that there is much about the lived experience of migration to São Paulo that falls out of forrozeiros' narratives. Survival in the diaspora is certainly possible, and if one has a network of support from family and neighbors also from the Northeast, one need not feel completely alienated from the place one settles, nor psychologically devastated by saudade for one's loved ones left behind. Taking into consideration these facts excluded from forró's narratives, one can better understand that traditional forró lyricists are representing a specific migrant standpoint that does not encompass the entirety of the experience of migration. They emphasize the movement of migration and return migration over and against the way of life in the destination city or region. This is part of a general critical orientation towards the manner in which Northeasterners have been forced to migrate for reasons of economic necessity. Their lyrics make it clear that most migrants would much rather stay in their home region, but due to the underdevelopment of the Northeast (or the hyperdevelopment of the Southeast), they are essentially forced to seek work elsewhere.

Yet even in academic studies and interviews that do, unlike forró, focus on Northeasterners' attempts to adapt to life in São Paulo, there are indications that migrants from rural areas continue to be influenced by a peasant standpoint after settling in a city. In this sense they are in tune with the typical standpoint of traditional forró singers, whose ideal is to be relatively independent or self-sufficient through working their own plot of land. The influence of this standpoint is particularly clear with respect to the kinds of jobs most prized by the Northeasterners living in Southeastern metropolitan regions. It is not so much that they wish to be farming plots of land in the middle of São Paulo city. Rather, what all of these jobs share in common is the sense of autonomy which the worker derives from them, a sense which rural-urban migrants especially tend to value. These kinds of jobs often involve self-employment or a low degree of supervision from superiors, ranging from merchant to taxi driver (Durham 1978). Some Northeastern migrants even derive a welcome sense of autonomy from factory labor despite close supervision. As explained by several interviewees, in this case it is the ability to be recognized by both employer and state as a worker in the formal economy that provides a sense of autonomy, since along with this recognition come certain guaranteed rights like regular health care and unemployment benefits (Oliveira 1982, 38; Medina 1989, 41).

Taking a social-psychological approach, Cardel theorizes a "sertão peasant ethic" (*ética camponesa sertaneja*) that is maintained amongst rural Northeastern migrants to the city (Cardel 2003). This ethic includes the desire for some level of autonomy as just noted, but more generally consists of a conservationist mentality with respect to Northeastern culture and identity. With a focus on migrants to São Paulo from the rural municipality of Olhos d'Água, Bahia, Cardel demonstrates the psychological state of liminality that is prevalent amongst virtually all migrants to some degree. Those who have come out of a rural background of subsistence farming, sharecropping, and/or day labor find themselves in a more intensely liminal psychological state once displaced into urban São Paulo. They are between two places in that they are continually considering the possibility of return to their place of origin—as Cardel terms it, this is both a feeling and a reality of eternal return, since many of the migrants find themselves shuttling back and forth between the two regions based on their economic and emotional-psychological needs (Cardel 2003). One special category of migrant that is particularly oriented towards return to the home region is what Cardel terms the "indivíduo migrante potencialmente herdeiro"—a migrant, usually the first-born son, who is likely to inherit his parents' plot of land when they are no longer able to farm it themselves due to old age or death. These men are also typically encouraged to marry within their original communities to solidify their roots there. Here we can recall the singer of "A volta da asa branca" who hopes to be able to return to his home region and get married to his beloved Rosinha by the end of the year—as long as the harvest does not spoil his plans. Thus the evidence that Cardel presents regarding recent migration to São Paulo is very much in line with the discourse of the forró canon. We can assume that many migrants, perhaps almost all Northeastern migrants to some degree, imagine the ideal conditions which would allow them to return to the home region and finally put down roots.

Another aspect of migration that forró has not been able to capture in its full complexity is the distinct experience of female migrants. Especially in the context of traditional forró or the forró canon, the perspective of the singer tends to be gendered male—whether or not the subject of the song is migration. Nevertheless, the reality is that for several decades women have often comprised the majority of internal migrants in Brazil (Medina 1989, 156). In Cardel's study, the number of female migrants from the community of Olhos d'Água, Bahia at the turn of the twenty-first century was nearly double that of male migrants (Cardel 2003). Cardel explains the greater number of women migrants in terms of the normative gender roles of their home community in the rural interior of Bahia. Men, especially men who are potential heirs of their family's land, are expected eventually to return and settle down in their place of origin. On the other hand, there is more flexibility with regard to women from the community who find husbands who are "good workers" and therefore putatively can provide for them. It is accepted that these women need to settle in the destination city (in this case São Paulo).

Yet there is a certain danger for women who choose to migrate on their own. Again, this is an issue that is overlooked in the discourse of forró. According to one interviewee from a small Northeastern community in the interior, women are judged to be prostitutes if they leave their community alone, unaccompanied by a male family member (Baptista 1998, 191). On the other end of their migratory journey, women like the aforementioned Luiza Erundina continue to have to battle against machismo if they seek to have a successful career (Medina 1989). Despite such obstacles, many—at times most—migrants have been women in recent decades (IBGE 2003, 54). In terms of economic opportunity, this is not surprising—there is more unskilled labor available for women than for men in the service sector thanks to the demand for female housekeepers, maids, and cooks. This situation has also led to a greater number of women becoming heads of household or providers for their families since the 1980s (Baptista 1998, 162; Clemente 1993, 53). In general, Northeastern women interviewed in various studies and surveys find a greater amount of freedom with respect to gender roles when they migrate to São Paulo. Comments made to interviewers reflect a general sense of more widely-accepted lifestyle choices for women, including support for, or at least tolerance of, women as workers and as single mothers (Santo André 2000, 77; Medina 1989, 80). Another woman's story highlights the relative lack of acceptance of single mothers in the Northeastern interior. This woman became pregnant in the Northeast and then migrated in order to give birth to her baby in São Paulo, due to her sense that she and her child would be shunned in her home town for not being part of a normative nuclear family (Medina 1989, 93).

Finally, there are indeed poor migrant women from the Northeast who, whether by choice or coercion, become prostitutes. These are likely the Northeasterners whose experience is furthest from that projected in forró discourse, since commonly they do not see the Northeast as a place to which they would prefer to return if possible. As explained in Pereira's study of prostitution in São Paulo, many prostitutes are migrants who have been forced out of their homes because of emotional, physical or sexual abuse (Pereira 1996). For these women and girls, migration is an escape from their traumatic pasts, and prostitution one of the few choices of employment open to them as homeless female migrants. Thus it is not surprising that one teen sex worker in São Paulo who had migrated from the Northeast was not very responsive regarding her biography when interviewed, commenting that she did not like to think about her past (Medina 1989, 58). Clearly, this standpoint is far from the typical forró perspective that longs for return and imagines the Northeast as a redemptive space. It is important to recognize that, especially in the context of migration, forrozeiros have not been able to represent these experiences of lower class women. Due to the largely male-gendered perspective of traditional forró, the genre has also failed to represent the more common experience of women who migrate on their own and find legal work in the service sector of the Southeast. Another reason for this lacuna in forró lyrics is that, as argued above, the genre has always resisted representations of the destination space of migration, focusing more on redemption through return migration to the Northeast. Even in the case of recent electronic and university forró, in which women participate to a greater extent in singing, lyrics and songwriting, the experiences and epistemes of women migrants have not yet found lyrical prominence.

Turning back to an issue that is of concern both in forró and in the interviews of Northeastern migrants, we can consider the necessity to preserve Northeastern popular culture. This conservationist attitude is something that most Northeastern migrants can identify with and was brought up by various interviewees. For instance, one migrant to São Paulo worried about the influence of mass culture on Northeastern popular culture, citing the influence of a Rio de Janeiro-produced soap opera on the popularity of certain kinds of Northeastern folk art (Medina 1989, 105). Others mentioned a desire to preserve Northeastern culture more generally, and in terms of music specifically, to maintain traditional forró's privileged status above innovations in the genre that are considered "forró moderno" (Santo André 2000, 66). In Galhardo's study of visitors to the event-space of the Center of Northeastern Traditions (CTN) in São Paulo, there is an almost universal sense amongst the interviewees of the urgent need for a *resgate* or rescue of Northeastern traditional culture in the diaspora (Galhardo 2003). Most interviewees surveyed, including both first-generation migrants and their children, saw the CTN (discussed in detail in Chapter Two) as an authentic and effective space for preserving Northeastern culture. They deemed it important to pass on a regional cultural patrimony to the next generation so as to keep ties to the Northeast strong. Galhardo argues that this conservationist orientation is a means of opting out of the more corporate, homogenized, mass-culture industry of São Paulo. Baptista, too, describes the residents of the Jardim Colombo favela as opting out of the mass-culture industry—but these residents, due to their poverty, tend to spend their leisure time within the confines of their own community and do not regularly visit the CTN. Like the attendees of celebrations at the CTN, though, Northeastern migrants in Jardim Colombo regularly gather together in events to commemorate important regional festivals with traditional food and dancing (Baptista 1998). As one might expect, forró takes precedence at such events as it does at the CTN. Thus in this case, forró's attempt since its inception in the 1940s to valorize, share, and preserve Northeastern popular culture continues to be a widely praised project amongst Northeastern migrants and their descendents.[2]

**Migration Policy and the Sociology and History of Migration**

According to urban and regional planning specialist Carlos B. Vainer,

> the history of the constitution and evolution of the Brazilian state has been, also, in good part, the history of ideas, institutions and practices directed at measuring and administrating the mobilization and placement of populations (Vainer 2000, 15).

In this second section of the chapter, I will seek to demonstrate the accuracy of this assessment by analyzing various shifts in modes of migration in Brazil since the nineteenth century as well as some related developments in state (read: elite) policies concerning migration. My intent is to ground the history of Northeastern migration detailed by forró lyrics in a larger historical and sociological context of population flows within and between the regions of Brazil. Having established such a context, we can then consider more specifically how forró musicians have positioned themselves with respect to the many and changing debates and policies concerning migration.

---

[2] For a relevant comparison of conservationist and renovationist approaches among Brazilian artists of the twentieth century, see Draper, 2008.

The earliest phase of post-Independence migration policy in Brazil revolved around a desire to import European migrants and thereby to Europeanize or "whiten" the country. The evidence of the Brazilian elite's Euro-centric immigration policies goes back to the very founding of the Brazilian Empire. A week after the establishment of Brazil's first constitution in 1824, the emperor Dom Pedro I signed a law demarcating the lands of the German colony of São Leopoldo, justifying the existence of the colony by explaining the "superior advantage of employing free white people, industrious as much in the arts as in agriculture" (Vainer 2000, 15). Later, this desire to encourage the immigration of free white workers would be combined with the desire of regional and national elites to prevent an exodus of Brazilian workers from rural areas. Frederico Neves labels this latter desire as a need "to keep the man in the country" in order, firstly, to assure sufficient labor for the landowners in the latifundia system and, secondly, to avoid the growth of conglomerations of poor migrants in the larger cities (Neves 1996). These latter groups were deemed as potentially dangerous mobs and indeed did increase crime in cities like Fortaleza when they traveled seeking refuge from the devastating drought of 1877 and later severe dry spells. Of course, in the twentieth century similar groups of poor migrants began to settle more permanently in the cities and form favelas. However, from the latter part of the nineteenth century through the first half of the twentieth, policies to discourage such internal migration were prevalent. In Ceará, Neves argues that the policies that were putatively developed in order to combat droughts (such as irrigation and public works projects in the interior) were in fact primarily attempts to prevent large-scale migration of rural workers (Neves 1996).

Furthermore, it is no coincidence that the earliest attempts to "keep the man in the country" occurred during the dying years of slavery. As more and more Afro-Brazilians found freedom after 1850, culminating with abolition in 1888, elites became increasingly concerned with keeping these newly liberated men and women in the country, specifically in the same municipalities in which they had been slaves. For example, the Saraiva-Cotegipe law of 1885 established that ex-slaves were required to remain in the same municipality for five years after their emancipation. Otherwise, according to the language of the law "he who absent[ed] himself from his domicile [would] be considered vagabond and apprehended by the police in order to be employed in public works or agricultural colonies" (Vainer

2000). This restriction on movement was only one among multiple restrictions on liberated Afro-Brazilians set forth in the Saraiva-Cotegipe law, however for our purposes it is the most relevant. It reflects the deep fears of the elites that slaveowners would lose all of their manual laborers and that former slaves would migrate and destabilize urban areas as drought refugees had already begun to do in the 1870s. As Neves demonstrates, this attempt to keep rural workers in their native municipalities heralded a paradigm that would be followed for much of the following century in Ceará and the Northeast more generally. This anti-migratory policy reached its final iteration in the so-called *frentes de trabalho* or work fronts organized by the state and federal governments in the 1950s and sixties (Neves 1996). Again, the aim of these public works and irrigation projects was to employ rural workers within or near to their native municipalities in order to prevent them from emigrating to more densely populated urban areas. Previously I have mentioned the "drought industry" which turned these work fronts into corrupt and politicized organs, manipulated by the local authorities to their own political and financial advantage. Whatever the effectiveness or legitimacy of the fronts with regard to the local infrastructure, they may well have had the unintended side effect of encouraging rural-urban migration by salarizing rural workers. These workers were then inclined to migrate to industrialized areas where they could more easily participate in the salaried workforce (Neves 1996). Despite continued efforts from elites at the local, regional and national levels, Northeasterners had begun to migrate en masse in search of economic security.

Yet the Euro-centric mentality of policymakers favoring international migrants lasted well into the fifties, even as the new post-war paradigm of internal migration took hold. At last in 1955, President Kubitschek had begun to acknowledge the phenomenon of rural-urban migration as inevitable and identified the "rural exodus" as a "symptom of progress" (Vainer 2000, 24). Of course, this judgement reflects Kubitschek's favored policy of import substitution through rapid urban industrialization. At the same time, it ignores what forró highlights—the often painful experiences of those forced out of their home regions in order to survive in the new economy. By the decade of the sixties, policymakers had recognized that internal migration was by far the primary source of migrants throughout the entire country. In 1980, when the rural exodus had been deemed excessive and a more totalitarian governmental approach to population flows had been established, the National Program of Support to Internal Migrations was created. Vainer details how a national "strategy of territorial rationalization of migratory flows" had been developed over the course of the military regime's years in power, leading up to this National Program and its sub-programs, SIMI and SAMI (the former being the System of Information on Internal Migrations and the latter Support Services to Migrants) (Vainer 2000). The institutional bases of SAMI became the so-called CETREMIs (Centers of Migrant Triage and Guidance), which continued to function in the post-dictatorship era. These centers provide migrants with temporary lodging and give them funds for travel to their place of origin or to locations of possible employment.

Yet Aranha argues that in practice, the CETREMIs (also called CETRENs, hostels, migrant assistance institutions, etc.) have functioned to discipline migrants' bodies and movement through São Paulo state in such a way that they are continually displaced, forced to travel from one CETREMI to the next with no real chance of settling down (Aranha 1996). Such temporary lodging for migrants is a key element amongst the strategies developed by municipalities in São Paulo to force poor migrants to be continually itinerant. These policies even include secret deportations of migrants from cities, with rented vehicles being used to transport them to other cities in the earliest hours of the morning. Rather than attempting to get workers to settle in the country as governing elites did in the past, these cities simply prevent them from forming favelas within their own borders, pushing the problem to neighboring municipalities. Vainer confirms that similar efforts are ongoing in other states such as Rio Grande do Sul, calling them "active policies of segregation and closure of urban territory to migrants" (Vainer 2000, 29). The same author argues further that these recent efforts to segregate migrants on the local level are related to the absence of a national migration policy in a neoliberal era. The social response to migrants' needs is only enacted in a piecemeal and short-term fashion that ultimately reinforces their constant migratory status.

Internal migration has continued to be the most significant source of population flows up to the present day in all the five major regions of Brazil. The part Northeastern Brazilians have played in this history can be seen if one considers the migration data for the past few decades, especially between the Northeast and its emigrants' preferred destination, the Southeast. In both the seventies and eighties, 3.5 million Northeasterners migrated to the state of São Paulo, for a total of 7 million over the course of two decades (Oliveira 1982; Della Monica 1992). During this same period, Santos demonstrates that about a third of Brazil's total population were internal migrants—31.7% in the 1970s and 33.6% in the 1980s (Santos 1994). Thus Northeasterners were part of a larger phenomenon of mass displacement within the country as rapid industrialization reached its zenith in the metropolitan centers and the so-called "agricultural frontiers" of the Center West and the North continued to draw workers (Cunha 1995). While the overall number of internal migrants relative to the national population has declined somewhat in more recent years[3], Northeasterners continue to migrate in large numbers and to favor the Southeast and São Paulo specifically as a destination. Even a cursory glance at a migration map based on Brazil's 2000 census confirms that population flows between the Northeast and Southeast (especially São Paulo) continue to represent the most significant migration between regions in the country (Fig. 4.1).

Before moving on to analyze the data from the 2000 census that confirm the continued significance of Northeastern migrants, let us consider the following broad overview of demographic developments in the mid- to late twentieth century:

> The principal tendencies of urbanization and of spatial redistribution of the Brazilian population, in the 1940-80 period, pointed [...] towards the multiplication of the number of cities, towards the growing concentration of the population in urban locales of great size, principally in metropolitan areas, and towards the concentration of economic and demographic activity in the Southeastern Region, especially São Paulo and Rio de Janeiro (Sales and Baeninger 2000).

Since 1980, all of these trends have continued to be significant, but with some important variations. These newer developments include migration from the center to the periphery of metropolitan areas, migration to mid-sized cities, and most importantly with respect to Northeasterners, return migration to their native region (IBGE 2003). Recent census data demonstrate both continued migration to the Southeast as well as increasing migration from the Southeast to the Northeast at the turn of the twenty-first

---

[3] According to census data for the period 1995-2000, 9.1% of the national population were internal migrants (IBGE 2003, 74, 76). Doubling this figure for the decade still results in less than 20% of the national population as internal migrants, a significantly lower percentage than that of the two previous decades noted above (31.7% and 33.6% respectively).

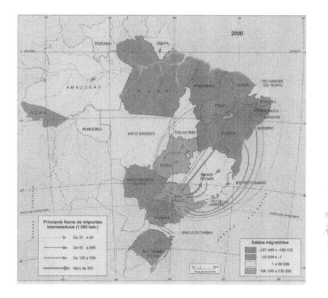

Figure 4.1: Map of net migratory flows between 1991 and 2000 (thicker
arrows indicate a larger group of migrants) [Source: IBGE 2003, 51]

century. For example, between 1986 and 1991, 917,482 Brazilians migrated
from the Northeastern to the Southeastern region of the country (IBGE 2003,
48). This figure represented the vast majority (67.7%) of the total number of
emigrants from the Northeast during the five-year period. A decade later, in
the period 1995-2000, the number of emigrants to the Southeast reached a
total of 969,435, that is, 68.7% of the total number of emigrants from the
Northeast (IBGE 2003, 48). Thus in terms of both absolute numbers and of
the percentage of total emigration from the region, migration from the
Northeast to the Southeast has remained significant and even increased
somewhat (5.7%) in recent years. However, despite being smaller in absolute
numbers, the relative increase in migration going in the opposite direction
has been far more significant. In the period 1986-1991, 332,434 Brazilians
migrated from the Southeast to the Northeast. A decade later, in the period
1995-2000, 462,628 people migrated in the same direction (IBGE 2003, 48).
Thus there was a 38.3% increase in migration from the Southeast to the
Northeast between the two decades.

   Therefore in relative terms, migration from Southeast to Northeast has
increased most dramatically. There remains the question of how one can
surmise that these figures represent a return of Northeastern migrants to the

home region rather than a new group of migrants from the Southeast. In fact, other data from the same census tend to support the former conclusion that Northeasterners are returning home in greater numbers. First of all, one needs to consider the profile of the Northeasterners who are leaving their home region. The plurality of these migrants are in their twenties, and as mentioned before, the majority of them are moving to the Southeast. Census charts taking the age and gender of migrants into consideration indicate that the number of emigrants from the Northeast gets smaller and smaller as age rises. Charts for the Southeast demonstrate an almost exactly inverse phenomenon—thus more and more people leave the Southeast (and less arrive) as they get older whereas people leave the Northeast in decreasing numbers (and immigrate in greater numbers) as they age beyond their twenties (IBGE 2003, 54-55). These data are consistent with typical behavior of Northeastern migrants, that is, leaving in their twenties in search of work and then returning in later decades to settle down in their native region. Migratory flows by gender do not differ much in these charts, confirming that, at least in the last few decades, migration between Northeast and Southeast has certainly not been a "male" phenomenon as one might surmise from some traditional forró lyrics.

The Brazilian government's census-taking body (the Brazilian Institute of Geography and Statistics or IBGE) confirms these conclusions in its own analysis of the census data. The IBGE describes typical emigrants from and then immigrants to the Northeast and the characteristic movements of both groups as follows:

[The most common emigrants] are young Northeasterners, principally from the semi-arid zones devastated by the constant dry spells, in search of new employment or business opportunities. In 2000, the group of 20 to 24 year-olds comprised 23.3% of the total of departures from the region and that of 15 to 29 year-olds, 53.1% [...] The behaviors of the structures by age of the departures and entrances are quite distinct. The departures are concentrated in the younger age groups and the entrances into the region present their greatest strength among older ages. Despite not being able to specify how much of the volume of entrances consists of natives returning to the region of origin (indicative of return migration), it is quite probable that an expressive portion of this flow is constituted by these movements. The elevated strength of entrances in the 5 to 9 year-old age group can be justified by the previous analysis. It is likely what is normally denominated as indirect contribution of migratory movements, that is, children that were born in the place of origin of the movement and returned with their parents (IBGE 2003, 55).

Thus we see a majority of the emigrants from the Northeast in the most recent year recorded, 2000, were under 30 years old. These migrants are affected by the shortage of agricultural work or other means of employment and decide to seek their fortunes outside of the region for the various reasons outlined earlier in this chapter. As Northeasterners move beyond the under-30 age group, they become much less likely to leave the Northeast and much more likely to return there, sometimes bringing their children back to the home region with them.

We can situate forró within this history of migration and migration policy as a still relevant subaltern response to economic and political pressures that have been placed upon Northeasterners in various regions of Brazil for at least the last century. Generally speaking, the perspective of forrozeiros that sing about the Northeastern experience of migration has been to agree with the old elite policy of keeping the man in the country, however with the insistence that this policy is only justifiable if the rural worker can lead a dignified life in the Northeastern interior. If not, then against all odds Northeastern workers will try to find that dignified life in other regions of Brazil where opportunities are more plentiful. However, they will always maintain a saudade for the Northeast and a desire to return when conditions allow, thus emphasizing the possibility of redemption for the region. To paraphrase Luiz Gonzaga in "Vida do viajante," the life of the migrant "is to walk through this country/ to see if some day [he or she] will rest happily" (Gonzaga and Cordovil qtd. in Ramalho 2000). Taking into consideration that the migration of Northeasterners in search of economic opportunities continues to be a nationally significant phenomenon, and that migratory flows returning to the Northeast are more significant than ever, it is clear that there are some strong socio-economic factors motivating forró's continued relevance and popularity.

Considering the 2000 census data on migration a little further, a relatively new development catches the attention that deserves specific analysis as it relates to forró's popularity. According to a chart that graphs the relative number of immigrants to Brazil's states coming from urban vs. rural areas, the vast majority of migrants throughout the entire country are now coming from urban places of origin (IBGE 2003, 57). In the context of migration originating in the Northeast, this development makes perfect sense when one considers that 69.1% of the population of the Northeast resided in urban municipalities as of 2000 (IBGE 2007, 19). Based on historical trends, it is reasonable to assume that the percentage of urban dwellers in the Northeast has surpassed 70% as of this writing. In fact, according to past census data the Northeastern population has been majority urban since 1980 (Sales and Baeninger 2000, 36). For historical comparison we can consider that in the era of forró's first rise to national prominence, around 1950, 26.4% of Northeasterners lived in urban areas and 73.6% in rural areas (Sales and Baeninger 2000, 36). Thus an almost complete reversal in the region's rural-to-urban population ratio came about over the course of the latter half of the twentieth century, in large part due to inter- and intraregional migration to urban municipalities.

So the continued popularity of forró with Northeasterners and Northeastern migrants in particular is not a question of people from rural areas assuaging their saudade—more important is the strong regional identity and history it invokes. There is also a saudade for that history and its authentic rural roots at work amongst many forró fans, if not for specific rural places of origin. Thus, on the one hand non-Northeastern forró fans and musicians enjoy the music as representative of authentic Brazilian popular culture and its ties to the Brazilian *povo* or people. On the other hand, urban Northeasterners throughout the country are appreciative of the music's ties back to the rural roots of their specific regional culture. Finally, one should not forget that, stylistically at least, forró has undergone some urbanization as a genre in recent years. The more recent innovations in forró along the lines of urban popular culture (such as electronic instrumentation and sophisticated stage production) seem much less surprising when one recognizes that Northeasterners have been a primarily urbanized population for several decades. In fact, as detailed in Chapters Two and Three, electronic forró as a genre emerged in the Northeast (in the city of Fortaleza, Ceará) in the late 1980s, the same decade that the region's population shifted to an urban majority. This population shift (and the related shift in lifestyles) should certainly be considered as one of the societal factors contributing to forró's evolution over the past few decades.

**The Social Psychology of Migration**

In this final section of the chapter I will consider forró's ability to explore the psychology of the migrant or diasporic subject. Through comparison with studies primarily in the field of social psychology, one can get an idea of this musical genre's perspicacity in its representation of migrant subjectivity. One particularly relevant song in this context is Gonzaga and Teixeira's "Que nem jiló," discussed previously in Chapter Two. This song addresses the key psychological element of memory and the subject's affective connection to and organization of that memory through saudade. Scholars in the field of social psychology and the subfield of intercultural psychology have covered the same ground and come to remarkably similar conclusions on the manner in which Northeasterners and other migrants deal with their connections to, and separations from, diverse places over time. Furthermore, this section will emphasize the key role that forró itself plays in both the elaboration of the trauma of migration and separation from home, as well as the celebration and remembrance of the regional culture brought into the diaspora.

Psychologist Taeco Toma Carignato studies the psychological impact of migration on Brazilians migrating to Japan, yet some of her conclusions are very much applicable to the internal migration of Northeasterners in Brazil. Carignato articulates the distinct ways in which a migrant may choose (or not choose) to deal with the trauma attached to separation from a place he or she considers home. She describes what the migrant loses as "principally the place in the familial, social and cultural constellation that [the migrant] occupied before leaving, a place which [the migrant] will never find again even if [he or she] returns to the land of origin" (Carignato 2005, 11). In this kind of situation, Carignato argues that a clean break with the past is impossible. Migrants cannot simply choose to forget the past, but rather must go through a process of mourning in order to elaborate their losses. Otherwise, "the traumatic experiences of separation and of the losses can reappear when the subject confronts impasses of a psychic or other nature, such as cultural conflicts or economic crises" (Ibid.). The return of this repressed trauma rooted in separation and loss can result in depression or even persecution complexes, of whose root cause the migrant may well be ignorant. Yet neither can migrants effectively close themselves up in the past, since they are constantly being bombarded by the new environment in which they live. According to Carignato, the act of migration thus commonly produces a subject who is "divided, contradictory, that desired to emigrate but denies that desire, that knows the reasons for [his or her] displacements yet refuses to take ownership of that knowledge" (Carignato 2005, 11-12).

There is a clear parallel here with the lyrical discourse of the aforementioned "Que nem jiló." Approaching the issue of separation from a loved one common to Northeastern migrants, this song attempts to differentiate between "good" and "bad" types of saudade. The good type is described as remembering "for the sake of remembering" in order to realize that one is happy in the present "because [one] did not suffer" ("Que nem jiló," n.d.). On the other hand, saudade is described as bad if it means that "we live to dream / of someone whom we desire to see again" (Ibid.). The singer deems this kind of nostalgia an unhealthy, perhaps obsessive connection to the past. As discussed in Chapter Two, the song concludes with the singer's affirmation that through music, he can transcend any sadness that remains associated with his memories—"saudade, my remedy is to sing." This model of psychologically managing one's memories of loss is close to that of the ideal migrant subject as suggested by Carignato. The subject must go through a process of mourning to work through his or her losses, but ultimately should be able to move beyond them to live in the present. "Que nem jiló" specifically asserts that singing, and by extension making or appreciating Northeastern music, is one way the migrant can be sure to be living in the moment without forgetting his or her personal history and regional roots.

Taking a somewhat broader approach than Carignato, Sylvia Dantas DeBiaggi presents migration as a psychological transition between cultures. She focuses on the process of psychological acculturation through which all migrants must go to one degree or another. DeBiaggi defines acculturation as "a succession of states in a process of resocialization resulting from a change in cultural context" (DeBiaggi 2005, 17). This process is subdivided by DeBiaggi into four varieties of acculturation: assimilation, separation, integration and marginalization. She defines these varieties as follows:

> We call *assimilation* the strategy in which the individual gives up his culture of origin and adopts the majority culture [...] In contrast, the strategy of *separation* occurs when one avoids contact with the majority society and there is an attachment to the original culture. [...] *Integration* represents a strategy in which a degree of maintenance of the culture of origin occurs simultaneously with the interaction with other groups. [...] *marginalization* occurs when there is little interest in or possibility of the maintenance of one's own culture and little interest in maintaining contact with other groups (Ibid.).

This typology of acculturation provides a revealing context within which to consider the adaptation of Northeastern migrants to a new social and cultural context in Southeastern Brazil. Where do Northeasterners fall along this continuum, and how do popular culture and forró factor into the equation? DeBiaggi clarifies that acculturation can occur to different degrees in the various areas of a migrant's life, and this variation certainly occurs in the case of Northeasterners.

In terms of labor and language, many of these internal migrants are best characterized as integrationists. In the case of economic pursuits, we have seen previously how Northeastern migrants are often informed by a sertanejo peasant ethic in their search for employment, seeking out opportunities that give them a sense of autonomy reminiscent of farming one's own plot of land. These jobs are connected to the economy of the area to which they have migrated, thus representing an integrationist mixture of work valued in the Northeast and the Southeast. In the linguistic case, there has sometimes existed for internal migrants a perceived need to learn a "new" language— that is, to adjust their lexicon and pronunciation in accordance with the regional variant of Brazilian Portuguese. As noted previously, some migrants have faced discrimination due to their regional accents. In the past a common response to such discrimination has been to assimilate linguistically, taking on a São Paulo or Rio de Janeiro accent as much as possible. This is an adjustment that is generally easier for better educated migrants and therefore varies according to class.

But thanks to genres like forró along with other efforts to valorize Northeastern culture, it is more socially acceptable in the present day to be a Northeastern linguistic separatist (or at least to take special pride in one's regional accent) than it was in the fifties, an era when migration to the Southeastern cities was on the rise and discrimination was at its height. Indeed, the arena of popular culture itself (including genres like forró and cordel literature) is where one finds the most promotion of a regional voice. Northeasterners also are often separatists (again in DeBiaggi's sense) in kinship and marriage. Intermarriage with others from the home region is probably the sphere of action within which this conservationist type of acculturation is most common. Baptista's study of the favela of Jardim Colombo demonstrates this phenomenon, noting the frequency of intermarriage among Northeasterners who meet within this diasporic community (Baptista 1998). In fact, the concentration of Northeastern migrants in certain neighborhoods and municipalities of São Paulo encourages such intermarriage. Endogamy is one means which descendents of migrants can employ to maintain attachments to the Northeast despite having assimilated to some degree to the urban, pluralistic culture of São Paulo or Rio de Janeiro. Thus integration, and to some degree separation, are the most apparent forms of acculturation amongst Northeastern migrants. On the other hand, the extremes of absolute psychological assimilation or marginalization are rarely evidenced in Northeastern migrant communities. In either instance, the collective maintenance of strong affective ties to the regional culture of the Northeast is the key factor. Obviously these ties would hinder a complete assimilation, but marginalization is also avoided since however alienated a migrant might feel in São Paulo or elsewhere, he or she always has the hope of a redemptive return to the Northeast. These hopes are fostered with the help of popular cultural traditions such as forró and songs like "A volta da asa branca" that celebrate a triumphant return to the region.

Cardel focuses on the liminal state of consciousness experienced by migrants from a rural area of Bahia's interior to the eastern periphery of São Paulo city (Cardel 2003). Her work proves without a doubt that the experiences of the migrant catalogued by Luiz Gonzaga continue to resonate in the minds and hearts of Northeastern migrants in the present day. Furthermore, Cardel's study highlights once again the profound, living, communal and familial ties that Northeastern migrants have established between their region and São Paulo. Forró's steadily growing heterogeneity, as described in Chapter One, reflects this trend of a regional people and their culture dispersing throughout the country and facing new experiences in the diaspora while still maintaining strong ties to home, a home which most would still prefer to return to if at all economically feasible (the feeling of "eternal return" noted above). In the diaspora, the people Cardel interviewed tended to glorify or mystify their original community. But upon returning to their village of Olhos d'Água, Bahia, this imaginary of home only seems to be confirmed on a psychological and even a physical level for these migrants. Many of those who had returned to the community spoke of feeling physical pain, weakness, or sickness in São Paulo and then regaining their health upon returning to their home village.

However, no informant, either in the receiving communities in São Paulo or having returned to Olhos d'Água, was able to be emphatic about staying in either place. This ambiguous state of mind confirms Cardel's theorization of a liminal state of consciousness, common among Northeastern migrants. This is frequently a negative liminality for migrants who feel forced to move to São Paulo simply to survive. The minority of rural-urban migrants who are potential heirs of their families' land, however, tend to experience liminality positively since they see migration as an option to capitalize on the time during which they await their inheritance, rather than as their only means for survival. Such states of consciousness have close parallels in the discourse of some canonical forró works like "Asa branca" and "A volta da asa branca." Clearly, in works like these the singer's mind (and heart) is in one place, the Northeast, while his body is in another, the Southeast or the diaspora more generally. If the (male) singer believes that the possibility of return is imminent, then he will express his liminal state positively. The singer of "A volta da asa branca" does exactly this, rejoicing that he will be able to return and get married in Pernambuco at the end of the year. Alternatively, the singer of "Asa branca" expresses a negative liminality (deeming his forced migration a punishment from God) since he sees return to his lover and his region as only a distant hope.

In addition to the transition between places and the resulting liminal consciousness, solitude is another experience of migrants with significant psychological repercussions. Rosangela da Silva Almeida demonstrates that, as with liminality, the psychic responses to solitude can have positive and negative valences for migrants (Almeida 2003). Solitude can be utilized as a time for contemplation and self-reflection, leading to an improvement in one's state of emotional and psychic well-being. However, the positive associations of solitude are limited by the fact that migrants often experience it as having been forced upon them. Thus a state of solitude experienced outside of the Northeast is often associated with a negative sense of isolation and alienation. Again we can refer to "Que nem jiló" and its recognition that one can use one's time for reflection in a self-constructive or self-destructive way. As suggested in the song, one constructive practice to deal with alienation in the diaspora is through music itself—"saudade, my remedy is to sing." Appreciation of forró as a singer, dancer or listener reaffirms one's ties to a larger regional community, whereever one might be living. This response to feelings of isolation or loneliness is a communal one, however, which does not preclude silent, individual contemplation but is not explicitly advocating it.

The reinforcement of ties to the home region through music could well be a part of the phenomenon Almeida describes as migrants becoming more "encapsulated in their identities" (Almeida 2003, 140). Almeida makes the liberal-democratic argument that this encapsulation is a troubling symptom of the lack of a welcoming public space in São Paulo where Northeasterners could be received as equal citizens and interact as such with their fellow Brazilians. But of course this is a problem that affects the urban popular classes in general. As Almeida and many others in the field of social psychology recognize, Northeastern migrants and their descendents have their own specific strategies of dealing with this shrinking public sphere, strategies based in social networks and regional-ethnic identity. Amongst these strategies are the stories of migration sung in forró lyrics, which offer a sense of solidarity and at times an opportunity for catharsis. The specific references to Northeastern popular culture in works like "Pau de arara" and "Baião" also enable remembrance and a feeling of belonging in the diaspora.

**Conclusion**

In this chapter we have seen ample evidence of the experience of migration from the perspective of Northeasterners and of those scholars who have interviewed them and analyzed their displacement into São Paulo and Southeastern Brazil. We have also considered the sociological data of Northeastern migration and the history of this migration and related migration policy over the last century. Finally, we took into account the psychological impact of migration and the variety of psychic responses resorted to by Northeastern migrants. In all of these areas, traditional forró musicians developed their own discourse to explore the significance of emigration from their region on both an individual and collective level. This discourse is one of departure and return, of loss and retrieval, of trauma and redemption. The genre has been gradually updated by subsequent generations, but the evidence from a variety of fields demonstrates that its focus on migration has remained remarkably accurate and relevant to the present day.

# Chapter Five

# The Synthetic Urge: Brazilian Narratives of National Development and Dependency in Global Cultural Studies

One of the major flaws in recent analyses of cultural production, including those of forró and Brazilian popular music in general, is the tendency to reproduce the closure of the potentially savage hybrid into its "tamed or cultural possibility" (Moreiras 2001, 296). The closure of the radical openness of the hybrid to change, in other words the neutralization of its ability to critique and destabilize identitarian categories, is quite common in mainstream postcolonial and cultural studies. This tendency is symptomatic of a *synthetic urge* that leads to an uncritical reification of the concept of cultural hybridity. Such reifications simply reproduce the current logic of global capital, as Michael Hardt and Antonio Negri describe it here:

> Many of the concepts dear to postmodernists and postcolonialists find a perfect correspondence in the current ideology of corporate capital and the world market. The ideology of the world market has always been the anti-foundational and anti-essentialist discourse par-excellence. Circulation, mobility, diversity, and mixture are its very conditions of possibility. Trade brings differences together and the more the merrier! Differences (of commodities, populations, cultures and so forth) seem to multiply infinitely in the world market, which attacks nothing more violently than fixed boundaries: it overwhelms any binary division with its infinite multiplicities (Hardt and Negri 2000, 150).

Thus hybridity qua mere cultural mixture (or the overwhelming of binary cultural divisions through synthesis) is one of the very conditions of possibility of the ideology of the world market. For this very reason one must be especially wary of the synthetic urge which leads one to participate in the reification and marketing/circulation of hybrid subject positions. Pace Hardt and Negri's dismissal of hybridity, however, such a wariness does not rule out a more critical, savage hybridity which destabilizes cultural hegemonies through its analytical process. My aim in what follows will be to analyze the production and intellectual discussion of subaltern music and culture in Brazil. At the same time, I will critique the analytical process by which a desire to merge cultural analysis into some master narrative of modernity can cause some thinkers to synthesize apparent contradictions into a stable or tamed hybrid, even where a savage hybridity emphasizing continued tension would be more appropriate. In the following chapter I will then narrow this discussion to forró, demonstrating how an emphasis on savage hybridity is particularly relevant for this regional genre.

### Gilberto Freyre, Fernando Ortiz and the Origins of the Synthetic Urge

Within the field of Latin American studies, one can trace back the synthetic urge to theorists of hybrid national identity like anthropologists Gilberto Freyre and Fernando Ortiz. As a beginning to my discussion and critique of the synthetic urge, it will prove revealing to analyze the seminal works of these thinkers of hybrid synthesis and transculturation, respectively, which were both written at a time when capital, and thus the reification of identities, were still functioning primarily on the level of the nation-state. However, it will become clear that even in these earlier thinkers' works, attempts to merge their theories into broader, international debates about modernity and national identity caused them to foreclose the critical potential of their conceptualizations of the hybrid. This introductory genealogy of the synthetic urge in Latin American thought will schematically address Freyre and Ortiz's seminal works, *Casa grande e senzala* (1933) and *Contrapunteo cubano del tabaco y el azúcar* (1940).

In terms of the anthropological discourse Gilberto Freyre utilizes to analyze Brazilian cultural history, we would have to consider him a disciplinary thinker attempting to come to terms with subalternity, that is, the constitutive outside of hegemony. As such, an analysis of his classic work, *Casa grande e senzala* (*The Masters and the Slaves*), has many important implications for both the field of cultural studies and subalternist projects in the present, be they in a Brazilian, Latin American or global context. A discussion of Freyre's work must certainly broach all of these various contexts, since he positioned himself as a thinker within an international, postcolonial debate. The subalternity which he attempts to explore, in fact, remains largely in this international context and does not substantially enter into his analysis of Brazilian history. By this I mean to say that Freyre sees himself as a third-world Latin American anthropologist coming from a subaltern perspective with respect to the dominant cultural constructs of Europe and especially North America. Freyre came into close contact with the metropole in his studies at Colombia University under the famed US anthropologist Franz Boas, and all of the ideas he develops in *Casa grande e senzala* are inflected by this contact.

The desire behind his cultural analysis is to distinguish Brazilian singularity (deriving from Iberian, particularly Portuguese colonization) with respect to race relations over and against the increasingly hegemonic model of racial conflict as exemplified by legal segregation in the United States, with its historical underpinnings in the whole history of English colonization. But in foregrounding his committment to valorizing the uniqueness of the "synthetic principle" behind the construction of the national imaginary in Brazil, Freyre inevitably excludes any thematization of subalternity *within* that imaginary (Freyre 1986). Freyre thus relinquishes any unambiguous claim to a phenomenological analysis of hybridity in Brazil and enters the realm of a performative discourse fulfilling the synthetic urge (at this historical juncture necessarily directed towards national synthesis). Thus he demonstrates the danger for any subalternist project of a lack of "rigorous theoretical *askesis* (self-disciplining)" with respect to the representation of the "multitudinous expressivities" secreted from any subaltern condition (Surin 2001). In a related essay on subalternity, Kenneth Surin describes the importance of such askesis in that it assures that "the inevitable outstripping of (subalternist) description by (subaltern) expressivity" is coordinated with a complementary movement of "displacement of the theorist rather than simply a displacement of the subaltern object of study" (Ibid., 50). Thus my argument is that Freyre commits himself to a theory of subaltern expressivity wherein the (racially) subaltern object of study is displaced in the service of the development of an (ultimately falsely subalternist) anticolonialist political project. I identify Freyre's project with what Alberto Moreiras describes as "melodramatic consciousness," or "the false consciousness of a real situation," which plays out a deceptive dialectic based on a subaltern reality which it must ultimately deny (Moreiras 2001). If we are to approach anything like a "critical regionalism" which takes a subaltern perspective and leads to a "real consciousness of multiple and always false situations," (Ibid.) then failed (but incredibly influential in terms of promoting an ideology of national miscegenation and synthesis) subalternist projects like Freyre's must be thoroughly critiqued and either discarded or reconstructed. Perhaps it is through precisely such a criticism that one begins to produce a critical regionalism as opposed to the hegemonic regionalism based in a Freyrean "fictitious alterity" (Santiago 2001).

Now I will provide a schematic outline of Freyre's development of the history of the "synthetic principle" mentioned above. The basic idea is that Portuguese colonists and their slaves intermixed sexually and culturally to a much greater degree than any other colonial populations did, especially the English. As opposed to the absolute oppression and subsumption in hegemony to which blacks in North America were subjected, the Portuguese had a much looser hegemony that involved an atmosphere of cordiality and an unwillingness or inability to radically emphasize and segregate or eliminate phenotypical, genotypical and cultural manifestations of Africanness. The result was that Africans and later Afro-Brazilians had some access to power and thus never came to identify as an oppressed racial group like North American blacks. Radical miscegenation eventually led to the Brazilian identity Freyre theorizes, based on racial (qua biological) and cultural harmony and hybridity. Left out of this equation is, of course, the indigenous population, which Freyre incorporates primarily as a vestigial element in the Brazilian nation that has contributed some important linguistic, nutritional and other cultural elements (called "native culture values") to the national synthesis, but is no longer (or perhaps never was) really a subject of Brazilian history.

To begin a more specific subalternist critique of Freyre, I will first analyze the manner in which he highlights the exceptionalism of the Portuguese and Portuguese colonization. Even prior to colonization, the Portuguese were favored towards racial hybridity and tropical colonization in their geographic and cultural environment situated between Africa and Europe. They were more used to a tropical climate than their fellow Northern European colonizers, and had much more exposure to African culture through the Moorish invasion and the favorable sea currents which made exploration of the continent quite feasible for a seafaring people. In fact, Freyre even speculates based on fossil evidence that the first prehistoric populations in Portugal may have been African, thus making even the Luso-Portuguese an African-descended population. For Freyre, in some sense the Portuguese were already a hybrid nation—despite being involved in the Inquisition and Reconquest like their Iberian neighbors.

But Freyre's great resolve in tracing back the Brazilian "synthetic principle" to Portuguese roots leads him astray in this case, displacing the subaltern object of study. Within Portugal, one example would be the case of the heretic, Jew, or Moor. At first Freyre acknowledges that this was perhaps the one area in which the Portuguese were profoundly intolerant, but then he points out the coexistence of various religions under the Moorish regime. When it comes to the transition to a Lusitanian regime through conquest, however, Freyre vaguely states that the "two great dissident bodies" of Jews and Moors were tolerated until "the majority came to feel that their tolerance was being abused," "At least by the Jews," who "had become holders of large peninsular fortunes...accumulated chiefly through usury" (Freyre 1986, 207). Here Freyre sounds like an apologist for the Inquisition, precisely because he does not allow himself as theorist of Luso-tropical exceptionalism to be displaced by any expressivity of the subaltern objects of study in question.

When it comes to the actual colonization of Brazil, we can see another apologia for the violence of conquest in his displacement of Indians. Although Freyre contributes substantial space to describing indigenous contributions to the nation, he also states that Portuguese imperialism "from the time of its first contact with the indigenous culture, struck the latter a death-blow" (Freyre 1986, 181). This would seem to describe the violence of primitive accumulation, however Freyre then states that "it did not strike it down suddenly, with the fury displayed by the English in North America" and thus "we may congratulate ourselves upon an adjustment of traditions and tendencies that is rare" (Ibid.). Thus Freyre seems to want his reader to believe that a slower imperial death-blow is somehow ethically preferable to a furiously rapid one. The only way that this could be the case, assuming we take Freyre seriously when he says the indigenous element is largely vestigial, is that the ethical superiority stems from the mere fact that it allowed some biological and cultural miscegenation to occur between colonists and natives, thereby making the colonialism essentially more indigenous. But here the expressivity of the subaltern in question is again displaced entirely, this time into the field of accumulation of the colonizer.

I will note here that Freyre also downplays the violence of slavery, at various points even referring to African slaves as "colonists" and "the masters of the land." Some of these characterizations border on the happy Sambo figure in the US, and in one specific case we can see how he plays this figure against the indigenous or Indian-descended population in order to give a picture of a sort of "good" or well-adjusted subaltern. "[Native] populations, which are chiefly to be found in the backlands of the Northeast, are gloomy, silent and reserved, sly and even surly, without the infectious cheerfulness of the [Negroid] Bahians and without at times their irritating petulance, without their grace, their spontaneity, their courtesy, their hearty and contagious laughter" (Freyre 1986, 285). This passage is intended to describe the contemporary situation in Brazil, and it is revealing not only of Freyre's privileging of Afro-Brazilians in the national imaginary but also multiple expressivities which he must erase in his depiction of that imaginary. The abjection of the Indian, his slyness and surliness, as well as the annoying petulance of the Afro-Bahians, are all indicators of subaltern desire that should displace Freyre and his theoretical production towards a more radical idea of savage hybridity. But his consistent focus on proving a more hegemonic, nationalist hybridity leads him to overlook such expressivity as "annoying" at best and pathological at worst. The melodrama which Freyre constrains himself to produce involves only the "contagious laughter"of the Bahian that infects the Portuguese master but not the doomed Indian. This is a synthesis which clearly does not leave room for expressivities like those produced in forró, those that trace the exclusion of the subaltern inherent in Brazil's nationalist narrative of modernization.

Freyre's portrayal of Brazilian culture and society as a hybrid synthesis reflects and reinforces what remains a dominant discourse to this day in Brazil, namely, racial democracy. This ideology is closely related to the project of national exceptionalism that Freyre propounds. Racial democracy is not so much a democratic ideology as one of "racial exceptionalism" (Hanchard 1994). Brazil is thought to have a profound intermixture of race and culture stemming all the way back to the miscegenation of female African slaves and their male Portuguese masters. Brazil's lack of a history of legal segregation such as the regimes that existed in North America and South Africa only confirms the unique harmoniousness of Brazil's race relations in the minds of many Brazilians. This perception remains a hegemonic ideology despite the efforts of many sociologists and other academics and activists in Brazil since at least the 1960s to point out the serious politico-economic inequalities faced by the country's African-descended citizens. The fixation on racial exceptionalism in the influential ideology of racial democracy is a near perfect example of the taming of hybridity. A savage hybridity would acknowledge that apparent racial mixture and social harmony in Brazil is disturbed and greatly complicated by issues of disproportionate poverty and general exclusion from the benefits of citizenship for poor Afro-Brazilians.

Recent scholarship has called into question the survival of racial democracy as a dominant national ideology in Brazil. The most salient example of such scholarship can be found in the work of Edward Telles. However, even as Telles argues that Brazilian scholars and the general public are now more sceptical of claims of racial exceptionalism, he signals repeatedly that if Brazil has entered a post-racial democracy era, this does not entail that the ideology has lost its considerable influence. Indeed, even Telles implies that it continues to represent the primary paradigm for thought on race relations in Brazil. Telles states that Brazilians still believe that "human relations" in Brazil "are superior to those of segregated countries" like the US (Telles 2004, 77). He further acknowledges that "[m]any Brazilians seem to still believe that elements of racial democracy are at the core of Brazilian values" (76). Despite its purported demise in the 1990s, according to Telles "[racial democracy's] legacy nevertheless continued to shape social relations in the following years" (46). In the end, Telles does not suggest that another racial paradigm has replaced racial democracy in Brazil. Rather, the amalgamation of racial uplift, affirmative action and pro-miscegenation public opinion as described by Telles gives one a sense of a society seeking to patch up the tattered flag of exceptionalism, projecting racial democracy as a "dream for Brazil's future" (76).

Fernando Ortiz, in an anthropological work with attention to detail on par with Freyre's, takes a quite different tack in outlining Cuban exceptionalism, ultimately allowing his own arguments to be displaced by the inherent ambiguity of his terms. Cuba is indeed globally exceptional in its cultural hybridity according to Ortiz, yet this exceptionalism is not the real focus of his analysis. It is the phenomenon of the tobacco plant, including its production and trade, that comes to represent Cuba's truly unique identity (and national potential) in Ortiz's *Contrapunteo cubano del tabaco y el azúcar* (*Cuban Counterpoint: Tobacco and Sugar*). Tobacco is originally a sign of subaltern nationalism over and against the exploitation of international capital that dominates the trade in sugar. Ortiz calls the sugar plantation and mill the "favored child of capitalism," and sugar comes to represent mass production, foreign ownership, and the exploitation of workers as opposed to the craftsmanship, small-scale operation, and independence that tobacco and its producers symbolize. However, with characteristic attention to the contradictions in his own argument, Ortiz eventually problematizes the dichotomy he sets up between national, native tobacco and international, non-native sugar. The initial characterizations of sugar and tobacco are eventually complicated by the working out of a dialectic between use value qua tobacco and exchange value qua sugar. According to Ortiz, tobacco is today much more like sugar than it ever was, demonstrating the increasing global dominance of exchange which makes all primary commodities interchangeable as mass-produced and internationally circulated (agro)industrial products.

But thanks to the concept of transculturation, Ortiz comes to the conclusion that Cuba has a sort of global reign in the world of tobacco. Cuban cigars or "Havanas" are internationally recognized as a symbol of quality and craftsmanship, lending the country an exceptional economic position in the production of this important commodity. Transculturation, Ortiz's most famous concept, is not thematically introduced until the second section of the book and not worked through analitically or in any depth until his chapter on the transculturation of tobacco. As noted above, in the first section of *Contrapunteo cubano*, Ortiz presents tobacco as a synthesis of all that is uniquely Cuban and subaltern vis-à-vis international finance capital. But for Ortiz, tobacco is simultaneously the perfect symbol of transculturation or cultural hybridity, to such an extent that its history as a ritual object and subsequent transformation into a commodity within global capital flows demonstrates a "universal transculturation."

Tobacco begins as a plant smoked in Native American religious rites, then comes to be smoked by sailors visiting Cuba and by Afro-Cubans for pleasure, thereafter is "transplanted" to Africa through the agency of the sailors and widely disseminated throughout the continent, and by the sixteenth century begins to be consumed by Europeans of various classes in Iberia, England and France. Thus the plant and its various varieties of consumption (cigar, pipe tobacco, chew) cross every conceivable racial, class, religious and national boundary. However, rather than inducing Ortiz to conclude tobacco loses its essentially Cuban quality through its new socioeconomic universality, the concept of "universal transculturation" leads Ortiz to a characterization of Cuban tobacco as "conquering" the world through an absolute synthesis with these global capital flows. This reversal brings about a reification of the hybrid wherein the subalternity essential to tobacco as a concept in the book's first section becomes subsumed under the sign of the plant's commodity form in the latter section, in which the theory of transculturation is developed. Ultimately, tobacco becomes synonymous with its commodity form in Ortiz's work, and thus he is forced, in order to prove its continuing Cubanness, towards speculations on traces of Cubanness in modern smokers' behavior. An example is his recollection of the island's indigenous tribes' manner of smoking tobacco, now supposedly evident throughout the world in certain characteristic ways of inhaling and exhaling smoke. Ortiz is reduced to searching for these mere traces of subalternity after his subject's universal transculturation is shown to be nothing more than a global commodification:

> As civil liberties triumphed and political constitutions were guaranteed, the cigar came into the ascendancy once more, coinciding with the advent of economic liberalism in Cuba, which threw the port of Havana open to all nations. And in this atmosphere of free industrial and commercial enterprise Havana tobacco, by the universal plebiscite of the world, was awarded the imperial scepter of the tobacco world. Havana tobacco from then on became the symbol of the triumphant capitalistic bourgeoisie. The nineteenth century was the era of the cigar. The ground is now being cut from under its feet by the democracy of the cigarette. But cigars and cigarettes are now being made by machines just as economy, politics, government, and ideas are being revised by machines. It may be that many peoples and nations now dominated by the owners of machines can find in tobacco their only temporary refuge for their oppressed personalities (Ortiz 1995, 309).

Havanna tobacco is shown to be an emperor of the tobacco world, and Havana cigars the symbol of the triumphant capitalistic bourgeoisie. But ultimately Ortiz is forced to conclude that these historical figurations of tobacco have nothing to do with Cuba, rather they are much more tied to a mechanized, industrial-capitalistic world order. Still, Ortiz cannot resist, in the final sentence of his work, the temptation to tie tobacco back to its thematic origins in the book's first section as a sign of Cuban individuality and freedom—now construed as a "temporary refuge" for the universally-oppressed proletariat. Nevertheless, under the conscientious anthropologist's full realization of the weight of global capitalism, this line of speculation can end in nothing more (or less) than a trope, a symbolic flourish, a puff of smoke.

Common to both Ortiz and Freyre is the taming of a potentially savage theory of hybridity by the increasing subsumption of the nation-state in a global structure of economic and political hegemony. Ortiz is more conscious of this transition, while Freyre plays a game of upmanship within the global system without recognizing the game's influence upon his own analysis. But both of their claims to national exceptionalism through synthesis, while resistant to certain forms of ideological hegemony, ultimately result in a concept of the hybrid that is a hegemonic synthesis. The forcing of such a stasis upon the hybrid precludes representation of the continual redistribution and reenactment of power that is occurring on the local, national, and global levels; thus this hegemonic synthesis leads to a masking of the work of domination in Latin America. The object of domination is necessarily the subaltern, who is essentially excluded from any notion of hybridity that loses its destabilizing, critical potential and moves towards a stabilized, reified synthesis of two static terms. These important thinkers, then, are emblematic of the dangers of the synthetic urge for even the most careful and thorough of cultural analyses.

**Contemporary Echoes: Symptoms of the Synthetic Urge at the Turn of the 21st Century**

A certain polemic around race relations in Brazil, involving four academics in France and the United States as well as a popular musician in Brazil, clearly demonstrated the ability of the synthetic urge to displace the subaltern object of study and to suppress subaltern expressivity and solidarity. In an article first published in French in 1998 and translated into English in 1999, Pierre Bourdieu and Loïc Wacquant make a wide-ranging attack on United States cultural imperialism and those "carriers" of US concepts who abet this empire throughout the world (Bourdieu and Wacquant 1999). Their polemical article, entitled "On the Cunning of Imperialist Reason," singles out several analytical concepts and terms which Bourdieu and Wacquant deem especially imperialist in their aspiration to universal applicability in all societies. These supposedly North American terms and concepts, such as "underclass," "minority," and "race," are subject, according to Bourdieu and Wacquant, to "the dehistoricization that almost inevitably results from the migration of ideas across national boundaries." This dehistoricization, along with the United States' ability "to impose as universal that which is most particular to itself," result in a colonization of the intellectual field and academic discourse of other countries such as Brazil and France (Ibid., 51). Subsequent to such a colonization, thinkers are divorced from the realities of their own societies (or the societies they analyze) by these foreign concepts commodified and circulated with the backing of multinational publishing houses. The end result, say Bourdieu and Wacquant, is "nothing but the semi-scholarly retranslation of the salient problems of the day into an idiom imported from the USA (ethnicity, identity, minority, community, fragmentation, etc.)" (Ibid., 50).

From a Brazilian studies perspective, Bourdieu and Wacquant's most egregious reductionism involves warping the concept of race to make it fit their schema, wherein it is merely a form of cultural capital traded by Brazilianists in Brazil and the US to increase their own intellectual and institutional prestige, if not simply to "[ensure] booksales, for lack of success based on intellectual esteem" (Bourdieu and Wacquant 1999, 45). The obvious irony of Bourdieu and Wacquant's stance does not fall far short of complete tautology here—not only do Bourdieu and Wacquant performatively reduce race and racism to a US phenomenon, they also perform a reductive, dehistoricizing synthesis of Brazilian society in order to prove its incompatibility with their simplistic concept of race. All of this while accusing scholars like Michael Hanchard of engaging in "brutal, ethnocentric intrusions" into Brazil using "North American racial categories"[1] to universalize "the US folk-concept of 'race'" (Ibid., 48).

As John French points out, Bourdieu and Wacquant show no recognition that there may exist multiple forms of racism in different social contexts. French demonstrates through a detailed literature review on race relations in Brazil that many Brazilian, North American and European scholars have already recognized this fact. Furthermore, they have demonstrated the existence of race relations, racial identity, racial nomenclature, and racial domination specific to Brazil's unique history (French 1999; French 2000). French notes Denise Ferreira da Silva's enumeration of some of the difficult questions Hanchard tries to address in his work:

How is racial exclusion possible without overt racial discrimination, and more or less explicit mechanisms of racial segregation? Why do such high levels of racial exclusion not entail the emergence of race consciousness, and the consequent political mobilization among black Brazilians? Why do black Brazilians lack a

---

[1] It remains unclear why Bourdieu and Wacquant require the continental epithet here, since they claim repeatedly that race is, in essence, a North American concept.

separate (racial) identity? (Silva 1998)

Hanchard recognizes the importance of these questions and the related ideologies of racial democracy and whitening, but also makes it clear there is indeed political mobilization of blacks (*negros*) and African-descended people in Brazil. His book explores how these activists in the Movimento Negro Unificado [Unified Black Movement] became the exception to the rule in Brazil, and what perspectives they share and disagree on with the larger Afro-Brazilian population.

Regarding racial democracy, Bourdieu and Wacquant never go beyond admitting its existence as a myth promoted by Freyre. This knowledge does not provoke them to question the myth more deeply along with so many other scholars, but rather to simply express their preference for the racial democracy myth over and against "the myth according to which all societies are racist" (Bourdieu and Wacquant 1999, 44). Here Bourdieu and Wacquant join ranks with Freyre in discursively performing a hegemonic, national-racial synthesis which necessarily precludes subalternist analysis and excludes both the racial subalterns and the political movements that reject this hegemony. Like Freyre, Bourdieu and Wacquant emphasize national unity and uniqueness in order to use their Brazilian imaginary itself to critique North American intellectual production. They do so at the expense of the real ambiguity and internal dissent over Brazil's self-image. Unlike Freyre, Bourdieu and Wacquant are guilty of simplification to the extent of completely ignoring white supremacism as it exists in Brazil, primarily in the form of placing higher social value on lighter skin color.

On the other hand, in an April 2000 *New York Times* article, Caetano Veloso does admit the existence of the ideology of whitening while critiquing Hanchard's work. Not only that, Veloso's critique is couched in a larger argument for more realist cinematic representations of Brazilian favelas, as exemplified by a film for which Veloso produced the soundtrack, *Orfeu*. Veloso stresses the importance of the appearance in the film of contemporary cultural manifestations of the African diaspora in Brazil, such as dreadlocks and rap music. But Veloso ultimately shares the Freyrean logic of praising miscegenation and upholding it as uniquely representative of Brazilian national progress. This clear synthetic urge leads Veloso into an apologia for the ideology of whitening, which he minimizes in Brazil by calling it "an inevitable dream of all the Americas" (Veloso 2000). He then proceeds to list four North American black performers (including Tina Turner and Michael Jackson) to prove his point that Brazil is no more backward than the United States in eliminating the discriminatory social value given to whiteness. So to uphold the primacy of cultural hybridity in Brazil through miscegenation, Veloso not only ends up making arguments about North American blacks based on questionable evidence (e.g. Tina Turner's hair), he also relativizes white supremacism throughout the Americas to the point of acceptance.

Caetano Veloso also mentions that Freyre "rejected the colonial presumptions of whitening while praising miscegenation" (Veloso 2000). But miscegenation was hardly a democratic process itself, especially in the oligarchic, slavery-based plantation society Freyre focuses on and analyzes as the historical progenitor of the modern Brazilian nation. Michael Hanchard says as much in his response letter to Veloso's NYT article, writing "miscegenation, in Brazil and in other former slave-holding societies, began as acts of dominance and not as an egalitarian principle that led to the erosion of unequal relations" (Hanchard 2000). The generally accepted historical argument that racial mixture began with the plantation patriarchs' sexual exploitation of their female slaves has even been backed up recently by the genetic research of a team of Brazilian and Portuguese scientists (Parra et al 2003). This reality is deemed unworthy of much criticism in Freyre, and the anthropologist even seems to accept or be mildly amused by the sexual exploits of the master or his legitimate sons. Veloso's synthetic urge to speak for what he calls "our blacks" leads him to a similar elision of the violent origins of miscegenation and their historical repercussions to this day (Veloso 2000). Michael Hanchard also notes in his response to Veloso that

> In Brazil, the celebration of miscegenation has occurred simultaneously in national popular culture and mythology with terminology that denigrates darker-skinned Brazilians, while upholding Northern European ideals of feminine and masculine beauty. Thus, miscegenation cannot be considered outside the lens of power and aesthetics. (Hanchard 2000)

Here we have an example of conflicting, but coexisting, ideologies within a national context. Veloso's synthetic urge leads him to discursively resolve this conflict and wrongly suggest that the ideal of racial democracy neutralizes the negative effects of the pigmentocracy in which whiteness both signifies and begets aesthetic and social privilege. Thus Veloso's and Bourdieu and Wacquant's visions merge through the reinscription of the hegemonic Freyrean synthesis.

## Questioning Anti-Imperialist Syntheses of Popular Culture

At this point we should begin to consider popular culture and cultural production within the lens of power and aesthetics, since Veloso broaches the issue of Brazilian music and its representation of the nation. Veloso calls the nationalization of carioca music a "very Brazilian project of making samba the medium of choice for expressing national identity" (Veloso 2000). Here Veloso puts the cart before the horse—it is only a *Brazilian* project because the carioca cultural industry put a great effort into making it so. If he really wishes to document popular culture in Brazil, or even just within the confines of Rio de Janeiro, he needs to recognize the Northeastern presence, especially that of forró, a music played throughout the city and the entire country. Forró was ignored in Marcel Camus's film *Orfeu negro* (1959) and continues to be ignored in Carlos Diegues's more realist Brazilian version, for which Veloso produced the soundtrack. Veloso critiques the older Camus film for misrepresenting samba, but not for its larger ideological framework in which carnival samba and bossa nova symbolize the entirety of the Brazilian musical soundscape. In the new version of the film, the soundscape is updated to include the rap music prevalent in Rio's favelas, but Veloso does not note the absence of any regional music like forró (or música sertaneja, *axé*, brega, reggae, etc.). Within Veloso's discourse on national music, there is no space left for the possibility of a savage hybridity that continually destabilizes identitarian syntheses—and would recognize the necessary exclusion from hegemony of forró and other regional musical discourses incompatible with a Rio de Janeiro-centered vision of Brazilian culture and cultural production.

It is no accident that Caetano Veloso, a famous musician, should weigh in on national identity as expressed in Brazilian popular culture. Music is a very important medium for the struggle to define national, regional and local identities in Brazil. Of course, this struggle always involves the attempt to establish or maintain a hegemony of certain genres as representative of Brazilian identity (with a corresponding dominance in the market for domestic music). For this very reason, music critics such as José Ramos

Tinhorão often use their analyses of certain musical genres in order to make more general arguments about cultural identity, the national culture industry, and economic and cultural imperialism in Brazil. Caetano Veloso himself, along with other members of the Tropicália and bossa nova movements, were labelled by Tinhorão as examples of North American imperialism in Brazilian music (since Tropicália was strongly influenced by trends in international rock, as bossa nova was by North American jazz). Ironically, in both his critique of Hanchard's monograph and of Marcel Camus's film, Veloso makes the same kind of conservative nationalist (i.e. misguided anti-imperialist) arguments that made him the target of Tinhorão's polemics.

To further deconstruct both Veloso and Tinhorão's hegemonic syntheses of national identity, we should consider some of Tinhorão's salient thoughts on popular music. Tinhorão's most detailed anti-imperialist critique is aimed at bossa nova (Tinhorão 1998, 25-47, 62-69, 72-87). He sees bossa nova as a bastardized samba, alienated from its roots as a cultural production of the popular or lower classes. This cultural alienation corresponds to the alienated economic position of bossa nova's creators, the middle- to upper-class youth of post-war Copacabana and Ipanema. These coastal neighborhoods comprise the so-called Zona Sul, where investment in real estate soared in the 1950s, causing a corresponding jump in property values. The resultant increase in the cost of living forced out the popular classes who had previously been able to afford housing in the area. Thus Tinhorão paints a picture of bossa nova musicians like João Gilberto and Tom Jobim as privileged youth, isolated in the Zona Sul, who thus had no interaction with musicians from other classes. The lower classes also tend to be of greater African descent due to systemic racism, so Tinhorão usually characterizes this as both an economic and a racial alienation from the mass of the Brazilian poor. The alienation of this young generation of musicians (between 18 and 22 at the end of the 50s) led to their desire to culturally mimic their equivalent class in North America. Since the United States' economy is more developed, their thinking supposedly went, then its culture must be similarly superior.

Thus according to Tinhorão's economically deterministic schema, the formation of bossa nova was essentially a Brazilian imitation of contemporary North American jazz. Tinhorão elsewhere tries to further this argument with technological determinism, claiming that from the moment the phonograph arrived in Brazil, "não era mais possível 'reinterpretar'," i.e.

it was no longer possible to reinterpret international music because the musician could now hear exactly the manner in which foreign music was played in its country of origin (Tinhorão 2001, 168). Of course, Tinhorão's determinism fails to recognize the ability of artists on the geopolitical periphery to appropriate forms from the center and reformulate them for their own indigenous aesthetic and political purposes. Even barring a strong, conscious subaltern agency, musicians are not machines that can exactly copy sounds they hear. Inevitably, any artistic form will be shaped by the socio-cultural context within which it is produced or performed.

Like Bourdieu and Wacquant in the intellectual sphere of production, Tinhorão borders on xenophobia in his implacable resistance to any cooperation or cultural exchange between center and periphery, or dominant and subordinate capitalist nation-states. One important difference, though, is that while Tinhorão acknowledges the predominance of North American influence, he does not claim there is a qualitative difference between European and North American imperialism in Brazil. Bourdieu and Wacquant, on the other hand, seem to be ignorant of, or unwilling to admit, France's long history of exporting cultural and intellectual production to the third world. Thus of course they do not problematize their own subject positions as European intellectuals working in French and North American universities. Tinhorão goes no further than the position that the technology of the record industry helped the United States's influence to gain preeminence in the 20$^{th}$ century. There is no doubt that this is true, but the middle-class artists of the bossa nova generation, along with Caetano Veloso's generation of Tropicalists, would prove that Oswald de Andrade's program of cultural cannibalism could be a fruitful way for subaltern artists to appropriate (eat) and transform (digest) international cultural production into a uniquely Brazilian product.

Considering Veloso's involvement in the cultural cannibalism of Tropicália, which helped to popularize national, regional and local transformations of international music, his conservative nationalism vis-à-vis Hanchard and Afro-Brazilian activists seems quite ironic. To be intellectually consistent, it would seem, Veloso would need to support African-descended Brazilians' efforts to reformulate North American anti-racist tactics in their attempts to combat prejudice and inequality in Brazil, just as he supports the appropriation of rap music by Rio's African-descended favela-dwellers. But if we recall the kind of nationalist cultural project Veloso advocates, then it becomes obvious there is no real contradiction in his thought. In his critique of Camus, Veloso accepts the cultural hegemony of Rio de Janeiro as a given. Cultural production in Brazil is only truly "Brazilian" once it has been reproduced by the carioca culture industry.

This is the key line of thought along which Veloso parallels Tinhorão. Tinhorão's polemics only make sense if one formulates Brazilian musical history as *a synthesis of the very musical forms which imperialism allegedly appropriates and bastardizes*. It is true that bossa nova and Tropicália are heavily influenced by foreign musical genres. However, there is virtually no interaction of forró with a world music industry, rather it was informed by the whole array of Northeastern Brazilian cultural expression (and much later in the 1970s, secondarily by rock). Tinhorão is forced by the logic of his discourse into a reiteration of the imperialist reality he is critiquing. This kind of discourse, like Veloso's, inflates carioca musical production into an exclusionary symbol of all the contemporary musical creativity in the country. Perhaps bossa nova (and by extension, samba) was heavily influenced by North American jazz. (To allow Tinhorão's claim, we must leave aside for the moment the problematic nature of characterizing influence as intrinsically imperialist, and the fact that bossa nova is only one among many subgenres of samba—not to mention the fact that bossa nova itself influenced North American music.) But this US influence does not represent an imperialist hegemony over all Brazilian popular music. Or rather, it only represents such a hegemony if one discursively upholds the hegemony of samba carioca over all other musical expression in Brazil.

### New Wave Hegemony: Samba Renationalized as International Symbol

It must be said, however, that bossa nova itself attempted to maintain this hegemony and in some respects succeeded. There is no doubt that bossa nova had aspirations to become a characteristically "Brazilian" form of music. What Tinhorão calls the bossa nova movement's effort to "denationalize" Brazilian music was in fact bossa nova musicians' attempt to nationalize their own particular brand of samba (Tinhorão 1998, 64). Through this *renationalization* samba could then represent Brazil to the world, becoming the "poetry for export" for which Oswald de Andrade had called in the twenties. In "Vaia de bêbado não vale," a song recorded on his most recent album, Tom Zé describes the history of bossa nova in these terms:

On the day that bossa-nova
invented Brazil [...]
It had to make it well
It had to make Brazil

When that year began, in the
Rains of March of 58,
Brazil was only exporting raw material [...]
And the world was saying:
What a retarded little people.
What a very backward people.

The surprise was in the end of that
same year
To all parts
The Brazil of The Duck
With bossa-nova, it was exporting art,
The highest degree of human
capacity
And Europe, admiring:
What an audacious little people
What a civilized people [...]


No dia em que a bossa-nova
inventou o Brasil [...]
Teve que fazer direito
Teve que fazer Brasil

Quando aquele ano começou, nas
Águas de Março de 58,
O Brasil só exportava matéria prima [...]
E o mundo dizia:
Que povinho retardado.
Que povo mais atrasado.

A surpresa foi que no fim daquele
mesmo ano
Para toda a parte
O Brasil d'O Pato
Com a bossa-nova, exportava arte,

O grau mais alto da capacidade
humana
E a Europa, assombrada:
Que povinho audacioso
Que povo civilizado [...]
(Zé 2003)

Musically, this song is inspired by bossa nova, led by its characteristic, subtly syncopated acoustic guitar sound but periodically disrupted by Ze's own idiosyncratic aesthetic. Tom Zé himself was involved in the Tropicália movement, and like many of the Tropicalists was influenced by the advent of bossa nova in the decade prior to Tropicália's birth in the sixties. From the lyrics, it is obvious that by the time Zé wrote this song bossa nova had become an international phenomenon and a source of nationalist pride for Brazilian artists and fans alike. The title is significant—it translates as "the boos of a drunk don't matter" and refers to a concert at which Tom Jobim responded to jeers from the audience with this very phrase. For whatever reason, some of the Brazilians present at this show were not satisfied with Jobim's bossa nova, but Zé suggests, by titling this song with Jobim's dismissal, that this dissatisfaction is irrelevant thanks to the international acclaim received by the genre and described in Zé's lyrics. Obviously, the advent of bossa nova was accompanied by a privileging of international desire, particularly that of "Europe" and other industrialized nations to which Brazil historically had exported primarily raw materials. This is another example of a nationalist, synthetic urge, however in this case rather than a conservative nationalism we find a liberal one focusing on investing a small amount of Brazil's newest cultural capital in global markets (as a commodity that symbolizes, and sells, the nation as a rapidly modernizing geopolitical and cultural force).

Due to the nationalization of bossa nova and then Tropicália and Brazilian rock, Rio de Janeiro's culture industry began to lose interest in Luiz Gonzaga's forró. Gonzaga was still popular throughout the Northeast and toured throughout the region (and elsewhere), but in the sixties he had been replaced in the national market by musical forms considered more "advanced" because they were in dialogue with, or at least responding to, international trends. Yet it was premature to call the baião, as Tinhorão does, an "ephemeral success" (Tinhorão 1998, 57). Baião and forró would return to national prominence upon several occasions, throughout the following decades, as an irruption of popular-regional desire into the national market and consciousness. Although other genres produced by the Southeastern culture industry often make claims to exclusive representation of Brazilian music, one should not confuse the discursive hegemony these forms may claim or achieve at any one point in time with the actually existing condition of popular music and desire.

# Chapter Six

# The Synthetic Urge and Forró: Against Hybrid Totalization

What of scholars who make the counterhegemonic effort to focus on regional genres like forró? We can expect them to have a more complex view of the national distribution of popular music. However, this more complex view does not necessarily allow these thinkers to avoid the synthetic urge with respect to forró's historical trajectory. It cannot be denied that forró is a result of a great synthesis of various Northeastern ethnic and musical traditions. The genre is a musical mixture of various Northeastern styles such as xote, *maracatu*, xaxado, baião and coco and incorporates European instruments like accordion and guitar, African percussion such as the large zabumba (drum), and sometimes also includes indigenous wind instruments and shakers. This synthesis of primarily European and African instrumentation and the third and lesser indigenous element corresponds to the national imaginary of miscegenation (*mestiçagem*) most famously theorized by Gilberto Freyre. Gonzaga himself would often perform in a more or less elaborate version of an ornamentalized costume evoking the Northeastern cangaceiro or bandit, an iconic figure of Northeastern marginality and resistance typically considered to be of mixed racial ancestry. The synthesis of all these elements of Northeastern culture has been duly noted by scholars analyzing forró and its greatest proponent, Gonzaga.

Yet the fact that Luiz Gonzaga began his career as a popular musician in the Southeastern metropolis of Rio de Janeiro has led several chroniclers and scholars of forró to assert that his music represents a synthesis of urban and rural life and cultural production. This assertion, however, is more a result of the synthetic urge than any supporting evidence from the forró canon. As discussed in detail in Chapter Three, forró generally resists any synthesis of its rural roots with urban realities. This resistance explains forrozeiros' failure to cognitively map the metropolises to which so many Northeasterners were migrating. The synthetic urge of forró scholars in this case is fueled by a grander narrative of modernization in Brazil which equates urbanization with development and thus progress. Gonzaga's success is attributed to his ability to "stylize" Northeastern popular culture for an urban audience, that is, to urbanize traditionally rural music. The developmentalist narrative excludes the demands of rural workers, and in this regard, it is notable that only one forró study thus far has attempted to draw connections between the landless workers' movement and the redemptive rural imaginary so common to forró (McCann, 2004). In addition to Bryan McCann's recognition of the MST's appropriation of Luiz Gonzaga's music (noted in Chapter Three), Silviano Santiago draws a parallel between the regionalism of the landless movement and that of música sertaneja (Santiago 2001, 172). But Santiago does not mention forró, limiting his discussion to a genre more prevalent in the Southeast.

**Luiz Gonzaga in the City: A Synthesis of Rural and Urban?**

At this point we should analyze some specific studies of forró in greater detail. Sulamita Vieira focuses on migratory movement in her work on Luiz Gonzaga's heyday in the forties and fifties, *O sertão em movimento: a dinâmica da produção cultural* (*The Sertão in Movement: The Dynamics of Cultural Production*). Vieira's focus on movement deserves a detailed analysis, since it very effectively reveals the social and artistic repercussions of the massive displacements of Northeasterners. As migrant workers and refugees from drought began to arrive in great numbers in Southeastern cities, the baião and other "satellite genres" from the Northeast, which would all come to be known as forró, made their grand arrival on the stage of Brazilian popular music (Vieira 2000, 48). Vieira makes the point that this wave of migration was no real solution for a systemic problem of exploitation in the Northeast, rather it simply contributed to the reproduction of the unchallenged power of the regional elites over the local populace, and to the expanding economic hegemony of the Southeast over the nation (Ibid., 200). Migrants were set into motion by the failure of corrupt and inefficient latifundios to employ a labor force during periodic droughts, but when these laborers were drawn to economic opportunity in São Paulo and elsewhere, these cities often "did not receive them formally as a labor force" (Ibid., 94). This lack of integration into the new urban environment, as discussed in Chapter Three, is reflected in forrozeiros' cognitive resistance to mapping the city in their lyrics.

Accordingly, Vieira cites various examples of this "confrontation between the sertão and the city" (Vieira 2000, 203). She mentions this confrontation in the context of her discussion of Humberto Teixeira and Luiz Gonzaga's "Estrada de Canindé [Canindé Road]." This song references the lack of automobiles (transformed into "Artomove" in Northeastern dialect) with the line "Artomove lá nem se sabe/ Se é home ou se é muié [Automobile there they don't even know/ whether it's a man or it's a woman]." As Vieira points out, these lines are followed by a transition signalled by the word "but," which leads to the closing verses in which the beautiful natural environment of the sertão is emphasized, in contrast with the city's modern technology. This technology ultimately has no use in the sertão, since nature deserves to be appreciated at a slow, rural pace: "Coisas que pra mode vê/ O cristão tem andar a pé [Things [i.e. nature's beauty] which to see/ The Christian has to go by foot]" (Ibid.). Obviously there is a turning away from the city, and a privileging of the rural Northeastern interior in this work. Yet here Vieira seems to be most interested in the fact that the description of resplendent nature in full bloom is part of another movement—that between the scarcity of drought, driving out sertanejos, and the fertility after the rains, welcoming them home again.

Vieira expands on the idea of confrontation when she notes a "certain tension" between Northeasterners and the city, despite their attempts to seek refuge there. She explains that "going there, even if [he] stays, the sertanejo will not be a *Southerner*, since in the end he is there provisorily." "[He] is in the big city," she continues,

> but he does not perceive himself as part of it and [he] feels the imposition of a 'new identity'—*baiano, pau-de-arara, nortista, paraíba*—, almost always with a depreciative connotation, which [he] resists embodying, nurturing the desire to return (Vieira 2000, 226).

The refugee from the sertão (usually gendered as male) is not attempting to become an urbane citizen of the Southeast, probably at least partly because the Southeast stereotypes and rejects him, but also because of an incredibly strong affective attachment to his idyllic rural home and the family or lover he has left behind.

It should not come as a surprise, then, that Luiz Gonzaga demonstrates some ironic distance from the phenomenon of "modernization"—although Vieira does not recognize it as such. Vieira cites a comment from Gonzaga on the *Proposta* television program in 1972, in which Gonzaga says, with a reportedly "malicious grin (*riso malicioso*)," that he was "modernizing" when he reduced his cangaceiro outfit to just a hat, thus representing only "the head of Lampião," the famous bandit by whom his costume was inspired (Vieira 2000, 233). Now, Vieira seems to take Gonzaga literally when he invokes modernization, which is representative of the manner in which her analysis falls under the sway of the synthetic urge. Certainly the synthesis of popular rural tradition with urban modernity makes for an attractive narrative in a country like Brazil where strong ideologies of miscegenation and development coexist. This narrative becomes all the more attractive at a time like the present in which syntheses of modernity and tradition, and scholarly accounts thereof, have obtained global recognition as common sense.

Nevertheless, we should not take Gonzaga seriously here, because his comment is an example of *malícia*, a kind of devilish tricksterism. Gonzaga is responding to the "poets" and "intellectuals" who insist that a sertanejo cannot be a true sertanejo without dressing up like a Northeastern cowboy or backland bandit. He says that "stylization is enough" to characterize one's own origins and identity (Vieira 2000, 233). Gonzaga's assertion of his own personal style, however, is not really an attempt to be more "modern," and this is why he grins. Being more "modern" is exactly what the "intellectuals" in question are accusing him of, and thus he feels a need to defend his own authenticity as a Northeasterner of humble, country origins.

Whether or not her misunderstanding of Gonzaga's comment is the prime motivating force behind her argument is difficult to say, but Sulamita Vieira describes the great sanfoneiro's music as if it were a project of "updating tradition" (*atualização de tradição*). It is as if baião, she continues, "were weaving, patiently and artistically, a third scenario, with pieces of 'there' and of 'here,' combined and regrouped to maintain the articulation of those two worlds" (Vieira 2000, 248). This "third scenario" is precisely a synthesis of the Southeastern urban metropolis, "here," with the backland country, "there" in the Northeastern sertão. Vieira goes on to emphasize this point with another synthetic trope, calling the articulation of sertão and city "a new language." But is this really Gonzaga's language? It is true that a few examples of lyrics can be found in which Gonzaga praises Rio de Janeiro, however these tend to be chronicles of his personal success (and that of his collaborators) in the carioca culture industry, rather than any general trend in the forró canon representing the Northeastern migrant experience.[1]

Another example Vieira uses, "Adeus, Rio," in which Gonzaga praises the beautiful morenas (brunettes, or brown-skinned women) of Rio de Janeiro, hardly seems to be an example of the "reordering of the world of the migrant" she makes it out to be (Vieira 2000, 252). The singer lightheartedly says he will miss the carioca women, but that his Rosa "is in first place," so he must return to her before she replaces him. The song is all the more lighthearted because the singer can apparently come and go as he pleases between the Northeast and Rio de Janeiro, which he calls a "good place for a caboclo to party." This narrative is hardly typical of the migrant experience, nor is it typical of forró lyrics, so Vieira's use of it as evidence regarding the migrant's point of view is suspect. She writes that the song demonstrates how the migrant no longer only has eyes for the sertão, but can now "see the city through the lens of someone who lived in it" (Ibid.). Not only is the song lightly humorous and atypical, though, it also contains no real image of the city as such. There is one mention of Copacabana, and of course the morenas, but nothing beyond this—in fact the song is markedly lacking in terms of spatial orientation and of a more general cognitive mapping of the social environment, especially for a song which directly addresses the city itself. Notably, there is no mention of the suburbs where many Northeastern immigrants live, nor of the large market of São Cristóvão where they congregate on weekends.

Further, what of the extended quotation from Humberto Teixeira which Vieira provides, in which the great Gonzaga collaborator calls urban life a mere deceit, a failure for the sertanejo? Teixeira states that the caboclo must "pretend to live" when he flees drought in his home region (Vieira 2000, 15). For the Northeasterner, life in the Southeast is equivalent to death, in the sense that all affective attachments are stripped away from his or her local environment. At one point Vieira calls this state of affairs "living the sertão within the city," since of course many attachments remain to the home region while the Northeasterner is in exile (Ibid., 159). However, the general state of consciousness represented in forró would be better described as living the sertão *against* the city, or at least despite it. Perhaps Dominguinhos (see Chapter Seven, Fig. 7.2), one of Gonzaga's most important artistic heirs, said

---

[1]See, for instance, my discussion of "Baião de São Sebastião" in Chapter Three.

it best when he commented that Gonzaga "urbanized forró, that is, he expanded the borders" (Silva 2003, 96). Historian Bryan McCann is also close to the mark when he states that Luiz Gonzaga "deliver[ed] the essence of the sertão to the urban center in a comprehensible and compelling package" (McCann 2004, 117). Gonzaga did produce and distribute Northeastern music within an urban market, on a scale never before seen. He helped to popularize many Northeastern genres nationally, and to dispel stereotypes about the backwardness of the Northeast. In this way, he certainly expanded the borders of the Northeast and brought forró into the largest urbanizing region of the country.

Ultimately, Vieira leaves us with an ambiguous vision of the Northeasterner's orientation after emigrating to the urban centers of the Southeast. The ambiguity arises from the urge to represent a popular music of rural origins, taken up by the urban culture industry, as a synthesis of rural and urban elements in Brazilian life. One could certainly argue that the recognition of Gonzaga's authorship and the distribution of his music are products of an urban environment, in the same vein as Dominguinhos's comment. But the manner in which Luiz Gonzaga and other forrozeiros made use of this medium to portray the Northeast and its people was hardly an attempt to incorporate that region and that people into the hegemony of urban, industrializing Brazil. Vieira is closest to the discourse of forró when she says that the Northeasterner is "in the big city, but he does not see himself as part of it." Often, he or she resists even seeing the city when producing Northeastern music. Even a subtle sociological analysis like Vieira's *O sertão em movimento* runs astray when dealing with sertanejos' cognitive block vis-à-vis the city. The urge to incorporate forro's subjects into a grander narrative of modernization and regional-national synthesis is too great. Here we are dealing with an alignment of various dominant Brazilian and Latinamericanist discourses on hybridity which reinforce each other.

**Traditional Forró: The Duel of Urban and Rural**

One way to try to avoid a reductive synthesis when discussing forró is to differentiate different subgenres or stylistic approaches within the genre. Such is the nature of Expedito Leandro Silva's analysis of São Paulo forró, *Forró no asfalto: mercado e identidade sociocultural* (*Forró on the Asphalt:*

*Market and Sociocultural Identity*). This is certainly more feasible for Silva since his work takes a broader historical perspective than Vieira's, which only covers the period of Gonzaga's professional apogee in the forties and fifties. To begin, Silva associates "traditional forró" with the legacy of Luiz Gonzaga. Silva provides quotations from Gonzaga, who first popularized forró in the form of baião, which prove that the famous accordionist was concerned both with appealing to a broader audience and with representing the popular classes of the Northeast. For instance, a citation from Assis Ângelo relates Gonzaga's comment that he "defined, urbanized, and refined" baião (Assis 1990, 53). This statement is Gonzaga's explanation of how he turned baião into a recognizable genre of Northeastern music, giving it a place in the national market through a clear commodification. It does not reflect an attempt to urbanize forró's discourse, however. Silva supplies another quotation which demonstrates that Gonzaga wished to take advantage of many elements in Northeastern folklore, and furthermore only those which he and his collaborators deemed were "made with the image of the people" (Dreyfus 1996, 121). It was important to Gonzaga to give these popular roots "a new wardrobe," that is, to make Northeastern music using his own personal style and creativity (Ibid.). But the common experiences of Northeasterners, both their struggles and their joys, remained the guiding principle of Gonzaga's oeuvre and the vast amount of related production in the forró canon.

In the context of discussing Luiz Gonzaga's musical production, Silva presents a schema that seems to produce the same type of synthesis we have seen in Vieira's work:

> The traditional and the modern character mix in Luiz Gonzaga's musical project. The traditional is attuned to the audience, while the modern relates to the market, to urban and industrial products. In that "duel" between the urban world and the rural, baião was the most appropriate music to consolidate the new and the old, its instrumentalization and the rapidity of the opening-and-closing of the accordion apportioned entertainment to all the social classes (Silva 2003, 87).

Silva describes the mixing of the traditional and the modern and the consolidation of the old and the new in Gonzaga's musical project, seemingly echoing the hegemonic discourse of hybridity. However, the author also describes the development of Gonzaga's music as a duel between urban and rural worlds. The ambiguity in this passage reflects the complexity of Silva's analysis, in which tradition is not reducible to the country nor modernity to the city. In fact, tradition stands for the popular nature of Gonzaga's work, that is, its attempt to capture the collective sufferings and celebrations of Northeasterners and its continual dialogue with that same collective through live performances. While attuning his music to a people and its folklore, Gonzaga also was attempting to establish a broader market for forró, not only for purposes of personal profit but also to dispel stereotypes against Northeasterners held by many Southerners. The only way this could be done was through the culture industry, which Silva characterizes as the modern character of Gonzaga's work. The carioca culture industry may well have influenced Gonzaga in choosing baião and creating a recognizable musical genre out of that element of Northeastern culture. Gonzaga also made full use of this same culture industry's media outlets to popularize his music on a national scale. All of this activity is certainly fully circumscribed within the modern industries of the Brazilian entertainment media and utilizes their relatively vast array of technological resources for reproduction, circulation, and publicity. The duel between urban and rural Silva mentions, then, is not won or lost by modernity or tradition. Simply put, the popularization of forró involved a promoter of rural, living tradition who made use of modern technology to gain the type of viable national audience samba carioca already had established. This exploitation of the modern culture industry to project his rural imaginary is what Gonzaga himself meant by "defining, urbanizing and refining" baião. To this extent, one could say the modern and the traditional mix together in Gonzaga's work, but the urban plays a very small part in shaping the discourse and worldview reproduced in forró.

Silva also describes how the musicians of today who have inherited Gonzaga's project of "traditional forró" have an astute and critical view of the media. Many perceive a lack of respect from the media and the big record companies, who see them as "folkloric and outdated" (Silva 2003, 98). While these traditional forrozeiros are not resistant to innovation in their music, they still insist upon maintaining strong ties to the popular traditions of the Northeast. They certainly cannot imagine giving these ties up to try to become modern pop musicians. They are also well aware that much of present-day pop music is simply "modismos" or fads. There is some concern as to whether this is true of other styles of forró, although generally these traditional musicians support the efforts of other forrozeiros to make inroads by stylizing forró for the contemporary national market. There are, however, some clear exceptions to this tendency, involving vehement traditionalists who see any changes for the purpose of a more successful commodification as a betrayal or perversion of the genre. Such traditionalists are more likely to be middle-class and/or residents of the Southeast who feel the loss of communal tradition more acutely since their link to it is attenuated by various economic and diasporic factors.

**University Forró: The Middle Class to the Rescue**

Thus we arrive at the other categories of forró Silva uses, "university forró" and "electronic forró." Silva chooses this terminology because these terms are in common usage (he himself would prefer "modern" and "postmodern" forró), although individual musicians sometimes have reservations about categorizing themselves in any specific subgenre of forró. These reservations are an indicator of how fluid these classifications are and the complex relationship between the modern music industry and the traditionalist, regionalist ethos shared by many forrozeiros. When one considers the categories of university and electronic forró, the added factor of class distinction further problematizes the very idea of a common ethos guiding the genre. While musicians in either subgenre share similar values about promoting Northeasterners and their cultural production, musicians in electronic forró ensembles are attuned to the demands of a national, pop-industrial market for regional music, while university forró is attuned more to a smaller, night-club-frequenting, middle-class audience that demands an aura of cultural authenticity.

Forró first became associated with the cultural capital of the university-educated middle-class youth in the late 1960s, when figures like Gilberto Gil began to valorize Northeastern music. Prominent Tropicalist musicians such as Gil and Gal Costa contributed to an album with Gonzaga at the time, reviving national recognition of his work. Such collaborations were part of a general atmosphere in which the promotion of the music of the popular classes was seen as part of a leftist project of solidarity and resistance to the intensifying power of a military dictatorship that suppressed these classes (Draper 2003; Draper 2008). At around this time, the term forró first arose, to describe the medley of popular Northeastern rhythms played by Gonzaga and other forrozeiros. Around this new genre rose up a whole array of musicians promoted by Gonzaga, including:

> Jackson do Pandeiro [...], Genival Lacerda, Trio Nordestino, Marinês, Os Três do
> Nordeste, Coroné Ludujero, Claudete Soares ("Little Princess of Baião"), Jair Alves
> ("Baron of Baião"), and Zé Gonzaga ("Prince of Baião") (Silva 2003, 96).

These musicians would continue to produce forró for decades, some to the present day, responding to the desires of Northeasterners even at times when the national media had forgotten them.

Luiz Gonzaga, his aforementioned colleagues, and other bands in the seventies and eighties whom they would foster predominated in the world of forró until Gonzaga's death in 1989. In the seventies, forró achieved national prominence again with the help of a new wave of Northeastern musical transplants in the Southeast, including Alceu Valença and cousins Zé and Elba Ramalho. This could be described as the first era when the Southeastern middle-class began to share a deeper interest in the full complexity of popular music in the Northeast. But the presence of Gonzaga was influential enough to maintain a general coherence of the genre across regional and socio-economic divides. His profound influence can still be seen in the continued prevalence of the forró canon. However, since his death different communities of forró fans and musicians have begun to distinguish themselves. These newly defined communities are based upon elements that have existed in much of forró musical production since at least the seventies, but now there is no single figure with the prominence of Gonzaga to emphasize the common ground of all these elements.

Thus in the early nineties, a new discursive space opened up which was filled by several different artistic tendencies or niche markets. *Forró universitário* or university forró is the niche which corresponds to those bands associated with the cultural capital of the university. This association comes through band members' own university degrees as well as the community of university students and graduates who make up much of their regular audience. Often the ethos of artistic production for university forrozeiros is one of "resgate," a project of recovery or revitalization of a genre considered to be under threat of extinction. This "return to origins," as Dominguinhos calls it, certainly involves entertainment, as it is an attempt to tailor forró to urban night-club scenes frequented by wealthier audiences, where it was previously absent (at least since the eighties) (Silva 2003, 106). At the same time, there is a didactic element which attempts to, as one triangle player put it, "channel" the traditional forrozeiros to teach today's youth the value of their own cultural heritage (Author Interview with Fernando Silveira, 24 March 2004). Forró musicians and entrepeneurs stress that entertainment value is paramount, however the forró canon continues to determine the horizon of possibility for innovation. Nevertheless, the aforementioned club scene, which exists throughout the country but is most extensive in São Paulo where Silva focuses his analysis, is probably the university forró phenomenon closest to the imaginary of rural-urban synthesis.

Especially in São Paulo, an entire cultural economy has been built up around forró universitário. The club-going audience in São Paulo is distinct from audiences in the Northeast in that the paulistas are almost exclusively younger fans (people in their twenties and teens). These fans have access to the largest selection of clubs devoted to forró in the country. This culture revolves around dancing, like forró in general, however many of the dance styles in São Paulo are far from the traditional two-step, close couple dancing of the Northeast. Silva calls the style a "samba-rock," but the more elaborate routines seem most inspired by ballroom dancing. However, despite these clear differences, Silva insists that "the product is the same, it is just that in the nocturnal houses of the Southern zone it is sold with a different clothing" (Silva 2003, 110). Obviously, there is a difference in bodily movement as well, but these differences have not resulted in any significant deviation from the forró canon in the lyrical discourse of the musicians. In Recife, the university forró audience (primarily to be found in performances at the Sala de Reboco club and formerly at the Skina 341 club) is much closer to the ethos of traditional forró, with similar dancing styles and a similarly large range of ages. This is still largely a middle-class club audience, however in Recife and the Northeast there is a much smaller and more ambiguous economic divide between middle and lower classes. Thus in the end, university forró throughout Brazil still reflects the rural subalternism of its basis in the traditional forró canon. In this sense, at least, forrozeiros of this niche have succeeded in channeling a Northeastern epistemology.

**Electronic Forró: A Northeastern Popular-Operatic Spectacle**

The final subdivision of the forró genre which Silva discusses is commonly known as "forró eletrônico," or electronic forró. In contrast to university forró, the electronic variety has a performance style that is markedly distinct from forró prior to 1990. The number of band members on stage tends to be at or above fifteen, including multiple guitarists on electric and bass, a keyboardist, as well as various percussionists, vocalists, dancers (typically female but sometimes male-female couples), an accordion player and sometimes a saxophonist. Lighting and special effects tend to be elaborate and dramatic, and costumes are flashy and revealing. In addition, although it is a less marked difference than in the case of performance style, the lyrical discourse of electronic forró shows an increased focus on interpersonal romance. Thus electronic forró presents a better case for a possible synthesis of rural and urban epistemes than either university or traditional forró. A different aesthetic is certainly perceptible, one that emphasizes romance and spectacle. As discussed in Chapter Three, this aesthetic is certainly influenced by Brazilian popular culture in general, including soap operas and national pop music, as well as other regional or urban genres like axé and brega that market themselves largely through displays of sexuality and/or melodrama.

The relationship between proponents of forró eletrônico and forró universitário is a revealing one. Some middle-class university forró musicians and a number of fans criticize electronic forró as derivative and a bastardization of the more authentic forró canon rooted in the legacy of Luiz Gonzaga. However, Silva cites two important forró DJs in São Paulo, the brothers Mano Véio and Mano Novo, who make the claim that forró eletrônico was necessary to revitalize the genre after Gonzaga's death (Silva 2003, 114, 124). Many traditional forró musicians and the older university forrozeiros tend to agree that this revitalization took place, and some even think that this translates into greater interest in every subgenre of forró—although Mano Novo himself doubts this (Author Interview with Mano Novo, 22 March 2004). Some, like Enok Virgulino of Trio Virgulino, see no fundamental difference between electronic forró and the other two categories, taking a position similar to Silva's on university forró, that the product is the same but is just packaged differently (Author Interview with Enok Virgulino, 24 March 2004). Positions like this are in stark contrast with the common middle-class disregard mentioned above. From Silva's description of one electronic forrozeiro's struggle to promote his music, it becomes clear that the demand for forró eletrônico arises from the urban poor living on the periphery of São Paulo, or in the case of other bands in the

Northeast, of Fortaleza or Recife. This audience appreciates the melodrama and sexuality of electronic forró bands without any strong demands for adherence to authentic, traditional roots.

But do all of these diverse and sometimes disputing desires and discourses signify that a radical departure has occurred within the electronic subgenre? Silva tells us that electronic forró replaces Gonzaga's rural costume of leather hat and jacket "in order to incorporate other attributes of the urban and modern youth" (Silva 2003, 125). These modern attributes are referenced "not just in the costume, but also in the introduction of female dancers and electronic equipment" (Ibid.). One might add that they are referenced in at least one band's very name, Caviar com Rapadura ("Caviar with Brown Sugar Candy"). This name, according to the band's website, refers to

> the mixture and the union between the rich and the poor, the bourgeoisie and the man from the country, sophistication and simplicity, the mixture of romantic, electronic, modern forró and the traditional pé-de-serra (Caviar com Rapadura n.d.).

I should note here that the very fact that many electronic and university forró bands are developing sophisticated websites to promote themselves is a recent, modern and urban phenomenon and still very uncommon among traditional artists. The band's name, as defined in the excerpt from their site, certainly indicates a desire for economic and cultural synthesis between dual elements coded as either urbane or folkloric. However, as some of Silva's comments about marketing suggest, many of the above-mentioned new phenomena are limited to the category of "packaging" or publicity and sales. On the level of production, these bands tend to adhere to playing songs with faster, simpler rhythms led by the base guitar to match their spectacular, phantasmagoric performances. The tempo in general relates to the danceability of the music, which Silva considers one of the prime requisites of the genre, along with thematic elements dealing with romance or marked with satire or humor. The danceability is often reemphasized by couples of professional dancers who dance throughout the entire front space of the stage while the musicians play their instruments and sing. These dancers are modeling a certain kind of exhibitionist, ballroom-inspired dancing that is most popular in São Paulo.

Taken as a whole, all these characteristics of forró eletrônico point towards the formation of a new cultural constellation. However, they are still well within the orbit of the forró canon with its roots in Luiz Gonzaga's baião. Most of the phenomena that are labeled as new are really only distinct from forró tradicional in degree, and additionally in their relative prominence within the genre as compared to the configuration of the same phenomena in traditional forró. For instance, the costumes, female dancers and electronic equipment Silva mentions were all included in performances by Gonzaga and many of his immediate successors. These elements are simply used on a much grander, quasi-operatic scale in electronic forró in its attempt to take its rightful place within the field of Brazilian modernity. But it is still taking its place as a music of poor Northeasterners, a music that places their values on par with those of the urban bourgeoisie. Further, there is no indication that the lyrical discourse is now synthesizing the urban world with the rural. The same lack of cognitive mapping of urban social space is prevalent. There is not so much a reorientation in this regard as an increased emphasis on the romantic lyrics of the forró canon in which a singer, typically male, addresses a woman whom he loves and from whom he has been separated for some reason. Still evident, although less so than in traditional forró, is the association of yearning for the lover (i.e. saudade) with the yearning for return to the beautiful sertão. It should not be surprising that electronic forró does not discursively strive for the bourgeois sophistication which Caviar com Rapadura's name is intended to invoke. After all, its audience is hardly bourgeois and does not demand this kind of musical production. The core audience values forró's regional identity while this core and a broader public enjoy the pleasures of the performance spectacle, the easily danceable rhythms, and the poignant sensuality or provocative sexuality of the lyrics.

Ultimately, Silva sidesteps the issue of what kind of dynamic there is between the rural identitarian roots of electronic forró and its urban locus of production. He emphasizes what appears to be the most "new" in this subgenre in order to distinguish it as a category. In this way he is following the example of the bands themselves, which certainly like to present themselves as being the vanguard of the genre. Silva's focus on marketing may be a hindrance here, since the marketing of electronic forró, and even many aspects of its production, are indeed quite similar to other urban genres with no rural ties. But these similarities make all the more remarkable the subaltern resistance to an epistemological integration of its discourse into the urban sphere of musical production.

## Forró and Tinhorão's Continuum of Cultural Literacy

In a work written about two decades after his analysis of bossa nova (discussed in the previous chapter), José Ramos Tinhorão lays out a schema of "cultural groups or classes" that is very much guided by the dynamics of interchange between country and city. These classes are based on levels of cultural literacy mapped onto a spatial urban-rural continuum. The very idea of a continuum which includes rural groups, if only in a general sense, is a large step forward from Tinhorão's earlier work, away from a Rio-based national synthesis and towards a recognition of alternative loci of musical production in Brazil. Such a step might allow him to perceive the manner in which the subaltern presence of forró manifests itself within each one of these strata of consumption.

The "regional culture" is the lowest stratum in Tinhorão's schema, and is "almost always connected to the reality of the rural world" (Tinhorão 2001, 157). He characterizes this as an illiterate group due to the lesser quality and availability of education in many rural regions. Tinhorão's suggestion, by stating that this is a "culture...called folkloric," is that the music produced and listened to by this group is folkloric, with all the connotations of tradition, oral culture, and anonymous or collective authorship that come with that label (Ibid.). The second stratum is the "popular culture of the small urban centers or of the peripheries of the big cities" (Ibid.). This cultural group is qualified by its close temporal relationship to the rural world, being largely of "recent rural origin" (Ibid.). Tinhorão specifically notes that this group consumes "subproducts" of both regional culture and urban mass culture. His example of regional culture is música sertaneja, which is popular in southern and central Brazil, and as Tinhorão notes, it is "composed by recording professionals" (Ibid.). He makes no mention of forró here, however elsewhere he inaccurately categorizes forró as música sertaneja, so one can reasonably assume forró would occupy the same position within Tinhorão's urban periphery cultural group (Ibid., 174). This is certainly a group that values traditional Northeastern music and consumes a large amount of forró, especially forró eletrônico.

Tinhorão's third group, continuing upward on the socioeconomic scale, is "illiterate urban popular culture" (Tinhorão 2001, 158). This group seems to be at a further remove from the rural world, since it is merely "eventually also impregnated with vestiges of rural culture," and is comprised of unskilled workers and the urban poor in general (Ibid.). Tinhorão provides the example of people in samba schools. Presumably this group interacts with the recent arrivals from rural areas and is thus impregnated with the culture of the lower stratum. The whole issue of interactions between rural poor and urban poor is an extremely important one in terms of the history of Brazilian music, especially forró. In Tinhorão's formulation, it is unclear how the rural poor are transformed into urban poor. Cognitively, forrozeiros in cities across Brazil continue to resist urbanizing their discourse in the way that sambistas did. Yet Tinhorão does not explore the interconnections of his strata to any significant extent, probably due to the influence of the relatively simplistic synthesis he moves towards from his own complex schema.

The step to the next stratum is less ambiguous, involving an increase in education and literacy. This group is literate to some degree, but remains "without the conditions to understand the superior culture" (Tinhorão 2001, 158). There is no longer any mention of rural influence, so one could draw the conclusion that it is literacy which leads to cognitive urbanization. This correlation is not proven by the example of forró, however. In fact, cultural literacy, as in the case of university forró, can lead to a cultural project of returning to and strengthening rural cultural heritage. The example of university forró also problematizes Tinhorão's next stratum, "the urban popular culture of the emergent middle class" (Ibid.). This class has "access to the University," and is "highly influenced by foreign models, by its connection with the idea of social ascension (which explains its obsession for the new, the modern, the trend, the hot etc.)" (Ibid.). Clearly, this description recalls Tinhorão's critique of the middle class in Rio de Janeiro for producing bossa nova. One could attempt a similar critique of university forrozeiros for transforming forró into the latest middle-class trend, however the duration of interest has been at least a decade now and these musicians insist that they will not let their "movement" die out. Perhaps this could be called a middle-class fetishism of popular culture, however Tinhorão himself cannot claim innocence in this regard. Further, it is unclear why an obsession with the new and the hot should necessarily lead to an attachment to foreign models. Certainly this is an inherent element in capitalism, however it is not limited to international markets, and the renewed regionalism of the 1990s in Brazil has certainly proven the viability of the domestic market in producing new trends. More than trends, however, the domestic market has provided a consistent income for the recording industry, as Tinhorão recognizes elsewhere with a quotation from Ariowaldo Pires comparing Brazilian music "from the rural area" to a plantation behind the house of the industry. This plantation provides a steady income which supports the maintenance of the house and the beautiful garden of foreign music and music by university youth in the front yard (Ibid., 177). Tinhorão's final cultural stratum is the official culture of the elite, essentially the firmly entrenched class that has the most cultural capital to establish the hegemony of its taste and to maintain the front garden of Brazilian popular music.

### The Mediating Role of Cultural Ambassadors

José Ramos Tinhorão attempts to localize specific genres within each cultural group he mentions. But such localization belies the complex realities of Brazilian popular music, which tends to reach a wide range of audiences, and thus is no more born out by Tinhorão's urban example of samba schools than it is by that of forró. Since at least the beginnings of the recording industry in Brazil and the commodification of samba as a national genre, popular music has been distributed to all social classes by a variety of cultural agents. One of the most common means of disseminating the musical production of the poor has been the intervention of cultural ambassadors. A cultural ambassador is an individual (or sometimes a group) who, through his or her own personal ties to a collective of musicians, is able to use a superior socioeconomic position or fame to promote that collective's music beyond its original sphere of production. Luiz Gonzaga himself was known as "The Ambassador of the Sertão." In the case of samba carioca, one of the most important ambassadors was Noel Rosa, who would attend sambas in poor neighborhoods and then reproduce this genre for the burgeoning music industry on records and the radio. Rosa's role does not involve a question of simply copying popular genres and then selling them, however, although this type of appropriation certainly existed—indeed, it received a masterful cinematic portrayal from the perspective of an exploited samba musician in Nelson Pereira dos Santos's *Rio Zona Norte* [Rio Northern Zone] (1957). But generally a strategy of mere imitation would not be able to appeal to a broad audience of consumers, not to mention the ethical conundrums related to claiming authorship for music in the public domain (or even, in some cases, music authored by relatively obscure musicians who were either paid a nominal sum for copyright or nothing at all). Thus the ambassador usually adds his or her own stylistic sense to the genre he or she represents.

Unlike Rosa, Gonzaga is a rare case of someone rising up to national prominence out of the collective which produced his genre, or at least its basis in Northeastern folk music. Donga played an equivalent role in the history of the samba, however he was not nearly as successful as Gonzaga in shaping the development of his respective genre. Nevertheless, even Gonzaga had the help of a long series of mediators, most notably two middle-class Northeasterners, Humberto Teixeira and Zé Dantas. These partners were able to help Gonzaga simplify and refine Northeastern music for a national audience that was not ready to receive the Northeastern imaginary in its full complexity. Thus the baião was born as an identifiable rhythm and musical genre. As a new genre, it circulated at every socioeconomic level of carioca society, and via the radio, eventually to most of Brazil. For the elites, the baião would be performed by an orchestra led by the voice of the "Queen of Baião," Carmelita Alves. For lower social classes, to whom Gonzaga preferred to perform, the characteristic trio of accordion, zabumba and triangle was most common. The key point is that baião, like samba before it, was able to penetrate into every socioeconomic sphere and gain an enthusiastic audience, albeit always strongly identified (or pigeonholed) as regional music in a way that samba was not. Tinhorão likely misses the significant reach which even subaltern forms like baião have achieved due to his exclusive focus on consumption as determined by social class. Such a focus necessarily underestimates the powerful influence of artistic creativity, cultural ambassadorship, diasporic populations, and innovative marketing on the national audience and the various regional and socioeconomic niches. We can see that thanks to these four elements, the three categories of forró are today reaching a wider array of social classes than ever, spanning Tinhorão's entire schema.

Unfortunately, Tinhorão does not consider the full complexity of his own schema. He is still too distracted by an anti-imperialist critique to avoid another national synthesis in which the international recording industry becomes his target again, contaminating the musical consumption of yet another generation of middle-class Brazilians. The continued popularity of forró and other regional musics proves that there is at the very least a strong transregional resistance to what Tinhorão terms the "status quo of cultural domination" (Tinhorão 2001, 163). He believes that the success of this domination derives from an association of "good taste" with "modernity" and thus, with the help of the mass media, taste on the global peripheries is determined by whatever cultural production is imported from the more developed, and thus more modern, "foreign centers" (Ibid., 161). Once again, the treatment of the problem of cultural-economic imperialism as a national one invokes a synthesis that wields its own hegemony over Brazilian culture, excluding the diverse subaltern voices within forró and other popular genres. Tinhorão underestimates the ability of subalternity to irrupt into different sociocultural spheres, disrupting any hegemonic class or aesthetic consciousness.

**Negative Register of National Synthesis: Forró's Double Consciousness**

In Chapter Five I discussed Gilberto Freyre and Fernando Ortiz's broader theoretical syntheses of their respective nations, and attempted to trace a general tendency in Latin American cultural studies. Using specific examples within the realm of popular culture in Brazil, in which music plays a pivotal role, both Chapters Five and Six have described the manner in which the cultural theorists in question have relied upon a hegemonic national synthesis in order to inscribe their thoughts within some of the master narratives of modernity. We can divide the primary narratives at work in this context into two major categories—that of progress and development, and that of dependency and anti-imperialism. These categories are of course symptoms of a larger modern phenomenon, the radical expansion of capital commonly known as globalization.

On the one hand, I have described how cultural theorists and producers like Sulamita Vieira, Tom Zé and Caetano Veloso demonstrate a positive synthetic urge in an attempt to insert Brazilian cultural production within national and international narratives of development and progress. These thinkers trace the development of certain cultural production in such a way as to bolster a cultural narrative of progress that reflects the equivalent hegemonic narrative in the economic sphere. On the other hand, I have described the critical tendency of other intellectuals like Pierre Bourdieu, Loïc Wacquant, José Ramos Tinhorão and again, Caetano Veloso, to synthesize Brazilian culture for the purposes of developing an anti-imperialist critique of dependency. Due to a hegemonic synthetic urge—in this latter case for the negative purpose of excluding certain phenomena from the national identity—these diverse critiques are in the final analysis little more than examples of conservative nationalism and its attendant *reductiones ad absurdum*.

Ultimately, a theory of culture should attempt to respond to the demands of any subaltern consciousness within its domain. In the case of forró, the expressivity of the subaltern could be described, to use W. E. B. Du Bois's term, as a "double consciousness" (Du Bois, 2007). We have seen a double consciousness at work in the performances and lyrics of Luiz Gonzaga, his contemporaries, and in the production of the many bands who have followed in their wake to this day. It is a double or multiple consciousness that does not seek a resolution or synthesis as Du Bois's own formulation does. The discourse of forró straddles some of the major cultural antinomies in Brazil, including the spatial duality of rural and urban zones and the related temporal duality of modern and traditional styles. At the same time that forrozeiros maintain a strong redemptive memory of the rural way of life, itself contributing to a continual attunement to popular tradition, forró as a genre has been able to develop a critical consciousness of the entertainment media that it must use to disseminate itself. In this antinomian viewpoint, this double consciousness, the apparent contradictions never engage each other, let alone become resolved. Rather, they remain as unique constitutive elements throughout the various subcategories of the genre, resulting in a Northeastern regionalism that painstakingly responds to the various stylistic trends and technology of the culture industry. The modern music media can be engaged and exploited to the extent that they further the recognition of forró's historical contribution to the collective struggles and celebrations of Northeasterners. But the roots of place and people remain a limiting factor on the extent to which radically cosmopolitan musical and lyrical elements can be incorporated into the genre. The recognition of forrozeiros' reticence to participate in hegemonic syntheses of the aforementioned antinomies constitutes an avowal of a subaltern subject position that does not conform to hegemonic cultural analyses of the hybrid. On the conceptual level, this avowal is a move towards savage hybridity, which according to Alberto Moreiras,

> turns a reticent understanding of cultural change into a principle of counterhege-
> monic practice, and...places it at the service of the subaltern position in the
> constitution of the hegemonic system. The hegemonic relation—any hegemonic
> relation—must then be understood, not as a full hybrid body, but as a (quasi-)

socioideological totality that is only made possible through the negation or exclusion of the subaltern other. The subaltern position structurally marks the failure of hybrid totalization: the remainder of the hegemonic relation, that is, its negative register. (Moreiras 2001, 296)

In this failure of hybrid totalization, in the cracks of cultural theory, lies the true productivity not only of forró, but of the subaltern other that underpins all popular culture.

# Chapter Seven

# The "Changing Same" and Redemptive Regionalism in the Evolving Popular Musical Form of Forró

In the Introduction, I outlined what tradition is *not* in forró (viz. a localized archive of the past). In this chapter, I seek to define what it is, namely, the living memory of the changing same. This conception of tradition from Paul Gilroy captures the true vitality of forró and the historicity of its tradition (Gilroy 1993, 198). Irrespective of trends in the national culture industry that have popularized forró or thrown it into relative oblivion, forrozeiros have always valued Northeastern cultural legacies and have respectfully, even deferentially, sought to reformulate these legacies in light of the situation of Northeasterners in contemporary Brazil. These reformulations are really a carrying on of the changing same through individual musicians' stylistic innovations and stage personas, as well as through continued collective (audience) participation in traditional celebrations that have both specifically Northeastern and universal significance. Each celebration, such as a dance or a ritual festival, has its own (re)productive power that it contributes to the genre as a whole, throughout Brazil. Beyond living memory's relevance for the stylistic evolution of the genre, it is also politicized in various ways to distinguish the subaltern, Northeastern changing same as a redemptive regionalism. In forró lyrics past and present, one can find critical prophecies of social justice and autonomy for Northeasterners and their marginalized region. These prophecies are much akin to Walter Benjamin's concept of weak messianism, since they reflect the belief that subaltern peoples of the past have a redemptive claim upon the present. In addition, forrozeiros often develop a ruralism, much like negritude's emphasis on blackness, that emphasizes the vitality, strength, and importance of the rural economy, its workers, and their cultural traditions, over and against the hegemonic urban economies in Brazil. Thus at its best, forró as a cultural tradition demonstrates that, in the words of Patrick Chabal, "modernity is not the reverse of tradition but rather tradition as it has changed and modernised" (Chabal 1996, 10). Tradition in forró is ultimately the collective narrative of Northeastern workers as they have faced the challenges presented by a rapidly modernizing Brazilian state.

## "Respeita Januário": Paying Respect to a Vital Patrimony

Arguably, the song that best captures the role of tradition in forró as an evolving musical genre is Luiz Gonzaga and Humberto Teixeira's "Respeita Januário," first recorded in 1950. The song tells the story of Gonzaga's return to his home in the backlands of the Northeast, after achieving success and national fame in Rio de Janeiro. Of course, one might expect the famous "King of Baião" to be treated like royalty on his return to the humble rural region of his birth. But as he nears home, the prodigal Luiz is confronted with the venerable local reputation of his father, Januário:

[…]They were soon telling me
"From Taboca to Rancharia
From Salgueiro to Bodocó
Januário is the greatest!"
Half-annoyed old Jacó:
- Luiz!... Respect Januário!
- Luiz!... Respect Januário!
- Luiz!
- You might be famous
- But your father is more stubborn
- And nobody can beat him, Luiz!
- Luiz!...
- Respect your father's eight-button, Luiz (repeat) […]

Foram logo me dizendo
"De Taboca a Rancharia
De Salgueiro a Bodocó
Januário é o maió!"
Meio zangado o véi Jacó:
- Luiz!...respeita Januário
- Luiz!...respeita Januário
- Luiz!
- Tu pode ser famoso
- Mas tu pai é mais tinhoso
- E cum ele ninguém vai, Luiz!

- Luiz!...
- Respeita os oito baixo do teu pai (bis) […]
(Gonzaga and Teixeira n.d., 12)

It quickly becomes clear that, although the song names both Luiz and his father Januário, their personal relationship is backgrounded. The real emphasis in the song is placed on Luiz Gonzaga's return to the sertão. This is a very special return, one undertaken after Luiz has made a name for himself, achieving national fame and enough success to be able to boast an expensive instrument. Towards the beginning of the song, Luiz (as he is repeatedly addressed in the lyrics) allows himself some vanity, describing the instrument in loving detail, and imagines a grand, prodigal return to the Cariri region where he grew up. The idea of returning in triumph holds a particular relish for Luiz since Gonzaga had had to leave Exu quickly and rather ignominiously years before because of some trouble over his involvement with a rancher's daughter (against the rancher's wishes). But Gonzaga describes how he soon has his bubble burst by the locals, who either fail to be impressed by his national reputation or at least put on a good show of failing to be impressed. A grumpy old-timer, Jacó, emphasizes to the young upstart that, despite Luiz's fame, his father Januário is still the baddest eight-button accordion player in this neck of the backlands.

The prior verses beginning with "they were soon telling me," though, make it clear that Jacó is speaking for the community, and the collective nature of the address to Luiz Gonzaga is emphasized by the fact that Jacó's words form the repeated lines of the song's chorus. The imperative to "respect Januário" is the most emphasized verse of the song, repeated many times in performance. This imperative is a clear claim upon Luiz Gonzaga based in the cultural tradition of the Cariri community. It could be called a claim from the past upon the present, but the main emphasis is upon the continued importance of the older musician and his music in the present. Whatever Luiz Gonzaga has done in the Rio culture industry in order to make Northeastern music nationally famous, the music still exists as a living, breathing cultural tradition in the Northeast itself, with all the complexity and richness that the many local talents like Januário bring to that tradition.

Of course, this song is not the unmediated voice of a Northeastern community, since it portrays Gonzaga's own perspective on his homecoming. We must then consider why he chooses to present it in this particular way. It is clearly important to Gonzaga to make his audience recognize that the Northeast has an existence entirely independent of Gonzaga's own musical career, more specifically an existence distinct from the portrayal of the region which has been one of the major hallmarks of that career. In the Northeast, Gonzaga seems to say, he is just another accordionist among many other great musicians with their own unique styles. This attitude corresponds to Gonzaga's early efforts to develop the genre from a mere fad or Northeastern cultural curiosity and symbol to a complex allegory of the region and its history. But the major focus is the imperative to "respect Januário," and by extension, to respect tradition. The song begs the question, what does it mean to respect tradition, to respect one's forebears? Especially if one has made a career of commercializing their cultural traditions for a national audience through the modern culture industry?

At face value, it seems like a simple injunction to respect one's father. But Luiz Gonzaga knew better than most how difficult a task this really was for a musician of rural Northeastern origins who wished to develop his cultural tradition into a new genre of Brazilian popular music. Is it respectful to market a genre of music that once, as tradition or folklore, was a collective production of a community? Or even to sell an old tune like that of "Asa Branca" as one's own personal creation, even if one did write the lyrics? Here we are dealing with the vexing, and perhaps ultimately irresolvable, questions of authorship and private property that come with any commoditization. Luiz Gonzaga demonstrates his respect for tradition by always acknowledging his debt to the Northeast, as he does in "Respeita Januário" itself through venerating the figure of his father. It is probably inevitable that he be accused of exploitation of the Northeast by someone since he was (not by choice) the most prominent musician representing the region for decades, but there have been remarkably few of such accusations. This general acceptance of Gonzaga as the "ambassador of the sertão" may well be connected to his continued efforts to promote other musicians from the Northeast and, later in his career, to broaden his musical genre into an allegorical form that welcomed a diverse array of Northeastern voices, instruments, lyrics, rhythms, and performance styles.

Yet there are other problems more unique to respecting tradition, such as authenticity and the related degree of representativeness. If we judge authenticity only by a musician's putative "purity," that is, by his or her rural or regional isolation from Brazilian popular culture, then one would have to judge Gonzaga and his music entirely alienated and devoid of authentic Nor-

Figure 7.1: A model "casa de caboclo [country peasant home]" at
the Luiz Gonzaga Museum in Exu, Pernambuco (The sign displays
one of Gonzaga's verses: "To dance with my sweetheart in a white-
washed room.")

Figure 7.2: Gonzaga's musical heir Dominguinhos plays accordion
at a concert in São Paulo

theasternness. In no way does Gonzaga represent a Northeast that is an island of cultural production unto itself, isolated from the national culture industry and the hyperindustrialized states of the Southeast. From the beginning of his career, Luiz Gonzaga used the hegemonic culture industry of Rio de Janeiro to promote baião and the many other rhythmic and lyrical traditions of the Northeast which would come to comprise the genre of forró. This fact belies the critiques regarding authenticity, made by some cultural producers and critics, of certain musicians and styles of forró that they deem too urban (especially "low-class" urban in the case of forró eletrônico), too commercial, or too Southeastern. In order to make these kinds of critiques, the critics utilize the figure of Luiz Gonzaga as the ultimate benchmark for authenticity. Yet Gonzaga himself could be accused of commercializing forró for a mass, national (largely urban) audience in any number of ways. Clearly, for Luiz Gonzaga tradition's demand to respect one's forebears does not mean one must live and play music exactly as they did. To respect Januário is to celebrate the "living memory of the changing same" that Gilroy describes in his discussion of black diaspora. One must pay tribute to tradition, but do so in one's own authentic way, as Gonzaga does in "Respeita Januário."

The song does not merely repeat the merits of old musicians like Januário, but rather sets them in dialogue with the next generation as represented by Luiz. In "Respeita Januário," Januário's greatness as an accordionist is presented as a living, dynamic memory in at least two ways. First, Januário is still playing and is seen as the best musician of the area, even if nationally famous musicians arrive from elsewhere. This local veneration continues to exist throughout the Northeast, such as in Recife where musicians like Arlindo dos Oito Baixos and Santanna o Cantador are upheld as stars along with other, more nationally known forrozeiros. But more importantly, Januário's skill and knowledge are presented as compatible with Gonzaga's baião, which at the time the song was written in 1950 had become a national phenomenon through its production and distribution in the circuits of the Brazilian culture industry. Gonzaga does not take the demand to respect his father as a limitation on his own creativity, but rather turns it into an opportunity to reveal the "changing same" of Northeastern identities as they interact with modernization, or the rapid industrialization of the Brazilian economy.

## Baião, In Style and Out

We can further trace the celebration and revelation of the changing same in forró by considering Gonzaga's works that relate to baião's apogee and decline on the national stage of popular culture. The baião, as discussed at length in Chapter One, was the rhythm and dance through which Gonzaga first introduced Northeastern music and culture to the four corners of Brazil. At its height, the baião symbolized the Northeast, and thus its success was understood by forrozeiros and other Northeasterners as a victory for the entire region and its diasporic population in the South. Luiz Gonzaga and Zé Dantas's "A dança da moda," a baião whose title translates as the stylish or "in" dance, exemplifies the time when baião had access to the elite halls of high culture in Rio de Janeiro, and of course through the radio stations in Rio to the rest of the country:

> […]In the middle of the street there are still balloons
> There are still bonfires
> One can see the fire, but on the dance floor
> The people just dance, just request baião […]

> […] No meio da rua inda é balão
> Inda é fogueira
> É fogo de vista, mas dentro da pista
> O povo só dança, só pede o baião […]
> (Gonzaga and Dantas n.d.)

Clearly this song celebrates the surprising success of baião, which had become the first significant market competitor for samba in the modern Brazilian popular music industry. The lyrics initially describe the previous state of affairs in Rio de Janeiro when non-Northeastern music like polka was played during the traditional Northeastern harvest festival of São João (described more fully in Chapter Two). While clearly baião takes on faddish qualities in this song, its omnipresence is certainly an advance beyond the previous vacuum of Northeastern cultural production that persisted even during one of the most important festival periods of that region. In Gonzaga and Dantas's lyrics, the singer invokes the festival of São João quite forcefully, and in performance these lines ("Ai ai ai ai São João") are repeated by a chorus. This emphasis clearly invokes Northeastern tradition and ritual celebrations, and appropriately so, for the song was first recorded in April 1950, the typical time of year for recording songs intended to be released during the the São João season.

Perhaps the key lines for the purposes of my discussion here are the fifth through seventh, "In the middle of the street there are still balloons/there are still bonfires/One can see the fire..." While the song seeks to celebrate the new-found universal popularity of a Northeastern cultural product, the phenomenon is represented as another example of the changing same of subaltern regional tradition. In other words, as the music is commodified and popularized in new ways, the musician continues to base his creativity in the epistemological ground of traditional ritual and the memory of countless celebrations past enjoyed with fellow Northeasterners. This ground is cemented by the use of the word "roda" or circle in the final verses. The circle dance is one of the most traditional forms of dancing and immediately invokes the folkloric, collective origins of popular culture. Yet "roda" is used here in an expansive sense to capture not just the lower classes whose productivity resulted in much of today's Brazilian popular music, but also the upper echelons of Brazilian society who consume and reproduce this music in altered forms. The phrase "in every circle/they only request baião" serves to nationalize or even universalize (through a transregional, transclass socialization of dance) traditional, particularly Northeastern, culture. The "changing same," however, must be invoked again here for this nationalization begins from the roda, from the most traditional of bodily, musical epistemologies.

At the opposite end of the spectrum thematically, "Pra onde tu vai baião [Where are you going, baião]" invokes the decline in popularity of this once nationally and even internationally acclaimed rhythm. This work is a baião written by João Vale and Sebastião Rodrigues, and released in a recording by Luiz Gonzaga in 1963. Gonzaga, whose name was synonymous with baião at the time, had experienced a decline in the national popularity of his music which corresponded to the rise in popularity of bossa nova. Politically, Vargas-style populism and the state's search for a national-popular culture which might suture the interests of the working class to that of the ruling elites had been succeeded by Juscelino Kubitschek's developmentalist goal of fifty years' progress in five. The bossa nova was the sound track for these high hopes, and all of a sudden the Northeast's backwardness, which had always been the dark side of its stereotypical charm for the rest of the country, impinged upon the baião's previously sterling reputation. Yet at the same time that the voice of "Pra onde tu vai baião" recognizes this reversal of fortune, it embeds itself all the more in a Northeastern identity and traditional culture which it had always claimed as its basic source of strength:

[these four lines sung once by Gonzaga and repeated by chorus, after each new verse]
Where are you going baião
I'm leaving here
But why baião
No one wants me here [...]

I'm going to my foot-of-the-mountain
Taking my sack
There in the forró are the people that count
And I'm the king of the sertão

In the clubs and bars
They won't let me enter anymore
It's just Twist, Bolero, Rock, and Cha Cha Cha
Knowing this, it's better for me to retire [...]

Pra onde tu vai baião
Eu vou sair por aí
Mas porque baião
Ninguém me quer mais aqui [...]

Eu vou pro meu pé de serra
Levando o meu matulão
Lá no forró são os tal
E sou o rei do sertão

Nos clubes e nas boates
Não me deixam mais entrá
É só Twist, Bolero, Rock e Tchá-tchá-tchá
Se eu tô sabendo disso é mió me arretirá [...]
(Vale and Rodrigues n.d.)

The singer ends the song by comparing himself favorably to a cuckolded husband, gendering his relationship to his national audience, which he compares to a beautiful woman. He refuses to be tied to, and consequently betrayed by, a public that is already running around with the next fad, bossa nova. The implication here is that the forrozeiro has a much more loyal muse, namely, the Northeast and its people. In fact, Gonzaga would continue to perform for this diaspora throughout the country, whether or not he happened to be more broadly popular to people from other regions during any given period.

Again, we are brought face-to-face with the changing same of Northeastern popular tradition. As baião and later forró have circulated in differing degrees and directions throughout Brazil from World War II to the present, they have been performed for, and appropriated by, a wide variety of audiences, dancers and musicians, not to mention politicians. This circulation has tended gradually to reorient the genre towards an allegorical, historicized Northeastern discourse that incorporates the phenomena of cultural diversity within the region as well as the cultural and political exchanges between Brazilian regions in the process of forming a national imaginary. Yet whatever the outside influences, a constant theme has always been the redemptive power of the idyllic rural world of the sertão. The first verse after the chorus in "Pra onde tu vai baião" describes this world in a few expressionist brushes: the figure of the vaqueiro or cowboy and his famous sack (which is filled with instruments in one seminal forró lyric), the foot of the mountain (an iconic metonym for rural space and now an epithet for authentic, traditional forró), and of course the forró itself—a festive, musical celebration and its participants. These are the people that really count for this singer, as opposed to the fickle fans of the Southeast. The voice in the song represents a performer who is happy to perform forró for appreciative audiences throughout the country, and to inspire non-Northeastern musicians as well, but who does not depend upon them and is always assured to receive creative, epistemological, moral, and economic support from that regional, subaltern population that both produced his music and is reproduced in it. Of course, such a performer reflects the standpoint of the many Northeastern migrants who were more or less rejected by the Southeastern economic powerhouses of Rio de Janeiro and São Paulo. For these surplus laborers, the Northeast represented a home to which they could always return, and which would welcome them back with open arms as prodigal sons and daughters. This vision of the Northeast as a protectorate of the migrant and his or her cultural identity and integrity was itself a new phenomenon, created in the diaspora but serving to reconstitute the changing same in one more iteration of living tradition.

## Weak Messianism, Sertanejo Style

Tradition in forró also serves the essential function of performing and reproducing the "weak messianic power" of the past which Walter Benjamin describes in his "Über den Begriff der Geschichte [Theses on the Philosophy of History]" (Benjamin 1991, Vol. 1.2: 691-704). According to Benjamin's conception, past generations have a claim upon us in the present since we are always already, potentially, their redeemers. Such a relationship to the past exists in the lyrics of many works within the forró genre, reflecting the strong prophetic traditions of the Northeast. One song recorded by Flávio José, a contemporary Paraíban forrozeiro, clearly demonstrates these intricate ties between the past and present by imagining a future moment with its own present upon which today's desires and prophecies will have a claim. "Utopia sertaneja [Sertão Utopia]," itself a prophetic work, makes these claims upon the future of the Northeast while recalling that our present has failed to live up to the claims of its past:

> [...]One day when the sertão does not forget its history
> commemorates its glories, shows that it is a valiant people
> dances on beaten soil, a forró, côco and xaxado
> the yard all decorated the accordion in full harmony
> triangle, zabumba, happiness it is the time of São João
>
> One day when the sertão is simply all this
> it will listen and not stay silent it will be able to fulfill its role
> it will no longer drink of this bile that is bitter like jiló [bitter fruit]
> it will make a great flight on the wings of manumission
> In the ovens of hypocrisy no longer will it see its earth burned
>
> Um dia quando o sertão não esquecer sua história
> comemorar suas glórias, mostrar que é povo aguerrido
> dançar em solo batido, um forró, côco e xaxado
> terreiro todo enfeitado sanfona em plena harmonia
> triângulo, zabumba, alegria é tempo de São João
>
> Um dia quando o sertão for simplesmente isso tudo
> ouvir e não ficar mudo puder viver seu papel
> não mais beber desse fel que amarga feito jiló

fazer um vôo maior nas asas da alforria
nas brasas da hipocrisia não ver queimado o seu chão
(José and Filho 2004)

The song musically weaves together its language of prophecy, both through instrumental and vocal performance as well as through repeated thematic references to forró. The prophetic language projects a socially just and self-sufficient future for the sertão, while the references to music emphasize the importance of keeping this redemptive imaginary present in Northeasterners' hearts and minds through performance, celebration and remembrance of the fact that the sertão now has, and indeed has always had, the unfulfilled potential to redeem itself. Through phrases like "triangle, zabumba, happiness it is the time of São João," the song ties the prophetic phrases in the future subjunctive together with the present-tense performance of forró and related collective celebrations. Furthermore, the rhyme scheme in the cited section and elsewhere in the song associates the diverse phenomena of forró, praise, redemption, São João, and rejuvenated earth. Clearly, for these lyricists one of the purposes of Northeastern music and festivals is to praise the perseverance and potential of the subaltern populations of the Northeast, while prophecying the necessity of egalitarian social relations in order to economically and politically fulfill the basic and higher-order needs of all these people.

The idea of Northeasterners no longer having to see their earth burned by hypocrisy is a unique one, in that it connects the cyclical climatic phenomenon of drought, a traditional topic of forró lyrics, to the social conditions created by elites which contribute to weather-related human tragedies that might easily have been avoided with proper preparations and infrastructure. The hypocrisy involved here can be seen in Mike Davis's description of the "triple peripheralization" to which the sertão has been subject since the nineteenth century:

> [...]the capacity of any layer of government to sponsor irrigation works was constrained by what might be called "triple peripheralization": the underdevelopment of the Brazilian financial system vis-à-vis British capital; the Nordeste's declining economic and political position vis-à-vis São Paulo; and the sertão's marginality within state politics vis-à-vis the plantation elites of the coast. Politicians endlessly proposed irrigation schemes, but none were built. Ironically, the State's impotence to develop the sertão was inverted by the littoral elite into the racist caricature of the indolent, backward sertanejo (Davis 2002, 388).

Forró has always functioned to combat stereotypes of the kind presented here by Davis, and "Utopia sertaneja" is no exception. It does so in a powerful way through its accurate political critique that places the blame for underdevelopment squarely on the shoulders of politicians who "endlessly proposed...schemes" with no results. The oven that burns the sertão's earth is not merely a natural one then, but rather involves a complex mechanism of politico-economic subalternization. Of course, within today's mechanism, which we could call "imperial" following Michael Hardt and Antonio Negri's model of Empire, British capital has been replaced by the flexibly coordinated, neoliberal regime of global capital including multinational corporations, international lending institutions like the IMF, the United States government, international non-governmental organizations, and the United Nations (whose delegates are now occasionally sent to witness the violent assassinations of rural workers and their representatives in the Northeast). It should also be noted that the "safety valve" of immigration to São Paulo, which did not exist in the nineteenth century, has relieved some of the misery related to the surplus labor pool, at least in the region itself.

My larger point here is that "Utopia sertaneja" highlights the fact that the regional elite's hypocrisy in begging for aid from the federal government was the major problem. The reference to hypocrisy suggests the multiple ways in which the begging of the elites failed to change the subaltern status of most Northeasterners in the twentieth century. First, any money that was attracted did not solve the larger structural problems of disparities in wealth, and only arrived after the droughts were at the worst stage. Secondly, the money that did reach the Northeast was not even distributed to the poorest but rather siphoned away to the regional elite's private projects and bank accounts. Finally, the fact that the hypocritical Northeastern ruling class had made these public requests for aid gave the impression to the rest of the country that something was being done about the Northeast's problems when in fact the opposite was the case. But the genius of this "Utopia sertaneja" is that it is able to invoke all of these factors contributing to subalternization with the use of the traditional imagery of earth seared by drought. Tradition is politicized and set in motion as the changing same when this tragic metonym for climatic disaster is causally connected to the hypocrisy of those in power.

Sertanejos have always strived for self-sufficiency and desired social justice, in the spirit of the traditional redemptive imaginary of the sertão. "Utopia sertaneja" reveals this spirit as a weak messianism and details the claims of the past on the present, and the present on the future. Beginning with the biblical reference "the last shall be the first," the song continues on to outline the weak messianic demands that must be fulfilled in the Northeastern interior: agricultural plenty, economic success, general education and higher intellectual achievement, finding a voice and autonomy through egalitarian politics that take a critical view of duplicitous elites. Of equal importance to these socioeconomic and political goals is that of "not forgetting," but instead "commemorating" subaltern history (that of the "povo aguerrido," or embattled/valiant people), a demand which is closely related to cultural production and traditional celebrations like São João in the fourth verse. In fact, the song itself is evidence that cultural production is a central means of commemorating the subaltern populations of the Northeast, of recalling the past's claims for justice, and of imagining redemption in a just future.

**Recalling a Northeastern Prophetic Tradition**

The attitude toward traditional cultural production and ritual embodied in "Utopia sertaneja" can be witnessed not only in the works of most forrozeiros, but also in those of other Northeasterners who identify with their cause. These musicians are all performing within a larger, prophetic tradition which imagines redemption through the media of cultural production and collective memory. Many Northeastern artists today continue to project the traditional prophecies onto the present in a critical manner, making use of the revolutionary or anarchic figures of Lampião and Antonio Conselheiro. Conselheiro (The Counselor) himself was a millenarian thinker who founded a community of poor Northeasterners who were outcasts from the rest of Brazilian society. His most famous prophecy involved the sertão; he envisioned a day soon when the sertão would become the sea and the sea would become sertão. This was interpreted as a divine promise that the troubles of the marginal Northeastern interior would soon be ended, and the Northeast would become a proverbial land of milk and honey. For many, especially those who identify with littoral society or Southern Brazil, Conselheiro represented (and continues to represent) a sad part of Brazilian history associated with backwardness and civil strife. However, in popular

Northeastern tradition, as can be heard in "Utopia sertaneja," Conselheiro is a prophet who criticized exploitation perpetrated by the elites of the coastal region and the federal government in Rio de Janeiro while imagining redemption for the afflicted region, especially for its most marginal economic and geographical section, the sertão. The final verses of a song by the Recife pop musician Lenine reference famous forrozeiros as part of this lineage of critical prophecy and imagined redemption, and the song's chorus repeats the name of the other folk hero (or anti-hero) mentioned above, Lampião:

> There's no Christian
> Learning from Saint Francis.
> No one is treating
> The Northeast like the South.
> Neither is there
> Lampião, Trovão, Corisco.
> There's no beans
> Instead of cactus, you hear?
> There's no nation
> Lighting its lantern
> There are no more Gonzagas
> Arriving there from Exú.
> There's no more Brazil
> Of Jackson do Pandeiro [...]

> Falta o cristão
> Aprender com São Francisco.
> Falta tratar
> O Nordeste como o Sul.
> Falta outra vez
> Lampião, Trovão, Corisco.
> Falta feijão
> Invés de mandacaru, falei?
> Falta a nacão
> Acender seu candeeiro.
> Faltam chegar
> Mais Gonzagas lá de Exú.
> Falta o Brasil
> De Jackson do Pandeiro [...]
> (Lenine and Pinheiro n.d.)

This work, like "Utopia sertaneja," treats lack in the present as both a claim from the past and the possibility of redemption in the future. In the original Portuguese, the lyrics cited are literally a list of things that are today lacking in the Northeast, and in Brazil as a whole vis-à-vis the Northeast. On the other hand, the song's title, "Candeeiro encantado [Enchanted Lantern]," invokes both the simple oil lanterns of rural laborers in the Northeastern interior, as well as the magic of Eastern folk tales like those of *The Thousand and One Nights*. The magical folk theme is reenforced by the repeated intonation of Lampião's name, which recalls the many tales of adventure associated with the famous bandit and anti-hero (Lenine also certainly intends the pun with the English word "lamp" and the beginning of Lampião's name repeated three times in the chorus). Lampião, like Conselheiro, was viewed as a menace by elites and Southerners, while poor Northeasterners, perhaps because of his bad reputation with the aforementioned groups, tended to see him as a sort of Brazilian Robin Hood. In folk songs (many of which would later be refashioned by forrozeiros) and especially in literatura de cordel, Lampião was portrayed in a thousand and one tales of his own, along with his lover Maria Bonita and comrades such as Corisco, mentioned in the lyrics of "Candeeiro encantado" cited above. Lampião would also provide the model for Luiz Gonzaga's most famous costume, including the instantly recognizable, ornamentalized cangaceiro hat with several stars of David and a crown decorating the front brim. Lenine's song, along with José and Filho's "Utopia sertaneja" and Luiz Gonzaga's whole career, combine the redemptive magic of traditional Northeastern folk tales with a Franciscan celebration of and concern for the poor and the downtrodden (as well as an appreciation of the natural environment in the cases of Filho/José and Gonzaga). In the final verse from Lenine's song, cited above, the last two names mentioned are Luiz Gonzaga and Jackson do Pandeiro, two famous Northeastern forrozeiros who together helped birth the genre of forró and here are placed at the end of a long lineage of critical prophecy, stubborn resistance and survival, and, of course, profound creativity.

**"Êta Baião": In the Circle with Jackson do Pandeiro**

Jackson do Pandeiro himself provides an example of a singer (and tambourine player) who often approaches tradition by vividly evoking a specific, collective cultural event. His music provides proof that tradition, as the changing same of cultural legacy, need not stifle the creativity of performer and participants in any traditional cultural event. There is a sameness, perhaps a universal Northeasterness, to all these events, but individual performers like Jackson do Pandeiro bring their own stylistic innovations and stage personas to their music, interacting with the audience to form a changing, gradually evolving genre of music that relies on the (re)productive power of each unique musical celebration. From this perspective, it becomes clear that popular tradition involves an indefinite series of these types of happenings, stretching back into the past towards the misty, anonymous, and of course communal origins of a specific genre or dance. At the same time, the emphasis in any performance of tradition is on the present moment of celebration. The title of the song "Êta Baião [This Baião]" invokes the specificity of the night of dancing that the lyrics proceed to describe:

How beautiful it is to see in the high sertão
The guitarists striking the first low note. [repeat]

The men face off, rhyme without losing the thread
And thus is born the baião [...]

The guys throw off their sandals, putting feet to the ground
And later when the circle is formed the foot-sliding begins. [repeat] [...]

From afar the stamping feet are heard, and also the women replying
With their clapping hands.

This baião...this baião.


Como é bonito ver no alto sertão
Os violeiros rasqueando a prima com bordão.

Os cabras fazem desafio, rima sem perder o fio
E assim nasce o baião [...]

Os cabra tira as alpercata, bota os pé no chão
E depois de formada a roda começa o rojão [...]

De longe se ouve o tropé, e a resposta das mulhé
Batendo palma de mão.

Êta baião...Êta baião.
(Araújo 2004)

This work, written by Marçal Araújo and recorded by Jackson do Pandeiro in 1954, subtly weaves together the thread of tradition with detailed imagery from a night of dancing and music. No sooner do the lyrics mention the first note of a song being strummed by guitarists, than do we hear a reference to the origins of the baião genre in the traditional Northeastern "desafios" or challenges between two guitarists. Baião itself was originally the name given to the introductory phrase strummed on the guitar prior to each singer's improvised verse. The song's usage of the category "baião" ranges from this remembrance of its origins in Northeastern tradition to a more general association (in the chorus) of the category with the night of collective celebration and performance captured throughout the song. "Êta baião" details various other images of celebration, especially dancing, along with some of the general, popular Brazilian cultural practices so prevalent in the Northeast: i.e. call and response, circle dances, and clapping rhythms. Throughout, the lyrics and fast-paced performance style capture the incredible enthusiasm and energy of the participants in the event (Araújo 2004). As opposed to some of the songs discussed in Chapter Two that are tinged with saudade, this work incorporates no emotional distance from the event described, but rather an immediacy that envelops the listener in the continued vitality of Northeastern tradition.

Traditional, popular music thus finds its continued vitality through both collective participation and personal, performative stylistic creativity or innovation as displayed by adepts like Jackson do Pandeiro. Forró, in its most traditional popular sense, is a cultural happening that does not define itself along a line of teleological progress and thus could be seen as static or even backwards from the perspective of a vanguardist notion of artistic development. Yet, as "Êta baião" and the other songs discussed above make clear, there exists another form of development, based on an epistemology of the changing same, that allows forró to carry on tradition while it responds to and represents the lives, desires, and of course the music of Northeasterners in the present day. Performers throughout the Northeast and Southeast today bring their own unique personas and performative innovations to the genre, and more generally speaking the three sub-genres of university, traditional and electronic forró develop diverse class, regional, and gender perspectives on Northeastern cultural tradition while maintaining its continued significance as a legacy of the survival and productivity against all odds of a subaltern Brazilian people. Nevertheless, many Brazilians, particularly in the Southeastern region of the country, continue to associate both forró and the Northeast with an idyllic rural past (a sort of mythical originary location for national culture). Such associations typically lead to an assumption that tradition is dead or merely a trace of a formerly vital artistic and cultural trend. This assumption is only strengthened by forró's privileging of the rural, despite the fact that this space and imaginary is often stigmatized in the society as a whole for its putative backwardness vis-à-vis the rapidly industrializing cities of Brazil.

**The Rural Remembered and Revitalized**

We can further examine this ideological struggle over the vitality of the corpus of Northeastern tradition by considering two songs that present the performance of traditional music in Brazilian urban space in contrasting ways. The first song we will analyze in this regard is Tom Zé's "São São Paulo." This work is essentially Zé's ode to his adoptive city, the metropolis of the Southeast to which so many Northeasterners like Zé have emigrated over the past fifty years. Yet for our purposes here the element that is most important is the periodic musical citation, in the background of "São São Paulo," of Luiz Gonzaga and Humberto Teixeira's "Asa Branca." This paradigmatic forró lyric is cited in a fragmented manner as the chorus "São São Paulo, quanta dor/São São Paulo, meu amor [São São Paulo, how much pain/São São Paulo, my love]" is repeated. Zé seems to be establishing a historical link between São Paulo's present-day residents and a Northeastern cultural heritage (Zé 2003). Yet here tradition is presented as a sort of historical trace of regional, rural identity in an alien urban setting. The song loses the pathos most famously expressed in Gonzaga's saudade-inspired, epic delivery, since Zé delivers bits and pieces of the lines with rapid, emotionless vocals. Since "Asa Branca" has no thematic connection to the lyrics of Zé's song, and due to its rather peripheral treatment as a fragmented background to the chorus, it becomes apparent that even though it is deemed to have some importance as a genealogical trace, forró (and the rural,

Northeastern world of the sertão presented in loving detail in "Asa Branca,"
hymn of the Northeast) ultimately holds a marginal role in Zé's vision of
contemporary São Paulo. Luiz Gonzaga becomes a ghost representing the
diasporic affect that is presented as largely extinguished or irrelevant for
immigrant populations of Northeastern origin in today's urban Southeast.

In contrast, we can consider Mestre Ambrósio's "Pé-de-calçada"
(already briefly discussed in Chapter Three). Mestre Ambrósio is a now
defunct Recifense band whose members, like Zé, have also performed and
recorded music in São Paulo, and who continue to perform individually in
Recife and elsewhere with other musicians and groups. The band would
probably be considered forró universitário since the members are university-
educated, middle-class musicians and tend to have a younger audience,
however their attitude towards tradition is attuned to the general
epistemology presented in the forró canon and still represented by the forró
tradicional subgenre. Also like Zé, they were probably better equipped than
the more traditionally-oriented musicians to consider Northeastern tradition
from an urban perspective, as can be observed in some of the lyrics of the
aforementioned "Pé-de-calçada":

> […]Today I do forró at the foot of the sidewalk
> In the middle of the bustle, against traffic
> I went there to the jungle and I returned to the city
> From the caboclo I know my situation
>
> Old rabeca don't abandon me
> Zabumba earth-shaker, eat the ground
> At the moment when time disappears
> Transform the sidewalk into foot-of-the-mountain
>
> Hoje eu faço forró em  pé-de-calçada
> No meio da zuada, pela contramão
> Eu fui lá na mata e voltei pra cidade
> De caboclo eu sei minha situação
>
> Rabeca véia não me abandona
> Zabumba treme-terra, come o chão
> Na hora em que o tempo desaparece

Transforma em pé-de-serra o calçadão
(Siba 1998)

This song clearly demonstrates the ideology of ruralism that is disseminated through much of the traditional and university forró canons. Here I am thinking of a parallel between the rural and the blackness that Jean-Paul Sartre describes in his analysis of negritude and the poetry of Aime Césaire:

> It is not a question of the poem becoming part of the calm unity of opposites; but rather of making *one* of the opposites in the "black-white" couple expand like a phallus in its opposition to the other. The density of these words thrown into the air like stones from a volcano, is found in negritude, which is defined as being *against* Europe and colonization. What Césaire destroys is not *all* culture but rather *white* culture; what he brings to light is not desire for *everything* but rather the revolutionary aspirations of the oppressed negro; what he touches in his very depths is not the spirit but a certain specific, concrete form of humanity. (Sartre 1969, 436)

The destructive force of blackness in Sartre's formulation here is much akin to that of ruralism in Mestre Ambrósio's "Pé-de-calçada," in which the final lyrical imagery depicts the instruments of forró "eating" the ground of the city in order to transform urban space into rural. Clearly, it is music which has the power to invoke the country even in the midst of the asphalt and traffic of the city, or rather over and against this urban space. Instead of Europe and colonization, forró's ruralism defines itself against urban developmentalism and the privileging of large-scale industry. Thus "Pé-de-calçada," like forró in general, demonstrates that rural tradition is fully embroiled in a historical struggle over the political future of Brazilian society. In passing, a distinction must be made here with the music of Luiz Gonzaga, which almost exclusively associates the rural with the sertão of the Northeastern interior. Siba, the rabeca player and singer from Mestre Ambrósio who wrote "Pé-de-calçada," refers in this song to the rural coastal regions of the sugar plantations in Pernambuco, known as the zona da mata. In the traditional forró canon, this rural zone is more often depicted in the cocos of Jackson do Pandeiro. It is also the home of *forró de rabeca*, which features the traditional fiddle rather than the accordion. Yet the message is the same as in any Luiz Gonzaga song about the sertão—we must remember the rural.

**Conclusion**

Indeed, the great ethical claim of the changing same is that we cannot forget Northeastern rural culture, or worse, stigmatize it as a backwards or dying way of life, a remnant from Brazil's past. For proof of its continued vitality one need look no further than the music of contemporary university and electronic forró groups, such as O Bando de Maria, Mastruz com Leite, and of course Mestre Ambrósio (whose members have gone on to separate musical projects), all of whom attempt to "channel" the ruralism of forró in the urban centers or to celebrate it in the smaller towns of rural areas. The most common themes, as described in the various songs discussed in this chapter, also reflect the continued vitality of rural tradition on a regional and national level: the respect for cultural legacy combined with the play of creativity, the continued redemptive power of ruralist regionalism, and the simultaneous immediacy and universality of Northeastern cultural happenings, specifically forrós and the festival of São João, in rural and urban, regional and national spaces alike.

# Conclusion

# Multitudinous Diasporic Production: Critical Regionalism, Global Cultural Flows, and the Case of Forró

Towards the end of *The Latin Tinge*, John Storm Roberts comments generally on the flows of Brazilian popular music into and within the United States. His observation provides a starting point for a discussion of the forms of mediation any music from a subordinate capitalist country must undergo in order to achieve international exposure and continued circulation:

> The absorption of Brazilian music was affected by a number of factors, the main one being that, absent a major Brazilian immigrant population or music catering to them as salsa has catered to U.S. Latinos, Brazilian music, from the samba through the bossa nova and on, has always almost immediately been taken over by jazz musicians concerned with giving themselves more musical options. After all, the very first major Brazilian-derived successes of the 1960s came in the form of jazz-bossa played by Americans with the help of Brazilians—whereas all the Cuban music reaching the United States was played or at least directed largely by Latinos, even when the audience was Anglo-American. Brazil, from the mellow subtleties of bossa nova to the tear-away ebullience of batucada, gave jazz not one but an entire range of new possibilities. (Roberts 1999, 252-253)

Thus from the perspective of the North American culture industry, Brazilian music is virtually non-existent as such, but rather enters the United States' music scene primarily as influences or "tinges" in native forms. This is certainly true of baião, which contributed to a short-lived form called "jazz-baião" that made an appearance on Bud Shank and Laurindo Almeida's 1953 album, *Brazilliance* (Ibid., 134). The main example of jazz-baião on the album is a song titled "Blue Baião," which is a fast-paced jazz instrumental version of Luiz Gonzaga and Humberto Teixeira's first national hit, "Baião." Shank on saxophone plays the melody, taking the place of Luiz Gonzaga's vocals, and the sax is backed by Brazilian acoustic guitarrist Almeida, a bassist, and a drummer beating out a rapid baião rhythm.

## Depopularization in the Global Market: The Baião Goes Abroad

But what remains of Luiz Gonzaga and the discourse of forró in this international version of the baião? Simply put, very little. Obviously, any lyrical expression of the Brazilian Northeast is removed by the absence of vocals. The song also entirely changes the instrumentation and the tempo is much less danceable. According to Roberts, this album is "an almost eerie prefiguring of the gentle almost chamber-music quality of the early 1960s jazz-bossa recordings of Charlie Byrd, Almeida, Stan Getz, and others, as well as of their Rio originals" (Roberts 1999, 134-135). Thus this North American-Brazilian duo of jazz musicians was doing with baião something much akin to what bossa nova musicians like João Gilberto and Tom Jobim would be doing with samba a few years later. This type of appropriation of popular rhythms by middle-class or foreign musicians receives harsh criticism from conservative nationalists like Brazilian music critic José Ramos Tinhorão. As detailed above in Chapter Five, Tinhorão sees this appropriation within the national context as an alienation of popular music from its authentic roots that should be valued far less than the "original" folkloric music of the urban and rural lower classes.

When one considers manifestations of Brazilian popular music in international markets like that of the United States, however, radically transformative appropriation seems virtually inevitable. Forró specifically, as a subaltern regionalist genre without much success on international markets, shows the high level of mediation necessary for even the rich cultural milieu of the Brazilian Northeast to reach foreign audiences. As Roberts points out in the passage above, there is not a significant population of Brazilian immigrants in the United States relative to that from other Latin American nations like Mexico, Puerto Rico and Cuba (although conceivably this situation could change as Brazilian expatriate communities continue to grow in cities from Boston to Dallas to Los Angeles). The other U.S. Latinos mentioned  here provide a constant niche market for music from their countries of origin, keeping the music alive regardless of North American culture-industry trends and nurturing and innovating with Latin American genres within a rough, transnational equivalent of their original national context. Consequently, genres like salsa and música norteña flow into and circulate within the North American market with much greater ease than anything Brazilian. I should stress here that this ease of flow is only relative to Brazilian music—it is clear that norteña and salsa often do not have great national exposure in the United States, but rather are still vital due to their continued popularity and cultural currency with their respective U.S. Latino and Latin American audiences.

If we consider baião's international circulation a bit further, we can see that it had much the same fate in Europe as in the United States. At about the same time that *Brazilliance* was released in the U.S., the baião was experiencing a brief wave of popularity in France thanks to a song on the soundtrack of the film *O Cangaceiro* (1952). The film received the Palme d'Or at the Cannes Film Festival and thus was well known. *O Cangaceiro* was also a potentially effective vehicle for promoting the baião since the film was set in the Northeast and featured the bandits after whom Luiz Gonzaga had styled his own costume (although not quite as great a vehicle as *Orfeu negro* would become for bossa nova in 1958, with a soundtrack of all bossa nova songs written by two of the best artists of the genre, Tom Jobim and Vinícius de Morães). Yet there seems to have been little attempt to invite any Brazilian forrozeiros to come perform for French audiences at this time. In fact, Luiz Gonzaga himself did not go to France until almost thirty years later in 1982, at the invitation of a Brazilian singer living in Paris, Nazaré Pereira. But in the early fifties the baião did gain enough recognition so that, according to Dominique Dreyfus, "some French composers even went so far as to compose another baião, that, in truth, was a baião in name only" (Dreyfus 1996, 297). As in the case of "Blue Baião" in the United States, various necessary elements were lacking for baião to be anything more than a short-lived fad in France.

First and most significantly, France did not have a significant population of Brazilian immigrants, which as noted above is a crucial ingredient for the long-term success of a genre in foreign national contexts. Another limitation on baião's circulation in both the United States and France was the lack of any easily comparable "sister genre," especially in terms of performative presentation (including instrumentation) and lyrical themes. Shank and Almeida attempted to fuse the genre with jazz, while the French composers attempted to write a pure baião (or rather "baion brésilien") themselves, but in neither case were the musical idioms used capable of furthering baião as a Northeastern Brazilian cultural phenomenon. There was also the related problem that baião lacked a cultural ambassador with enough desire and symbolic capital to place the genre at center stage of First World culture industries, like Carmen Miranda and Hollywood musicals did for samba carioca, for instance. In the case of bossa nova, on the other hand, there were several famous North American and Brazilian expatriate jazz musicians who could shepherd the genre into great popularity. Naturally, they were willing and able to do so because bossa nova had a sister genre in the United States, and thus fit so nicely into the market for jazz in the early sixties. Finally, there were no other marketing categories, such as those of Afro-pop or Latin music mentioned in the introduction, into which baião could easily fit. This continues to be a significant limitation for forró in the present day, despite the rise of a global market for "world music." Indeed, while in the fifties there was not yet any "world music" as such, even with the advent of this category as well as Afro-pop and others, forrozeiros have had a difficult time finding a niche. One important reason for this difficulty with respect to world music categories is that this market tends to commodify artists as either authentic producers of folklore, or as avant-garde mediators and synthesizers of global flows. Any group of musicians that falls in between, like forrozeiros, must decide whether or not it is worth the possibly alienating effort to shift their production towards one of these poles.

**The Significance of Diasporic, Popular Roots: A Comparative Review of Forró in The National-Regional Context**

In contrast to baião's failure to enter global cultural flows to any significant degree, we can consider its great success in the Brazilian national market via the Rio de Janeiro culture industry. Here of course, baião and later forró had several important cultural ambassadors, including Jackson do Pandeiro and Luiz Gonzaga, who could contribute to shaping the genre as well as presenting it to audiences outside of the Northeast. The baião had a sister genre in samba, with which it shared a similar rhythmic structure (especially with the rural samba de roda from Bahia). In the forties, Gonzaga was able to utilize some of the same orchestration used for radio samba and choro to disseminate his baião (including accordion, cavaquinho, guitar, shaker, tambourine), with the addition of a few key instruments like the zabumba and later the triangle. Forró also has a certain national political relevance in that it can suggest a regionally integrated nation. However, the primary reason for forró's continued relevance on the national stage is the Northeastern diaspora in the Southeastern centers of industrialization.

Northeasterners of all generations in São Paulo, Rio de Janeiro, and elsewhere have consistently provided large audiences to more and less famous forrozeiros outside of forró's native region. These audiences were loyal even during forró's fall from the national stage in the years of bossa nova's hegemony. This constant support has allowed forró to return again and again to national prominence, thereby making it universally known in the country as one of the most important forms of Brazilian music. Thus on the national level, the example of forró supports Roberts's implication that a diasporic or migrant population with extant ties to the musical genre's original locus of production—or context of production—is necessary for the genre to transcend the status of fad.

I take the opportunity here to reemphasize the phrase *context of production*, because it is important not to forget that, despite some musicians' and critics' claims to the contrary, music often cannot be linked to one specific locus of production. In the case of baião and forró, the beginnings of the music as a popular genre are already within the diaspora in the figure and discourse of Luiz Gonzaga. The Northeast was of course always imagined as the original locus of production for the folkloric origins of forró, but many of the major works were first produced, recorded, and distributed from the diaspora, as exemplified by the common lyrical usage of the word "there" to indicate a separation from the Northeast or the sertão. As discussed in Chapters Two and Three, Northeastern artists from the beginnings of the genre have demonstrated a diasporic affect and a strong sense of cultural identity through their discursive commitment to the redemptive imaginary of the sertão, and their related cognitive resistance to substituting urban, Southeastern imaginaries for a Northeastern, rural one.

**Samba-Reggae's Repopularization: Returning the World Music Gaze**

Having considered the difficulties that a genre like forró/baião faces in reaching a significant audience abroad, without a diaspora, sister genre, or cultural ambassador to call upon for support across the border, it will provide a revealing contrast to analyze a recent example of a Northeastern Brazilian genre that has all three. I am referring here to the Afro-Bahian genre of *samba-reggae*, produced along with a variety of other genres of Afro-Brazilian music in Bahia's capital city of Salvador. Salvador is one of the greatest centers of production of regional music in Brazil, and certainly the best known in the Southeast of the country and abroad. One reason for this celebrity is samba-reggae, also known in its "electronic," pop-oriented form as axé. Samba-reggae has its local roots in the *blocos afros*, musical groups that traditionally perform during carnival, but as its name suggests, the genre is influenced by the Afro-diasporic music of the Caribbean. Clearly this connection to other African-influenced music in the Western hemisphere automatically gives the genre a large potential audience in the Black Atlantic and beyond. While it would be a stretch to call reggae a sister genre of samba-reggae, the huge groups of drummers that are featured in samba-reggae make the genre an easy sell on the percussion-inclined market for Afro-pop. The only element we have thus failed to consider is the availability of a cultural ambassador to the genre.

Enter Paul Simon. Simon toured through Bahia in 1990 looking for instrumental talent to back his vocals on *Rhythm of the Saints*. He found the samba-reggae drum troupe called Olodum, which would achieve international acclaim and recognition when the album won a Grammy and went platinum. Even within Brazil, Olodum and samba-reggae only became known on the national stage after the great success of Simon's album. But thereafter the genre became Brazil's most famous and best-selling regional music, leading to the commercial fad of axé music.

Since we know that samba-reggae had most of the necessary elements to enter into global cultural flows and circulate with relative ease, it is tempting to assume that the group's eventual international success was virtually inevitable. It is all the more tempting to assume this inevitability when comparing samba-reggae to a genre like forró that is largely restricted to the confines of Brazil. Some of the language in Goli Guerreiro's study of samba-reggae reflects this feeling of inevitability:

> The multiplication of cultural contacts in the globalized world facilitates the penetration of local production in the international music market. In the first half of the twentieth century, the contacts of the musical environment of Salvador were primarily with Africa and with Rio de Janeiro. In the sixties, seventies, and eighties, at the height of the negritude movement, exchanges expand in the direction of the Caribbean and North America. In the nineties, the globalization of musical exchanges occurs, [and these] exchanges materialize in world music (Guerreiro 2000, 159).

Globalization here appears to be an abstract phenomenon that transcends individual agency and tends to make global exchanges of culture a common occurrence. All of which is true, but only to a certain extent. The main flaw in this vision of globalization is the implied teleology from restricted access to open access to foreign cultural markets for artists from subordinate capitalist countries. What Guerreiro's picture of increasing global cultural flows leaves out is that, rather than becoming more democratic and naturally-occurring, global cultural flows continue to be highly mediated by multinational communications industries. It is not surprising that this fact is often overlooked by cultural producers and critics, since part of the purpose of this mediation is to give an aura of naturalness and inevitability to cultural exchanges among a diverse array of international musicians and other artists.

As indicated above, levels of mediation are particularly high when there is no diasporic collective to revitalize the music and it is entirely dependent upon the multinational culture industry for survival outside its original locus/context of production. This is forró's predicament, however even in the case of samba-reggae there is nothing "natural" about its ability to flow back and forth across national borders. For example, the entire global enterprise of Afro-Bahian music was largely contingent upon Paul Simon's initial desire to seek out first African rhythms and then rhythms in the African diaspora. It is entirely possible that had Paul Simon chosen to tour through French Guiana, or even Pernambuco, rather than Salvador, Olodum would never have received any recognition outside of its own region. Indeed, even Bahian groups like Olodum cannot be called international successes, according to Guerreiro himself, for it is "with difficulty [that] they sustain themselves in foreign markets for long and, in the majority of cases, they perform for audiences composed of Brazilians that live outside the country" (Guerreiro 2000, 163). Note the shift in language here from the passage cited above: "the international music market" has become "foreign markets" when the author considers Bahian artists' real ability to perform internationally and circulate their musical production globally. In truth, one must recognize that there is no one, El Dorado-like "international music market" that, once gained, will provide subaltern artists with permanent access to global cultural flows. Access to these flows is always a question of highly mediated distribution of recorded works and performing bodies. It should also be noted here that even an Afro-diasporic music like samba-reggae, aided by sister genres, an (admittedly non-Brazilian) diasporic population, and more than one influential cultural ambassador, is dependent upon Brazilian audiences abroad to sustain itself for any significant period of time, and thus it too is fundamentally limited by the relatively small number of Brazilian migrants to North America and Europe (these being the dominant markets for "world music," i.e. music outside these regions).

After the initial, rather utopian, presentation of the phenomenon of globalization in Guerreiro's account of samba-reggae in international markets, in which it appears that Bahian music is in an equal dialogue with other cultures across the world, the author reveals the problematic nature of such a global imaginary. Guerreiro demonstrates that the category of world music itself, and the desires it represents, can have a profound influence upon cultural production that enters their sphere of influence. Explaining recent trends in Afro-Bahian music vis-à-vis world music, Guerreiro states that

> Samba-reggae interests the producers of *world music* [English in original] due to the singularity of the percussive instruments used by the bands. The language of the drums is the differentiating element and only through it can Bahian musical production fit into the atmosphere of *world music*. For this very reason, when this production begins to circulate in the international panorama, there is a return to the percussive origins in the musical content of albums, as a form of legitimation of the musical product.
>
> Listening to the recordings of Olodum and Timbalada, one notes that the latest CDs of these bands reinvest in percussion. In addition to a lesser presence of electronic effects, leaving the percussive base much more audible, the references to candomblé and African ancestry rise to prominence, through the responsive technique of clapping and the content of the song lyrics. (Guerreiro 2000, 187)

Here we can see the mediation of international markets, or "the producers of world music," at work. These markets expect an authentic version of Afro-pop from Bahia, with an aura of folkloric authenticity. This authenticity is evoked by the predominance of drums and the illusion, due to the apparent lack of studio production or digital mixing of the music, that samba-reggae has somehow remained outside the influence of the modern culture industry. In other words, the music is commodified as organic folklore through a concerted effort on the part of its producers to elide the music's own real conditions of production. The category of world music creates a situation in which songs must be produced from a singular location in order to be commodified as authentic, but they can only be produced in such a manner that any cultural singularites of that locus that fall outside of the requirements of global desire are technologically and musically suppressed. Ironically, this suppression can only occur by means of continued international mediation and subsequent (re)production of the music, pulling it ever further from its mythical cult value as authentic cultural artifact. Thus subaltern cultural production in international markets often derives its legitimacy from satisfying a foreign desire that it can never explicitly acknowledge. "A guy that is born today is already globalized, he is naturally international," says Carlinhos Brown, one of the major cultural ambassadors of Bahian music and conductor of the group Timbalada (Ibid., 170). True, and yet globally, he can never market himself as such, at least not if he wishes to be considered a legitimate folk musician.

**No Thanks, Paul! : Critical Regionalism and an Emerging Musical Multitude**

The foregoing discussion of Afro-Bahian music qua world music is meant to provide not just a contrast to forró's relative isolation from international markets, but also to suggest the possibility that forró might follow a similar avenue of global commodification in the future. There is nothing to prevent Paul Simon or some other cultural ambassador from the dominant capitalist countries from doing for Santanna O Cantador or Elba Ramalho and forró what Simon did for Olodum and samba-reggae. But as in the case of Afro-Bahian music, it is very unlikely that current international markets for subaltern music (i.e. music from subordinate capitalist countries, or even from subordinate regions of those countries in the case of forró and samba-reggae) would allow forró to circulate in its full, tripartite, allegorical-multitudinous complexity. In fact, this feat would be structurally impossible due to the necessary imperial mediation of foreign demand through multinational corporations. The popular music industry  is dominated by six global corporations, and in the United States, these corporations control more than 95 percent of the market (Barnet and Cavanagh 1994, 26, 113). Without a diasporic population to provide economic and moral support for allegorical representation of the home region and its culture, musicians are at the mercy of these corporations and their marketing regimes. These regimes are inherently antithetical to multitudinous production due to their hierarchical juridico-economic frameworks, including restrictive copyright laws and inequitable accumulation of surplus value qua multinational cultural capital.

The impetus behind the present study can be understood as a critical regionalism that celebrates forrozeiros' potential for membership in a global multitude of cultural producers which bypasses these imperial markets of world music. According to Moreiras, critical regionalism is

> an enterprise of thinking that takes the subaltern perspective, formally defined as the perspective from the constitutive outside of hegemony, as the starting point for a critique of contemporary consciousness. Its goal is twofold: on the one hand, to continue the enterprise of deconstruction of melodramatic consciousness, whether local, regional, national, or global, understood as the false consciousness of a real situation; on the other hand, to move toward alternative, non-hegemonic local and regional histories that will seek to constitute themselves as the real consciousness of multiple and always false situations. (Moreiras 2001, 53)

The critique of melodramatic consciousness entails a step outside of false dialectics: between urban and rural, modernity and tradition, and generally between the folkloric-popular peripheries and the cosmopolitan centers imagined by the agents of imperial culture industries. The concept of false consciousness should not need much further explication, and false consciousness is precisely what lies behind the world-market epistemology that finds authenticity in the elisions of subaltern music's real conditions of production. Falsity in the context of "the real consciousness of multiple and always false situations," however, should be further explained as not untruth, but rather the denial of the necessity of truth claims underlying all discourses and epistemologies of authenticity. With an a priori denial of such truth claims, one can understand flows of culture *in flux* rather than always attempting to see them as ontologically representative of some coherent cultural region, people, or nation or as a synthetic symbol of some completed historical process such as the union of modernity and tradition.

In this study of forró, I have sought to further the enterprise of critical regionalism in two major ways. First, I have attempted to critique various forms of melodramatic consciousness that seek to suture forró's discourse into larger hegemonic discourses of modernity. The synthetic urge, critiqued at length in Chapters Five and Six, is constantly at work producing melodramas of national synthesis, of the union of tradition and modernity, of the resolution of differences between urban and rural spaces, and during Luiz Gonzaga's heyday, of the synthesis of Northeastern cultural diversity into one coherent symbolic representation. Secondly, I have advanced a subalternist presentation of the alternative history of forró as the real consciousness of multiple and always false situations. Forró's redemptive imaginary points out the falsehood of a nationalism based upon the dominance of Southeastern, urban industrialization. The genre's allegoricization highlights the falsity of a sovereign symbol that seeks to represent the many singularities of the Northeastern collective. Forrozeiros' emphasis on the historicity of tradition reveals the imaginary of the pure, untouched, rural locus of production as a melodrama. Northeasterners' diasporic affect, or saudade, as well as forrozeiros' cognitive resistance to mapping urban space reveal the falsity of Northeasterners' and other marginal populations' integration into the Southeastern economy. Utilizing the terminology I develop in Chapter One, combining insights from Benjamin and Hardt/Negri, we could call the subaltern epistemology revealed throughout this study of forró an allegorical-multitudinous consciousness. The Northeastern collective represented by forrozeiros is structurally egalitarian, allowing collaboration between diverse members of the group. It is also discursively allegorical, generally avoiding attempts by more famous musicians to claim exclusive, symbolic representation of the genre. Thus forrozeiros are always potentially members of a multitude of cultural producers.

Returning to the issue of the global circulation of cultural flows, we can conclude that because forró insists so much on its singularity, its regional specificity, it is likely to enter these flows to a significant degree only if allowed to do so without being required to give up that singularity. One way in which this has been done in the case of other Latin American music is through diasporic/immigrant populations, but forró's lack of such a population begs the question, is it possible to circulate subaltern music globally without the circulation of a corresponding community of listeners? The answer is that the possibility exists with current information technology, although the transnational mass media, including the big record companies as well as national radio and television, will have to become a lot less hierarchically structured, or they will have to be bypassed altogether by independent media. The internet provides one such possibility, but flows of Brazilian culture via digital file-sharing networks such as Kazaa or YouTube can only happen as piracy until artists begin to circumvent the more restrictive copyright laws reproduced in their contracts with multinationals. This is not a problem, though, for younger or lesser-known musicians who have not signed such contracts.

One example of endeavors in this vein in contemporary Brazil is the advocacy of Gilberto Gil, Northeastern musician and former Minister of Culture in President Lula's government, for Creative Commons. Gil has released songs through this organization, which helps artists to circumvent restrictive copyright laws and contracts with multinational corporations. Other artists who sign with major record labels, such as the forrozeiro eletrônico Frank Aguiar, are insisting upon affordable pricing of their CDs so that they can at least reach the subaltern regions and populations from which they receive their inspiration and loyal support (Silva 2003, 118-119). Perhaps projects such as Creative Commons, combined with pressure on record labels to accept a more democratically-oriented market, can help to disseminate the cultural production of the global multitude of subaltern artists. Of course, this process would also rely more upon international audiences to actively seek out foreign music, rather than just having it marketed to them by multinationals. But a more participatory attitude among audiences worldwide might not be such a bad thing, if we really want to make forró "for all."

# Works Cited

Albin, Ricardo Cravo, ed. 2006. *Dicionário Houaiss ilustrado da música popular brasileira*. Rio de Janeiro: Paracatu.

Albuquerque Jr., Durval Muniz de. 1999. *A invenção do nordeste e outras artes*. São Paulo: Cortez Editora.

Almeida, Rosangela d. S. 2003. *A solidão intimista na cidade mundial: Uma análise da experiência da migração*. Unpublished doctoral dissertation, Pontifícia Universidade Católica-São Paulo, Social Psychology.

Alzugaray, Paulo. 2000. "Ping-pong: Roberta de Recife." *ISTOÉ Gente*. Retrieved 19 August 2004, from <http://www.terra.com.br/istoegente/59/divearte/musica_pingpong_robertarecife.htm>.

Ângelo, Assis. 1990. *Eu vou contar pra vocês*. São Paulo: Ícone.

Anhembi Turismo e Eventos. 2004. "Agenda de eventos." Retrieved 10 August 2004, from <http://anhembi.terra.com.br/dspMostraMat.asp?idMat=399>.

Aranha, Valmir. 1996. "Os albergues dos migrantes no interior do estado de São Paulo: Programas de ação social ou políticas de circulação de população?" *Travessia* May-August: 25-29.

Bacon, David. 2004. "Be Our Guests." *The Nation*, 27 September. Retrieved 24 September 2004, from <http://www.thenation.com/doc.mhtml?i=20040927&s=bacon>.

Bando de Maria, O. 2004. "Sobre a banda." Retrieved 14 August 2004, from <http://www.obandodemaria.com.br>.

Baptista, Dulce M. T. 1998. *Nas terras do "Deus-dará": Nordestinos e suas redes sociais em São Paulo*. Unpublished doctoral dissertation, Pontifícia Universidade Católica-São Paulo.

Barnet, Richard J. and John Cavanagh. 1994. *Global Dreams: Imperial Corporations and the New World Order*. New York: Touchstone.

Benjamin, Walter. 1991 [1974]. *Gesammelte Schriften*. Ed. Rolf Tiedemann. Frankfurt am Main: Suhrkamp.

Berlinck, Manoel T., & Hogan, Daniel J. 1974. "O desenvolvimento econômico do Brasil e as migrações internas para São Paulo: Uma análise histórica." *Cadernos Do Instituto de Filosofia e Ciências Humanas da UNICAMP*.

Bourdieu, Pierre and Loïc Wacquant. 1999. "On the Cunning of Imperialist Reason." *Theory,Culture & Society* 16 (1).

Braga, Liliane P. 2001. *Forró "universitário": O "pé-de-serra" made in Pinheiros*. Unpublished graduate thesis, Pontifícia Universidade Católica-São Paulo, Journalistic Communication.

Bull, Malcolm. 2001. "Hate is the new love." *London Review of Books* 23 (2). Retrieved 7 September 2004 from <http://www.lrb.co.uk/>.

Burdick, John. 1998. *Blessed Anastácia*. New York: Routledge.

Cardel, Lídia M. P. S. 2003. *Migração, liminaridade, e memória: Um estudo sobre o choque entre imaginários e (re)construção de identidades*. Unpublished doctoral dissertation, University of São Paulo, Anthropology.

Carignato, Taeco T. 2005. "A simbolização das experiências de migração." *Travessia* September-December: 11-15.

Caviar com Rapadura. N.d. "A História." Retrieved 28 April 2004, from <http://www.bandacaviarcomrapadura.com.br/>.

Chabal, Patrick, ed. 1996. *The Postcolonial Literature of Lusophone Africa.* Evanston, Illinois: Northwestern University Press.

Clemente, M. L. 1993. *Um pensamento, uma lembrança: A mulher migrante nordestina na dinâmica do seu grupo familiar: Um estudo socio-histórico.* Unpublished master's thesis, Pontifícia Universidade Católica-São Paulo, Social service.

Cunha, José M. P. d. 1995. "A mobilidade intra-regional na metrópole: Consolida-se uma questão." *Travessia* September-December: 5-10.

Davis, Mike. 2002. *Late Victorian Holocausts: El Niño Famines and the Making of the Third World.* London: Verso.

DeBiaggi, Sylvia D. 2005. "Migração e implicações psicológicas: Vivências reais para o indivíduo e o grupo." *Travessia* September-December: 16-20.

Della Monica, Laura. 1992. *Nordestino no Brás: Uma questão cultural.* Unpublished master's thesis, University of São Paulo, School of Communication and Arts.

Dent, Alexander S. 2007. "Country Brothers: Kinship and Chronotope in Brazilian Rural Public Culture." *Anthropological Quarterly* 80(2): 455-495.

Diário de Pernambuco, O, ed. 2003. "Forró poético de Roberta do[sic] Recife." *O Diário de Pernambuco* 24 August. Retrieved 19 August 2004 from <http://www.pernambuco.com/diario/2003/08/24/viver3_0.html>.

Draper, Jack A. 2003. "Politicizing the Popular in Música Popular Brasileira: The People and the Region in Brazilian Musical Production, 1950-2003." *Annals of the Southeastern Council of Latin American Studies* 35(1).

———. 2008. "Renovation and Conservation in Brazilian Literature and Music." *Journal of Latin American Cultural Studies* 17(2): 167-184.

Dreyfus, Dominique. 1996. *Vida de viajante: a saga de Luiz Gonzaga.* São Paulo: Editora 34.

Du Bois, William E. B. 2007 [1903]. *The Souls of Black Folk.* New York: Oxford University Press.

Dunn, Christopher. 2001. *Brutality Garden: Tropicália and the Emergence of a Brazilian Counterculture.* Chapel Hill: University of North Carolina Press.

Durham, Eunice R. 1978. *A caminho da cidade: A vida rural e a migração para São Paulo.* São Paulo: Perspectiva.

Echeverria, Regina. 2006. *Gonzaguinha e Gonzagão: uma história brasileira.* São Paulo: Ediouro.

Ferretti, Mundicarmo Maria Rocha. 1988. *Baião Dos Dois: A música de Zedantas e Luiz Gonzaga no seu contexto de produção e sua atualização na década de 70.* Recife: Massangana.

French John D. 1999. "The Missteps of Anti-Imperialist Reason: Pierre Bourdieu, Loïc Wacquant, and Michael Hanchard's *Orpheus and Power.*" *Working Paper Series of the Duke University Center for Latin American and Caribbean Studies* 27.

———. 2000. "The Missteps of Anti-Imperialist Reason: Bourdieu, Wacquant and Hanchard's *Orpheus and Power.*" *Theory, Culture & Society* 17 (1).

Freyre, Gilberto. 1986 [1933]. *The Masters and the Slaves: A Study in the Development of Brazilian Civilization*. Trans. Samuel Putnam. Berkeley: University of California Press.

Galhardo, Soledad. 2003. *A formação de novos sentidos na cidade*. Unpublished doctoral dissertation, University of São Paulo, School of Communication and Arts.

Gilroy, Paul. 1993. *The Black Atlantic: Modernity and Double Consciousness*. Cambridge, MA: Harvard University Press.

Guerreiro, Goli. 2000. *A trama dos tambores: a música afro-pop de Salvador*. São Paulo: Editora 34.

Hanchard, Michael. 1994. *Orpheus and Power: The Movimento Negro of Rio de Janeiro and São Paulo, Brazil, 1945-1988*. Princeton: Princeton University Press.

Hanchard, Michael. 2000. "Legacy of Domination." *New York Times*, 3 September. Sec. 2: 4.

Hardt, Michael and Antonio Negri. 2000. *Empire*. Cambridge: Harvard University Press.

———. 2004. *Multitude: War and Democracy in the Age of Empire*. New York: Penguin.

IBGE (Instituto Brasileiro de Geografia e Estatística). 2003. *Censo demográfico 2000: migração e deslocamento*. Retrieved 30 July 2008, from <http://www.ibge.gov.br/home/estatistica/populacao/censo2000/migracao/censo2000_migracao.pdf>.

IBGE. 2007. *Tendências demográficas: uma análise da população com base nos resultados dos censos demográficos 1940 e 2000*. Retrieved 30 July 2008, from <http://www.ibge.gov.br/home/estatistica/populacao/tendencia_demografica/analise_populacao/1940_2000/default.shtm>.

Jameson, Fredric. 2004. "The Politics of Utopia." *New Left Review* 25.

Jannuzzi, Paulo d. M. 2000. *Migração e mobilidade social: Migrantes no mercado de trabalho paulista*. Campinas: IFCH/UNICAMP FAPESP.

McCann, Bryan. 2004. *Hello, Hello Brazil: Popular Music in the Making of Modern Brazil*. Durham, NC: Duke University Press.

Medina, Cremilda, ed. 1989. *Forró na garoa*. São Paulo: CJE/ECA/USP.

Moreiras, Alberto. 2001. *The Exhaustion of Difference: The Politics of Latin American Cultural Studies*. Durham, NC: Duke University Press.

Moretti, Franco. 1996. *Modern Epic: The World System from Goethe to García Marquez*. London: Verso.

Moura, Fernando and Antônio Vicente. 2001. *Jackson do Pandeiro: O rei do ritmo*. São Paulo: Editora 34.

Neves, Frederico d. C. 1996. "A seca e o homem: políticas anti-migratórias no Ceará." *Travessia* May-August: 18-24.

Oliveira, Antônia A. d., ed. 1982. *Os nordestinos em São Paulo: Depoimentos*. São Paulo: Ed. Paulinas.

Ortiz, Fernando. 1995. *Cuban Counterpoint: Tobacco and Sugar*. Trans. Harriet de Onís. Durham, NC: Duke University Press.

Parra, Flavia C. et al. 2003. "Color and genomic ancestry in Brazilians." *PNAS* 100 (1).

Pereira, Nancy C. 1996. "A estrada, a rua e a zona." *Travessia* September-December: 31-34.

Ragland, Cathy. 2009. *Música Norteña: Mexican Migrants Creating a Nation Between Nations*. Philadelphia: Temple University Press.

Ramalho, Elba B. 2000. *Luiz Gonzaga: A síntese poética e musical do sertão*. São Paulo:

Terceira Margem.

Roberts, John Storm. 1999. *The Latin Tinge: The Impact of Latin American Music on the United States*. New York: Oxford University Press.

Sá, Sinval. 2002. *Luiz Gonzaga: O Sanfoneiro do Riacho da Brígida*. Fortaleza, Brazil: Realce Editora.

Sales, Teresa and Rosana Baeninger. 2000. "Migrações internas e internacionais no Brasil: panorama deste século." *Travessia* January-April: 33-44.

Sandroni, Carlos. 2001. *Feitiço Decente: Transformações do samba no Rio de Janeiro (1917-1933)*. Rio de Janeiro: Jorge Zahar Ed.

Santiago, Silviano. 2001. *The Space In Between: Essays on Latin American Culture*. Ed. Ana Lúcia Gazzola. Trans. Tom Burns et al. Durham, NC: Duke University Press.

Santo André, Prefeitura Municipal de, ed. 2000. *De todos os lugares, histórias de migrantes*. Santo André: Prefeitura Municipal.

Santos, Regina B. 1994. *Migração no Brasil*. São Paulo: Ed. Scipione.

Sarno, Geraldo, dir. 1965. *Viramundo*. Prod. Thomaz Farkas. Rio de Janeiro: FUNARTE/RIOFILME. 40 min.

Sartre, Jean-Paul. 1969. "Black Orpheus." In *Black and White in American Culture: An Anthology from the Massachusetts Review*. Trans. John MacCombie. Ed. Jules Chametzky and Sidney Kaplan. Boston: University of Massachusetts Press.

Schwarz, Roberto. 1996. *Misplaced Ideas: Essays on Brazilian Culture*. London: Verso.

Sharp, Daniel B. 2001. *A Satellite Dish in the Shantytown Swamps: Musical Hybridity in the "New Scene" of Recife, Pernambuco, Brazil*. Austin: University of Texas.

Silva, Denise F. d. 1998. "Facts of Blackness: Brazil is not (Quite) the United States...and Racial Politics in Brazil?," *Social Identities* 4 (2): 201-234.

Silva, Expedito L. 2003. *Forró no asfalto: mercado e identidade sociocultural*. São Paulo: Annablume / Fapesp.

Surin, Kenneth. 2001. "The Sovereign Individual, 'Subalternity,' and Becoming-Other." *Angelaki* 6 (1).

Taylor, Timothy. 1997. *Global Pop: World Music, World Markets*. New York: Routledge.

Teles, José. 2000. "Roberta do[sic] Recife levanta a poeira no Rio." *Jornal do Commércio*, 12 October. Retrieved 19 August 2004 from <http://www2.uol.com.br/JC/_2000/1210/cc1210c.htm>.

Telles, Edward. 2004. *Race in Another America: The Significance of Skin Color in Brazil*. Princeton, NJ: Princeton University Press.

Tinhorão, José R. 1998. *Música popular: um tema em debate*. 3rd ed. São Paulo: Ed. 34.

———. 2001. *Cultura popular: temas e questões*. São Paulo: Ed. 34.

Vainer, Carlos B. 2000. "Estado e migrações no Brasil: Anotações para uma história das políticas migratórias." *Travessia* April: 15-32.

Veloso, Caetano. 2000. "Orpheus, Rising from Caricature." *New York Times*, 20 August. Sec. 2: 29.

Vieira, Sulamita. 2000. *O sertão em movimento: a dinâmica da produção cultural*. São Paulo: Annablume.

Yúdice, George. 2003. *The Expediency of Culture: Uses of Culture in the Global Era*. Durham, NC: Duke University Press.

# Musical Works Cited

Alves, Nanado and Ilmar Cavalcante. N.d. "Cheiro de Nós." Perf. Santanna O Cantador. In *Xote pé de serra* [Liner notes]. Somax.

Araújo, Marçal. 2004. "Êta baião." In *Jackson do Pandeiro: 50 anos de ritmos* [Liner notes]. P&C EMI Music Brasil.

Assaré, Patativa. N.d. "A triste partida." In *A vida e os 60 maiores sucessos do rei do baião*. Recife: Editora Coqueiro: 18-19.

Filho, João and Juarez Jr. N.d. "Meu pé-de-serra, minha vida." In *Mastruz com Leite: Do forró do grilo a New York* [Liner notes]. Fortaleza, Brazil: Somzoom.

Gil, Gilberto and Dominguinhos. 2000. "Lamento sertanejo." In *Gilberto Gil e as canções de Eu tu eles* [Liner notes]. Gegê.

Gonzaga, Luiz and H. Cordovil. 2000. "A vida do viajante." In *Luiz Gonzaga: a síntese poética e musical do sertão*. Ed. Elba Braga Ramalho. São Paulo: Terceira Margem.

Gonzaga, Luiz and Zé Dantas. N.d. "A dança da moda." In *Luiz Gonzaga: Despedida* [Liner notes]. Curitiba, Paraná: Revivendo.

———. N.d. "Minha fulô." In *Luiz Gonzaga: no meu pé de serra*. [Liner notes]. Curitiba, Paraná: Revivendo.

———. N.d. "Vozes da seca." In *A vida e os 60 maiores sucessos do rei do baião*. Recife: Editora Coqueiro: 17.

———. 2000 [1950]. "Adeus Rio de Janeiro." In *Luiz Gonzaga: a síntese poética e musical do sertão*. Ed. Elba Braga Ramalho. São Paulo: Terceira Margem: 93.

———. 2000 [1952]. "Tudo é baião." In *Luiz Gonzaga: a síntese poética e musical do sertão*. Ed. Elba Braga Ramalho. São Paulo: Terceira Margem.

———. 2000 [1950]. "A volta da asa branca." In *Luiz Gonzaga: a síntese poética e musical do sertão*. Ed. Elba Braga Ramalho. São Paulo: Terceira Margem.

Gonzaga, Luiz and Miguel Lima. N.d. "Penerô xerém." In *Sanfona dourada* [Liner notes]. Curitiba, Paraná: Revivendo.

Gonzaga, Luiz and Humberto Teixeira. N.d. "Qui nem giló." In *Luiz Gonzaga: Despedida* [Liner notes]. Curitiba, Paraná: Revivendo.

———. N.d. "Baião." In *Luiz Gonzaga: 90 aninhos* [Liner notes]. Curitiba, Paraná: Revivendo.

———. N.d. "No meu pé de serra." In *Luiz Gonzaga: No meu pé de serra* [Liner notes]. Curitiba, Paraná: Revivendo.

———. N.d. "Respeita Januário." In *A vida e os 60 maiores sucessos do rei do baião*. Recife: Editora Coqueiro.

———. N.d. "Juazeiro." In *Xodó* [Liner notes]. Curitiba, Paraná: Revivendo.

———. 2000. "Asa Branca." In *Luiz Gonzaga: a síntese poética e musical do sertão*. Ed. Elba Braga Ramalho. São Paulo: Terceira Margem: 94.

———. 2000 [1950]. "Baião de São Sebastião." In *O sertão em movimento: a dinâmica da produção cultural*. Ed. Sulamita Vieira. São Paulo: Annablume: 242.

Gonzaga, Luiz and Marcos Valentim. N.d. "Baião Grã-fino." In *Luiz Gonzaga: Verônica* [Liner notes]. Curitiba, Paraná: Revivendo.

José, Flávio and Miguel Filho. 2004. "Utopia sertaneja." In *Flávio José: Pra amar e ser feliz* [Liner notes]. Recife: LBC Gravações.

Lenine and Paulo C. Pinheiro. N.d. "Candeeiro encantado." In *O dia em que faremos contato* [Liner notes]. Rio de Janeiro: BMG.

Mazzilli, Thiago and Celso Rocha. N.d. "Terrinha." *O Bando de Maria: tiro de bodoque* [Liner notes]. Apache Records.

Morais, Guio de. 2000 [1950]. "No Ceará não tem disso não." In *Luiz Gonzaga: a síntese poética e musical do sertão*. Ed. Elba Braga Ramalho. São Paulo: Terceira Margem: 114-115.

Nascimento, Bete. N.d. "Vou tentar te esquecer." In *Mastruz com Leite: Do forró do grilo a New York* [Liner notes]. Fortaleza, Brazil: Somzoom.

Recife, Roberta d. N.d. "Aquela estrela." In *aquela estrela* [Liner notes]. Special.

Recife, Roberta d. and Naife Simões. N.d. "Quando um amor." *aquela estrela* [Liner notes]. Special.

Siba. 1998. "Pé-de-calçada." In *Mestre Ambrósio: fuá na casa de Cabral* [Liner notes]. São Paulo: Sony.

Vale, João and Sebastião Rodrigues. N.d. "Pra onde tu vai baião." In *Luiz Gonzaga: Despedida* [Liner notes]. Curitiba, Paraná: Revivendo.

Zé, Tom. 2003. "Vaia de bêbado não vale." In *Imprensa cantada* [Liner notes]. São Paulo: Trama.

Zé, Tom. 2003. "São São Paulo." In *Imprensa cantada* [Liner notes]. Trama.

# LATIN AMERICA
Interdisciplinary Studies

Gladys M. Varona-Lacey
*General Editor*

*Latin America: Interdisciplinary Studies* serves as a forum for scholars in the field of Latin American Studies, as well as an educational resource for anyone interested in this region of the world. Themes and topics encompass social, political, historical, and economic issues, in addition to literature, music, art, and architecture.

For additional information about this series or for the submission of manuscripts, please contact:

Dr. Gladys M. Varona-Lacey
Ithaca College
Department of Modern Languages & Literatures
Ithaca, NY 14859

To order other books in this series, please contact our Customer Service Department at:

(800) 770-LANG (within the U.S.)
(212) 647-7706 (outside the U.S.)
(212) 647-7707 FAX

Or browse online by series at:

WWW.PETERLANG.COM